Spirit and Gospel

The Power of God for Salvation

Roland J. Lowther

Copyright © 2017 Roland J. Lowther

First published 2017 by Paternoster
Paternoster is an imprint of Authentic Media Ltd
PO Box 6326, Bletchley, Milton Keynes MK1 9GG.
authenticmedia.co.uk

The right of Roland J. Lowther to be identified as the Author of this Work
has been asserted by him in accordance with the
Copyright, Designs and Patents Act 1988.

All rights reserved.
No part of this publication may be reproduced, stored
in a retrieval system, or transmitted in any form or by any means,
electronic, mechanical, photocopying, recording or otherwise, without
the prior permission of the publisher or a licence permitting restricted
copying. In the UK such licences are issued by the Copyright Licensing
Agency, Barnard's Inn, 86 Fetter Lane, London EC4A 1EN.

British Library Cataloguing in Publication Data

A catalogue record for this book is available from the British Library

ISBN 978-1-84227-886-4
978-1-84227-880-2 (e-book)

Unless otherwise indicated, Scripture quotations are taken from The Holy Bible, New
International Version Anglicised Copyright © 1979, 1984 by International Bible Society.
Used by permission of Hodder & Stoughton Publishers, a division of Hodder Headline
Ltd. All rights reserved. 'nivuk' is a registered trademark of International Bible Society.
UK trademark number 1448790.

Scripture quotations marked (esv) are from the ESV® Bible (The Holy Bible, English
Standard Version®, copyright © 2001 by Crossway, a publishing ministry of Good News
Publishers. Used by permission. All rights reserved.

Cover design by Pete Barnsley (CreativeHoot)
Printed and bound by Lightning Source

It is the same to say: 'The gospel is the power of God,' that is, the gospel is the power of the Spirit, or the riches, weapons, adornments, and every good thing of the Spirit, from whom it has all its power, and this from God.
                                    (Martin Luther, *Lectures on Romans*)

Contents

	Introduction: The Power of God for Salvation	1
1	**Where Has the Power Gone?**	9
	Disempowered by Culture	10
	Disempowered by Context	16
	Reclaiming the Power (Romans 1:16)	24
	Reclaiming the Spirit (Romans Introduction)	30
	Conclusion	38
2	**Temple and Spirit: Revealing Unrighteousness**	39
	Universals, Particulars and Romans	40
	The Temple and the 'Real' Problem (Romans 1:18 – 2:24)	51
	The Spirit, Sin and the 'Heart' of the Gospel (Romans 2:25–9)	59
	Conclusion	65
3	**Law Court and Spirit: Acquitting Sin's Penalty**	66
	Courtroom and Condemnation (Romans 3:1–20)	67
	Righteousness, Faith and the Law (Romans 3:21ff.)	73
	Abraham and Crediting Righteousness (Romans 4:1–25)	81
	The Spirit and 'Real' Justification (Romans 5)	88
	Conclusion	96

4	**Slavery and Spirit: Emancipating from Sin's Power**	97
	Union and Slavery (Romans 6)	98
	Law and the Christian State-of-Being (Romans 7)	106
	Spirit, Power and Life (Romans 8:1–13)	116
	Conclusion	126
5	**Adoption and Spirit: Conquering Sin's Presence**	127
	Perfection: Penultimate or Permanent	128
	Spirit, Sonship and Inheritance (Romans 8:14–16)	135
	The Spirit and the Hope of Perfection (Romans 8:17–25)	142
	The Spirit and Confidence (Romans 8:26–39)	149
	Conclusion	155
6	**The Righteous Shall Live by Faith**	157
	Saving Faith, Salvation and Righteousness	157
	Saving Faith as Rational Assent	163
	Saving Faith as Faithfulness	166
	Saving Faith as Perpetual Trust	170
	For Everyone Who Believes . . .	177
	Conclusion	179

	Conclusion: Power and Glory	180
	Bibliography	185
	Endnotes	197

Introduction: The Power of God for Salvation

That which is assumed is seldom examined. Until I was shaken from my dogmatic naivety by a stream of assertions that the gospel does not encompass a wider scope than the individual forgiveness of sins through the bestowal of the 'legal' benefits of Christ's righteousness to the penitent sinner, I simply took its meaning for granted. This 'shaking' clearly signalled to me that embracing such a crucial doctrine on the grounds of naive adherence to religious tradition or pragmatic pastoral maxims was unhelpful at best and erroneous at worst. Given I was reflecting on the Holy Spirit's role in Paul's ethics / theology at the time of this personal conviction, and fully realizing the gravity that the Spirit held in Paul's thought, it seemed most pertinent to revisit St Paul's gospel through this pneumatological lens.

Returning to Paul's landmark letter to the Romans with a renewed conviction and openness to the Spirit, I encountered a grounded, holistic and powerful message of divine deliverance, and a message that offered far more than the means of assuaging a guilt-burdened conscience before a just God. I rediscovered a powerful truth, originating from a gracious and loving God, channelled through the practical convictions of a faithful apostle, holistically engaging the 'real' needs of fallen and fallible humans (Jews and Gentiles). Indeed, I found a message of deliverance extending beyond the acquittal of past sins, encompassing power over present sin, establishing the presence of God's reign and offering an indefatigable hope that brings the eternal 'not yet' into the existential 'now'. Above all, I came to see that the Holy Spirit offered not just a fresh vision of salvation, but also the wisdom to understand it, the courage to embrace it, and the power to live it!

Without question, the 'beating heart' of the gospel is Jesus Christ, but its 'lifeblood' and animating power is the Holy Spirit. Without the Holy Spirit, the good news of the gospel is little more than a good idea. For Paul, the Spirit's influence in the gospel's provenance, delivery and acceptance authenticates it. Moreover, through the Spirit, the gospel is able to solicit a holistic response from its adherents. Sin is abhorred as a personal offence to God; Christ is embraced with a heartfelt trust; repentance manifests itself as real change; and life is joyfully surrendered to God. In fact, the gospel doesn't promote, nor does the Spirit produce a religion of fear and guilt. On the contrary, as the Holy Spirit unites believers to Christ, connecting them with the essence of his redeeming work, they joyfully and willingly embrace a life of devotion to him. This realistic identification with Jesus' crucifixion and resurrection forms the basis of a life of faith, moral conformity and joyful service. Neither quantity nor quality of human effort cannot emulate such a result; eloquent preaching may instil inspiration, law-based doctrine may incite moral reformation, but only the empowering presence of the Holy Spirit grants divine transformation.

While the Holy Spirit's work is not made quite as explicit as Christ's, this should not be taken to mean that the Spirit's role in Paul's gospel formulation is less important – far from it. The Spirit inspired Paul's understanding of the gospel and, in endowing him with the capacity to communicate it, had no small part in shaping the nature of the message itself. Many of Paul's interpreters read him through the structured frame of dogmatic categories; yet in truth, his soteriology does not so readily fit the pattern of preconceived theological constructs. Rather, the Spirit inspired Paul to reveal the truth of the gospel within the context of a 'dynamic' life, expressing and applying the truth in a way that engages the practical concerns of his readers within pastoral and missional life, and this is what we witness in Romans. In considering the gospel in the 'native setting' of the epistle, we more easily identify the Spirit's 'hand' at work; providing logic, making connections and giving substance to Paul's argument. Indeed, even something as seemingly innocuous as the metaphor is powerfully employed by the Holy Spirit as the means of giving structure and a sense of organic flow to the gospel's message.

The gospel, at least as Paul presents it in Romans, represents a powerful action on God's behalf to bring about the salvation of humanity for the glory of his name (Rom. 11:36). However, the message of 'salvation' is more than an abstract affirmation of one 'central' doctrine with various ethical or pastoral applications. It represents a singular, though multifaceted, revelation of salvific truth unfolded through a sequence of highly applicable metaphors. For Paul, the metaphor has a communicative power that abstract rational propositions simply cannot rival. Metaphor engages the human consciousness at a deeper level, conveying abstract ideas by appealing to the store of familiar meaning-rich ideas resident in the human memory, readily accessible to the imagination. Because of this inherent effectiveness, Paul uses multiple metaphors to set forth a holistic picture of salvation; disclosing unfamiliar spiritual concepts through familiar material symbols from the ancient world – temple, law-court, slave market and adoption, and others.

It would seem that from the outset, Paul's original target audience is clear. He described the gospel in Romans 1:16 as 'first' for the Jew (then for the Gentile). In fact, the letter is written to chiefly engage those struggling with Jewish-oriented doctrinal views. Using a Socratic style, Paul invites his readers to reflect on the gospel by way of a 'personal identification' with a hypothetical inquirer. Paul's interlocutor is most probably a Jewish convert or Gentile convert sympathetic to Jewish practices – one of 'the weak' in Romans 15. So Paul addresses his implicit audience through this idealized reader, methodically revealing the gospel in a way that engages his or her doctrinal concerns (Rom. 1 – 8), as well as laying a foundation for his subsequent pastoral instructions (Rom. 12 – 16).

The gospel addresses the deepest and oldest human problem: moral unrighteousness (and its universal and eternal consequences). Paul knows that all humans are morally alienated from God, consequently denying him the glory he deserves. Convincing those with Jewish sympathies that Gentiles are wrath-deserving sinners was not difficult for Paul; but convincing those who considered themselves privileged and above the standard of Gentile sinners that they too fall short of God's standards was significantly more difficult. Yet one symbol reaches deep into the Jewish religious consciousness, unearthing the true moral state – the temple. Temple stands as a stark reminder that God is holy, and humanity, no matter how religious or privileged, is not!

For the Jew, the temple represents the tangible point of contact between God and his people. Paul's use of the temple metaphor in Romans 1 – 2 represents an effective means of convincing a Jewish-oriented audience that religious privilege does not excuse sin. In fact, it reminds those who presume to enter God's holy presence that an approach cannot be made without paying serious attention to one's moral standing. To bolster this, Paul introduces an associated symbol – circumcision. In evincing that external religious privilege is of no value, he stresses that an inner transformation is required; 'heart' circumcision. In this new regime, the Mosaic Law and its associated symbols have become technically redundant. A deeper symbol of privileged membership is now required – the Spirit-transformed heart of faith!

If the revelation of the gospel uncovers universal guilt, where then can the guilty turn? For those used to relating to God on legal grounds, perhaps the law might offer clemency?[1] Paul uses a legal metaphor to provide the 'scaffolding' for his discussion on rectification and reconciliation. Using the familiar symbol of the law-court, Paul places his law-oriented interlocutor in the witness 'dock', and then prosecutes the case on God's behalf; in so doing he reveals the futility of law-based works' righteousness. Paul's uses of the scriptural indictments are irrefutable; no case stands on 'its own merit'. The law, which might have defended, even justified, now only condemns. Yet the gospel offers a hope beyond law.

Having established the incontrovertible guilt of even the most devout religious person, Paul introduces a new manner of *being set right with God*; a new way that bypasses a reliance on law – faith in Christ. Paul reminds the Jewish-oriented component of his audience that justification on the grounds of faith has its heritage in their own pre-law tradition. In using Abraham's example, the apostle argues for abandoning hope in *works of the law* and embracing Christ by faith; faith granted as a gift of the Spirit. Jesus' atoning death and empowering resurrection is fully sufficient, and consequently through faith in him sin's penalty is fully acquitted. This metaphor is used to further effect by addressing the commensurate aspect of existential guilt. Through the Spirit, the exonerated sinner can experience peace with God – genuine reconciliation. Those previously excluded from God's favour on account of guilt now confidently descend the steps of the courthouse righteous and exonerated – guilt-free.

But how far does the grace endowed in the gospel extend? Does the gospel merely acquit *sin's penalty* only to ignore *sin's power*? The outworking of this new 'legal' standing with God is one of Paul's primary concerns in his gospel presentation. Should redeemed sinners, presuming on grace, simply dismiss moral imperatives? Should they return to their familiar law ethic? For Paul, neither solution is satisfactory. In Romans 6:1 – 8:13, the apostle frames this liberating aspect of salvation through the primary metaphor of slavery. The apostle is clear; the gospel addresses deliverance from the power of *the flesh*, and the basis for this deliverance is the radical concept of 'union' with Christ. Christ not only *died for* sinners, but these same sinners were *crucified and raised with him*, breaking the 'present' reign of sin over their lives.

Paul's radical concept of identification *with Christ* enables the sinner to be emancipated from sin's power. In 'dying with Christ', believers previously allied to the law have now died to that 'old' allegiance. They are no longer bound to it, they are bound to a new moral alliance where the desire to conform to God comes from a new heart-motivation. Under a new Spirit-enabled solidarity with Christ, believers now walk in the 'new way' of the Spirit. This is a powerfully liberating way of living (Rom. 7:6). While the law did little more than remind sinners of their defects, the Spirit provides both the moral content for a God-honouring life and the power to actually perform it! In this dimension of the gospel, the Spirit's role is *practically* most powerful, releasing sinners from the slavery of sin, and establishing them as servants of righteousness.

It seems that many Christians are fearful of claiming the life-transforming power of the gospel, believing a life free from the controlling presence of sin is presumptuous. In fact, some adopt such a defeatist view of life that they only find consolation in a 'rational' reflection on the forensic benefit the cross brings – the acquittal of sin's penalty. But, in dismissing the possibility of substantive transformation, the power that enabled Jesus' resurrection is effectively denied. The gospel actually delivers from the presence of sin, and God supplies the means of enabling it – the Spirit's power. Rather than 'adopting' defeat, Christians are called to embrace the reality of their 'adoption' by God!

In fact, Paul's use of the adoption metaphor is aimed at encouraging believers to appreciate their new standing in Christ; no longer slaves, but sons – family. Sonship is confirmed by granting the Spirit of adoption, a deposit guaranteeing the eventual experience of salvation in eternity. Invariably, Christians are torn between two realities: this current age influenced by sin and evil, and the age to come, where all malevolent influences are extinguished. As such, the Spirit-enabled perfection that Christians claim in this age is incomplete, whereas the perfection they aspire to in eternity is absolute. The sanctifying Spirit, in enabling the 'real' removal of sin's presence, foreshadows final perfection and deepens the believer's appreciation of Christ as they joyfully anticipate the eternal glory to be revealed.

Paul advocates that salvation can only be obtained by faith. Though faith itself is simple, the 'nature' of saving faith is not always so. For some, faith represents nothing more than a rational decision, a mere assent to propositions about Jesus Christ. Still other Christians frame faith as faithfulness; a variety of saving faith that incorporates the notion of initiating trust with enduring perseverance, which has the proclivity to incorporate human effort into the attainment of salvation. Both views present problems. Given the potential pitfalls, how shall we understand the manner of the saving faith that lays hold of the salvation offered? I will argue that the Spirit, in initiating and sustaining faith in Christ, awakens the unbelieving heart to embrace Christ and then empowers the believer to remain in a state-of-faith 'in' Christ. The faith that saves manifests itself as a perpetual state of trust; it is an enduring state of belief that unites the believer to Christ. This is trust that keeps on trusting; a perpetual state of totally relying on the all-sufficient person and the work of Christ – from salvation's initiation to its final consummation.

But what is the gospel's ultimate purpose? The Lord originally created humanity to reflect his perfection and to manifest his glory; yet intoxicated by the lust to become 'like' God, they stole from their Creator what was rightfully his – glory (Rom. 1:23). The unrighteousness that embedded itself in the human heart in Eden, instigated a fall: a fall from divine favour, a fall into sin, a fall that corrupted the divine order, and a fall from humanity's greatest calling – the glory of God (Rom. 3:23). In response, the gospel's ultimate purpose is expressly the restoration of the divine order, returning to God what is rightfully his – the full manifestation of his glory. Furthermore, the purpose in redeeming humanity and the created order from futility is to restore them to their *specific role* within the compass of that primary purpose. Therefore, the gospel, in concert with the deliverance of humanity, is ultimately oriented toward the [re]establishment of a [eternal] divine order (Rom. 8:18–21), where 'all' creation fulfils its original ultimate destiny – the glorification of God.

The gospel proved so manifestly powerful that Paul defined it as 'the power of God for salvation'; a message rich in truth, deeply challenging, and powerfully transformative. It exposed human unrighteousness in light of God's holiness. It granted the acquittal of sin's penalty through Christ's atoning sacrifice. It enabled deliverance from the power of sin through identification with Christ. It empowered life-transformation anticipating the consummation of God's eternal kingdom. Oriented around the supreme truth of divine righteousness, this message endowed forgiven sinners with the confidence to stand in the *righteousness of Christ*, to live out this *righteousness like Christ*, and to embrace a new life in expectation of eternal *righteousness with Christ*.

Yet, the gospel promoted by many present-day representations of 'first-world' Christianity seems to lack the potency of Paul's gospel. In the place of a message animated by divine power often stands a form of religious proclamation that evinces little more than a notional commitment to Christ, conditional devotion to holiness, casual affiliation with Christian community, and provisional involvement in God's mission. Yes, the gospel once had power, but within the contemporary first-world context, the divine energy that animated the courage, conviction and devotion emanating from Paul's powerful salvation message appears to have dissipated, and it would be remiss of us not to ask why.

1

Where Has the Power Gone?

There was a time when I was oblivious of the things of which I am about to write; a time when I was simply content to uncritically accept the religious beliefs that were presented to me, and practise them in a way that granted apparent success. For me and many like me, we had the best of both worlds; a strong evangelical concern for the things of God, and (apart from obvious immorality) unimpeded access to the benefits of this world – just as long as we didn't become too 'radically' Christian. Of course, I was not 'ashamed' of the gospel (mostly), and believed that my Christian life was relatively effective. Yet something kept gnawing at my mind; a question kept nagging my conscience: why did the life and ministry of the New Testament saints have a power and vibrancy that mine lacked? Why did I fall short of their bold, selfless approach to serving God and promoting his gospel? Even though 'I' was Christian, why did my life seem so different from these ancient believers? And then, God in his providence allowed me to encounter the Holy Spirit in a meaningful way and in a fresh light. Through a set of circumstances, I was prompted to take the idea of 'obedience' more seriously than I ever had, and the Spirit of God powerfully awakened my heart to a new dimension of Christian experience. Then everything changed!

At first, I was simply content to examine the circumstances of my own life, and consider the personal factors that had limited the Spirit's power. But I soon discovered there were deeper issues at stake; cultural issues and theological issues; tenets within the tradition I embraced that had limited my full appreciation for the gospel, and the

Spirit's power within it. As a consequence, my questioning took a new form: why had my theological beliefs not alerted me to the problem, and how could I hold the beliefs I did, yet not access the Spirit as I should; in short, where had the power gone, and why? In seeking to answer this, the following chapter will briefly consider two issues. The first relates to insights on culture and context; why contemporary Protestant Christians (those who derive their theological heritage from the sixteenth-century Reformation) can hold so strongly to theoretical doctrines about Christ, yet remain relatively unperturbed by their own complicity with the world and its values. The second relates to the solution, and engages with the first chapter of Romans to discuss Paul's interpretation of the gospel and the powerful role of the Holy Spirit in shaping it. The power may have gone, but this does not mean it cannot be reclaimed!

Disempowered by Culture

Even for those within the Protestant tradition who proudly affirm doctrines built on Pauline theology, there appears to be a weakness with respect to manifesting a powerful and consistent profession of the gospel. I want to suggest that the limited capacity of many Western Protestant Christians to consistently and powerfully express obedience to Christ, in accord with the gospel they profess, may actually lie in an undiscerning appreciation of their own sixteenth-century tradition in its connection with the 'modern' world, and the application of it within this new context. As such, I will briefly reflect on the role of the Protestant movement in influencing Western culture, and how its seminal influence on it may 'now' be acting to immunize contemporary adherents of tradition from identifying the malevolent effects of modern 'worldliness' on their faith; thus, allowing believers to rationally assuage their consciences into believing they are *right with God*, even though they uncritically adopt lifestyles that fundamentally contradict that confession.

The gospel is a life-transforming truth. Yet life-transforming truths threaten those with vested interests in maintaining the status quo. Perhaps that is why many, challenged by Christianity's claims, often cite the mantra: 'A little religion is good, but you can't let it control your life.' Yet for deeply committed Christians, such as Paul, their faith in Christ could never be a peripheral attachment to their otherwise 'worldly' lifestyle. The gospel translates as the all-consuming reality of Jesus Christ and his lordship, with all its radical implications. When Paul wrote the words 'I am not ashamed of the gospel' he knew it would be offensive to Jewish sensibilities, confronting to Gentile wisdom, and potentially controversial on a political level.[1] Being 'not ashamed' of the gospel was not without significant cost. In fact, Paul's catalogue of sufferings and trials, outlined in his second letter to the Corinthians attests to this: 'I have worked much harder, been in prison more frequently, been flogged more severely, and been exposed to death again and again' (2 Cor. 11:23).

But, why did Paul's 'offensive' gospel remain so powerfully effective, whereas many present-day presentations of allegedly 'the same' message seem relatively powerless? Paul's gospel had integrity. It offered more than knowledge about Jesus; it offered a clear challenge to subdue every dimension of the believer's life to the authority of Christ. It was an uncompromising, powerful and holistic message, all-embracing in its extension and application. Paul did not promote an intellectual gospel that allowed an unimpeded pagan lifestyle, tacitly embracing a public adherence to Caesar's lordship – privately recognizing Jesus. Paul's gospel was shaped and empowered by the Spirit, such that its message boldly countered the ethos of the world.

In contrast, many modern Christians allow their 'worldly' lifestyle to impede their confession of the gospel. In mirroring society around them, they deny the gospel's truth and empty their profession of any substantive support![2] It is as Ronald Sider laments, 'What a tragedy for evangelicals to declare proudly that personal conversion and new birth in Christ are at the centre of their faith and then to defy biblical moral standards by living almost as sinfully as their pagan neighbours.'³ But how could such an incongruity go relatively undetected by the contemporary Christian conscience? How could Protestants, who have a strong heritage of boldly standing against the status quo, become so weak? Is there something in the modern world that bewitches them?

Indeed, the influence of the modern 'western' world may be more influential on the Christian consciousness than many realize. Craig Gay believes that the construction of the modern world is so materialistic and 'this-worldly' oriented, that even Christians are deceived into giving excessive attention to the exigencies of 'the here and now': 'Indeed, we are tempted to live as though God did not exist, or at least live as if His existence did not practically matter. In short, one of the most insidious temptations fostered within contemporary secular society and culture, a temptation rendered uniquely plausible by the ideas and assumptions embedded within modern institutional life is the temptation to practical atheism.'⁴

How then is it possible for the Western world to move away from a social construct where disbelief in the divine was virtually impossible at the time of the Reformation? How is it that 500 years later, belief in God, or at least its substantive significance, is seriously questioned?⁵ More importantly, why are those who 'claim' to believe in God so complicit with this new status quo? One answer to this conundrum lies in understanding the modern world and its historical connection with the sixteenth-century Protestant movement.⁶

Charles Taylor in his masterful work *A Secular Age* proposes that Protestant thinking had a significant role to play in the construction of the reality we now encounter as secularity; the phenomenon now eroding that form of Christianity! Taylor argues that within the 'enchanted' world of medieval Catholicism everything was conceived of in terms of the spiritual or the supernatural. The world was controlled by spirits, of which God was the most powerful. In such a context, the very thought of denying God seemed simply implausible, as Taylor indicates, 'In general going against God is not an option in the enchanted world.'⁷ An appreciation of the supernatural was ubiquitous. This was evidenced in Martin Luther's 1505 impassioned plea to St Ann for deliverance in the midst of a violent thunderstorm, as well as in the words of his hymn, 'A mighty fortress': 'and in this world with devils filled'. In the medieval reality, patent differentiation or partitioning between 'my' private inner life and the public external reality was simply inconceivable. After all, where could a person hide from the spirits?

Taylor argues that in the latter Middle Ages the Catholic Church began to emphasize the notion that each person would individually face the judgement of God immediately following their death.[8] This increasing emphasis on personal 'assurance' of salvation provided fertile ground for the binding of the popular religious conscience, which was subsequently capitalized on by the church, being used in the burgeoning indulgence 'trade'. Coupled with sentiments of a rising 'middle' class, seeking an individual destiny, a greater sense of individual spiritual consciousness developed.[9] As such, Taylor posits that within the sixteenth-century context, personal salvation (principally conceptualized as justification) was central to the religious consciousness. Yet, given the means of attaining this salvation had a heavy 'works' orientation, many sensed that this burdensome form of religion was not right.

As a result, Martin Luther's justification 'by faith' powerfully touched a 'raw nerve': 'In raising his standard on this issue, Luther was onto something which could move masses of people, unlike the humanist critique of mass piety, or the rejection of the sacred.'[10] In challenging the Catholic Church's corrupt practices, Luther called into question the church's capacity to wield God's *spiritual power*. Of course other renaissance factors have a role to play, but within the constellation of a sixteenth-century 'spiritual' universe, Luther's challenge fractured this enchanted world-view.[11] Luther, and those like him, had responded to the primary need of their time, yet had unwittingly sown the seeds of a more 'rational' approach to life. This approach placed greater value on the individual 'self', decoupled from the constraints of a sacred order. It was a 'self' free to order things as seems best – albeit, to the glory of God![12]

Once the controlling aspects of this enchanted reality were substantively challenged, the religious consciousness could be decoupled from this all-encompassing spiritual reality. The possibility of an existence free from the influence of a *spiritual realm* controlled by a domineering institutional religion began to emerge. However, the downstream effect would prove damaging, as Peter Berger remarks, 'Here lies the great historical irony in the relation between religion and secularisation, an irony that can be graphically put by saying that, historically speaking, Christianity has become its own gravedigger.'[13] Protestantism played a part in creating the secularizing monster that now challenges the form of its existence in the new secular order!

Of course, the rise of Protestantism wasn't the only 'secularizing' influence, nevertheless it assisted in opening a door that allowed many more nefarious elements to enter; elements that would wield a more destructive power. By the late seventeenth century, the rationalism of Descartes began to make serious inroads, being reified within the eighteenth-century Enlightenment with its many sociopolitical revolutions. Secularizing forces became more ubiquitous in the nineteenth and twentieth centuries, with manifold atheistic influences rapidly gaining traction within Western society – even defining it!

Modern secularization conspires to provide plausibility to the value of the individualized self. Through ideologies such as *economic rationalism* (the rationalization of conduct according to the benefits of economic exigencies), *human therapeutics*[14] (my need to feel good), and *society's division* into the private and public spheres[15] (I am free to act as I please in my sphere e.g. church), it accomplishes its goal. In the medieval enchanted world, meaning, significance, value and truth all existed outside of the individual self and potentially could impact on that self; the 'outside' world could 'not' be quarantined from 'my' internal reality.

In the modern disenchanted world, the *buffered self* (to use Taylor's term) is able to disengage from the reality of the outside world. As Taylor posits, the modern self is able to exclaim: 'My ultimate purposes are those which arise within me, the crucial meanings of things are those defined in my responses to them.'[16] Therefore, it is possible to extrapolate how the individualizing Protestant DNA, now resident within our modern secular world, could numb the malevolent effects of worldliness acting on the modern Protestant Christian conscience. In such a conceptual framework, the gospel is only given permission to become good news for *the interior self*, while simultaneously meeting stiff 'subconscious' resistance if it attempts to express open personal devotion to Christ in the external world. As such, the contemporary 'first world' Protestant consciousness is now caught in a 'catch-22' scenario. It is trapped between adherence to a sixteenth-century theology that it wants to confess, and a gospel-denying 'modern' secular world (birthed by proto-Protestantism) that it is subconsciously inoculated against denying!

Is there a way out of this conundrum? In practice, many adherents divide up their 'worlds', such that they can affirm the theological formulation of the gospel of the Reformation in the private realm and the company of like-minded adherents, while only whispering the gospel in the public domain! Should we then be surprised that the gospel is evacuated of power? Despite the temptation to seek ready-made answers in the past, Craig Gay suggests the way forward is not necessarily back: 'The gravedigger hypothesis suggests that resisting the distinctively modern form of worldliness may require more than a recovery of sixteenth or seventeenth century Protestant spirituality. It may well require reforming certain aspects of the Reformation tradition itself.'[17]

What is required is recapturing the gospel in all its potency, a gospel that is more than informative good 'news' for the individuated 'buffered self', but rather, a gospel of transformative power for all of life: public, private, theoretical, practical etc. Those wanting to face the challenges of the secularized future may find the comfort of the past too tempting. However, embracing past doctrines disengaged from a present context may prove a fool's errand, and there is no guarantee the future will be a rerun of the past. This 'new' reality cannot be countered by simply reviving a socio-theological construct, designed to address the primary concerns of a sixteenth-century Roman Catholic-dominated world. Surely, another approach is required?

Disempowered by Context

Our prior analysis has offered a brief explanation of why many in the Protestant tradition can embrace a view of the gospel that allows 'practical' incongruities to coexist, limiting the 'power' of the gospel, by muting the practical obedience of its adherents. Another element that serves to augment this phenomenon is an uncritical overemphasis of key theological concepts within a new 'secular' context; most notably, overemphasizing the doctrine of personal justification by faith. The 'primary' emphasis of justification by faith in a medieval culture served as a healthy and necessary corrective to the all-prevalent sixteenth-century error of justification by religious works. However, failing to appreciate that original context, and stressing the same doctrine (to the 'same degree') within a twenty-first-century secular culture, actually serves to exacerbate the problem in the popular religious consciousness, identified in the previous section; thus providing a doctrinal legitimation for severing the necessary connection between faith in Christ and obedience to Christ.

Therefore, the Protestant interpretation of the gospel, and its strict connection with personal justification, must be first understood in its own historical context. In a tradition reaching back from before the Reformation to Augustine, the concept of justification incorporated a wider view of the Christian life – that of acquitting the penalty of sin. For Augustine, justification was more than an act or pardon; it was incorporated in a 'new way' of living for the believer.[18] In this view, righteousness of the believer was also viewed as inclusive of an ongoing process, rather than 'exclusively' an instantaneous act.[19] Broadly following in this tradition, Thomas Aquinas took into account the 'ongoing' consequences that pertained to justification. Framed around Aristotelian logic, Thomas' system of justification comprised an instantaneous but ordered event, made up of four separate elements:

the infusion of grace, the free will's movement towards God, the free will's movement toward sin (repentance), and the remission of sin.[20] 'We might say that, for Thomas, justification is an instantaneous event in which, by an act of sheer grace, the sinner is led to turn to God in faith, repent of their sins and receive divine forgiveness.'[21] In this system, the believer is not simply deemed right; they are made right through an infusion of grace (usually initiated at baptism).

For Aquinas, justification is initiated by God's grace, an unmerited gift that ends with final glorification (the end result of justification). It is nevertheless granted as a reward to the righteous that *persevere* through this life; of course, with ecclesial assistance. Aquinas conceptualized the ongoing Christian life as a pilgrimage, where the ungodly are justified at the beginning and the just saved in the end.[22] However, like many theologies, this system struggled to adequately address the issue of ongoing sin (especially the concept of mortal sin). Ordinarily, through the principles of contrition, confession and satisfaction, sin was addressed by the sacrament of penance – administered by the clergy. However, at this very point the system revealed its greatest weakness. Within Aquinas' schema, justification is instantaneous. Remaining in that state of rightness required drawing on the means of Grace in an ongoing sense, i.e. the sacraments.[23]

However, any system that views a perpetual status of justification being wedded to a system of merit-oriented conduct within a religious process has a proclivity for righteousness through works. With the development of the doctrine of purgatory to account for the problem of unconfessed sins, the system of penance – that was originally designed to assist the Christian – failed. It morphed into a complex sacerdotal system ripe for the next level of religious dysfunction, the most obvious being the popular granting and selling of indulgences (eternal pardons). It was against this backdrop that Martin Luther set justification by faith 'alone'.[24]

Martin Luther appeared as a champion for the gospel in his time, and his primary weapon was the doctrine of justification *by faith*. Luther formulated his understanding of the gospel in response to the practices of medieval Catholicism. He countered a system that placed a great stress on salvation by works: 'It is an undeniable, and unobtrusive fact that, whatever was the doctrine of the church at this time, her practice had reduced the economy of individual redemption to an almost purely mechanical process of debit and credit for evil and good works.'[25] Against this culture of personal merit salvation, *justification by faith alone* represented a liberating and comforting truth, as Mark Reasoner suggests, 'The anxiety level regarding human attainment of righteousness would go down.'[26] In fact justification, in such a context, could be deemed such good news that it could be equated with the gospel, as Alan Spence remarks, 'So too, the classical doctrine of justification can only be interpreted right within its own context. It is good news for those who find themselves standing silent in the dock, convicted by divine law, and aware that they stand guilty before God, deserving of His condemning judgment.'[27]

Negatively, the flawed aspects of medieval Catholicism aided Luther's *justification by faith* in gaining acceptance. Positively, the influence of the *via moderna*, a 'new way' of thinking building on the philosophy of nominalism, also gave it traction. Nominalism suggests there is no objective identity in 'things', that is, not in the things 'themselves'; a thing is a thing, a particular is a particular, and an individual human soul is a human soul – not part of a giant cosmic soul, etc. The impact of this ideology had two effects: first, it established the principle that a person is truly an individual, and second, that this individual could engage with God in an unmediated or direct sense: 'Within the framework of God's absolute power, they [the theologians of the *via moderna*] emphasized that God was at liberty to justify man by other means than an infused habit of Grace.'[28]

On the basis of a *covenant or pact* between God and humankind, justification could take place. In employing 'covenant causality', the imputed value of righteousness could be willingly bestowed on the sinner by God, in much the same way a government could *impute* monetary value to coins of greater worth than their intrinsic value. Grace, therefore, could no longer be imparted or infused, it could now be imputed! Indeed, so important was this ideology's influence, that Jane Dempsey Douglas (a Roman Catholic) argues, 'Thus nominalism can be said to have played a preparatory role for the errors of the Reformation.'[29]

By the early sixteenth century, Luther's reflections served to consolidate his grasp of the concept of righteousness, leading to the conclusion: 'That man might become conscious of his need for another, strange righteousness – and thus turn to God in the humility of faith to receive this righteousness, which alone is valid.'[30] However, Alister McGrath observes that, from 1530, Luther's concept of justification, slightly modified by Philip Melanchthon, became enshrined in Reformation thinking, as:

1. A declaration that the Christian is righteous, as opposed to a process by which he is made righteous. It involves a change of status, not nature;
2. A deliberate and systematic distinction between the concept of justification and the concept of sanctification or regeneration; and
3. The formal cause of justification understood to be the alien righteousness of Christ, imputed to man in justification.[31]

Thus, within soteriology, the technical 'hegemony' of justification with respect to the 'individual self' was formally and firmly established. It became the highest and brightest star in the Reformation galaxy. In fact, it is not difficult to see how a sinner, having embraced Christ's righteousness in this manner, could be led to believe that justification was ostensibly 'all' there was to salvation. Moreover, it is also not difficult to see why contemporary Christians in this tradition might interpret the gospel in this same exclusivist manner.

Nevertheless, despite the need to stress justification by faith, the Reformers' 'own' testimony in their 'own' time, was not crippled by a lopsided emphasis of justification by faith at the expense of a commensurate life of conformity with Christ. While the doctrine of justification 'by faith' was the flagship doctrine of the sixteenth-century Reformation, we should not suppose that good *works* were dispensed with, as a commensurate aspect of the Christian life. In fact, Luther does not remove good works from his scheme at all.[32] Well aware of Roman Catholic claims of legal fiction, Luther knew that if good works don't flow from saving faith, then the nature of that faith should be called into question. In this respect, McGrath claims that Luther concurred with Augustine that justification encompasses the beginning, the development and the perfection of the Christian life.[33]

Of course, popularist slogans such as *sola fides* (faith alone) in reference to justification, have given rise to the notion that people like Luther held to this as an 'absolute' or a stand-alone maxim.[34] In fact, Luther has been popularly promoted as 'so emphasizing' justification 'by faith' that a moral life of holy obedience (sanctification) is largely discounted.[35] Yet for Luther, faith was far from an 'abstract' notion, as Walter Lowrie suggests, 'It was not mere assent to a doctrine, devil's faith without love, but involved faithfulness and trust (fiducia).'[36] Justifying faith also must give credence to the believer's ongoing state throughout life. For Luther the believer was *simul iustus et peccator* (justified yet a sinner): 'Therefore we are all born into iniquity, that is, in unrighteousness, and we die in it.'[37] Yes, Luther was a realist regarding sin, but he still positively embraced holiness within the Christian life.

For Luther the justified sinner had a new life: 'For the flesh or the old man must be coupled with the law and Works: the spirit or new man must be joined with the promise of God and his mercy.'[38] Theodor Dieter describes Luther's view on the ongoing moral life in this manner, 'Its starting point is the unrighteousness of the person who is totally a sinner and in no way righteous. The final point is the person who is totally righteous and in no way a sinner, which will happen after death.'[39] Thus, the believer is righteous with reference to his starting point in justification, but a sinner relative to his finishing point in eternity. In this view, the believer is always justified before God, even as they are on the continuum. Faith is 'vindicated' by a state of progress, as Dieter suggests, 'If the motion ends of a person who is righteous, but not without still being a sinner, then this person becomes only a sinner. Being a righteous or justified person is only possible if this person is becoming a righteous or justified person.'[40] Despite the potential to confuse Dieter's wording, Luther is not promoting justification by progress. Properly understood, he could only be interpreted as advocating that the believer's justification is *vindicated* by sanctification – proving its validity, not causing it.

For the German Reformer, active obedience did not cease to be part of his schema: 'This I say to the end that no man should think we reject or forbid good works, as the Papists do most falsely slander us.'[41] Although a tireless champion of justification by faith, Luther never 'practically' *divorced* justification and sanctification: 'It is well known that the new obedience in the justified brings with it daily growth of the heart in the Spirit who sanctifies us.'[42] In fact, he would view the believer who casually ignored sanctification as 'effectively' denying justification. Faith was not merely a rational engagement with God, but a *heartfelt relational devotion* to God, that honours and vindicates God's grace through holy obedience.

Similarly, the Swiss reformer, John Calvin, also viewed justification as the divine acquittal of human guilt against God's just condemnation of sinfulness. Yet for Calvin, justification was only one dimension of God's saving action toward humanity: 'Those whom He enlightens by His wisdom He redeems; whom He redeems He justifies; whom He justifies He sanctifies.'[43] Calvin had an integrated approach, in which (for example) the dual benefits of justification and sanctification in Christ are to be apprehended simultaneously: 'By partaking of Him, we principally receive a double grace; namely, that being reconciled to God through Christ's blamelessness, we may have in heaven instead of a Judge a gracious Father; and secondly, that sanctified by Christ's spirit we may cultivate blamelessness and purity of life.'[44]

Calvin made a clear 'logical' distinction between justification and sanctification (preventing them from becoming logically confounded).[45] But the Christian's justification does have a 'necessary' connection with sanctification, and the former lacks validity without the corresponding aspect of the latter:

> Why then are we justified by faith? Because by faith we grasp Christ's righteousness, which alone reconciles us to God. Yet you could not grasp

this without at the same time grasping sanctification also . . . Therefore Christ justifies no one whom He does not at the same time sanctify . . . us it is clear how true it is that we are justified not without works yet not through works, since in our sharing in Christ, which justifies us, sanctification is just as much included as righteousness.[46]

Ever the theologian of the Holy Spirit, Calvin could confidently assert the necessary connection between justification by faith and the sanctification that produced works of obedience in conformity with Christ: 'Everyone justified will be made holy and do good deeds. Both of them flow out of a union with Christ and logically imply one another. Eternal life is given to those who do good deeds, but the ground of their acceptance with God is the righteousness that is found in Christ, not the deeds which they have done.'[47]

The theologians of this era had every reason to stress justification by faith to the exclusion of a life of obedience, but they did not. They recognized the necessity for a concomitant manifestation of moral obedience, as a means of validating the gospel's testimony, and in this regard, to their credit, they were attempting to be consistent. However, a wholesale transfer and uncritical adoption of their doctrinal 'emphases' into an entirely different context fails to appreciate that the sixteenth century is a very different creature to the twenty-first century. In fact, uncritically reinforcing key emphases, such as an exclusive focus on justification by faith from one context, may actually work against the cause of the gospel in another context!

Simply, convincing ourselves that the doctrinal vessel that withstood the torrents of the sixteenth century will sail on regardless, despite time or circumstance, will not mitigate the severity or magnitude of the threat of the new 'secular' context we now face. In fact, a ubiquitous religious culture of works-righteousness has now been replaced by a ubiquitous social culture devoid of Christian moral imperatives. The mighty dam wall of Christendom and its quantifiable moral context – for which the Reformation vessel was so perfectly designed, and into which it was so effectively launched – has now ruptured. The theology which fortified itself in effectively sailing against the cultural currents of religious works-righteousness – conditioned by this ubiquitous moral culture of medieval Roman Catholicism – now finds itself disempowered and vulnerable to strange new currents; *an ideological and practical deluge from the opposite direction.*

Indeed, emphasizing the 'exclusivity' of justification by faith to the point that it 'equates' with the gospel may well be having the opposite intended effect in a contemporary twenty-first-century context. It may serve to legitimize the previously discussed problem of 'worldliness', granting the comfort to retreat inwardly, when just the opposite is required.

Without question, there is a new threat against which this sixteenth-century vessel is ill-equipped to navigate (and possibly even identify): a ubiquitous secular culture, powerfully augmented by technology, working relentlessly and often unperceivably to draw everyone (Protestant Christians included) into its ever-widening vortex of moral depravity and 'practical' atheism. It represents a challenge of unprecedented proportions.

The Reformation forms of theology were designed to address the problems of the sixteenth century; principally addressing a religion system interpreted as advocating justification before God being augmented by human merit, as the means of human salvation. In countering this, *justification by faith alone* was emphasized and morality (by law) was tenuously attached – though logically separated. Although this system appeared to work within an ostensibly religious / moral context, an engagement with the relatively new phenomenon of modern secularism has revealed the *systemic weakness* with this form of soteriology. A weakness pertains to the 'effective' relationship between faith and obedience within the matrix of salvation. Yet if this key relationship can be correctly reinterpreted, the gospel's power can be 'theoretically' restored; ignored or interpreted wrongly, the twin evils of legalism and licentiousness will perpetually plague Christianity, weakening its testimony. What is of supreme importance at this point, then, is not lamenting the plight we now find ourselves in, but seeking to find a solution to these flaws, and reclaim the gospel's power.

Reclaiming the Power (Romans 1:16)

Reclaiming the power of the gospel begins with asking the right question(s). Many think the right question to begin with might be: 'What is the gospel?' Of course, the ensuing answer usually advances a definition of the term *euangelion* (glad tidings or a message of good news), connecting its meaning to something like a military victory or an escape from a plague etc.[48] All this is valid and true, but referring to 'news that is good' invariably necessitates paying closer attention to the *inferred content* of this particular 'news'. Using texts such as Romans 1:16, attempts are often made to associate adjacent words in the text with the term *euangelion* to ascertain its specific religious meaning. However, determining 'which' words or concepts take precedence vis-à-vis this *inferred content* is less straightforward.

Many popular Protestant formulations selectively associate the gospel with some key terms, while ignoring others. The 'key' term *salvation*, sequentially included in the 'gospel defining' sentence in Romans 1:16, is often passed over in favour of, or morphed into, the concept of righteousness (occurring later in Rom. 1:17). As such, the gospel is defined 'exclusively' with reference to *righteousness*, and this usually in its technical / legal sense – focusing on justification. Commensurate with classical Reformation formulations, previously discussed, these 'gospel' definitions stress the technical and/or rational view of justification by faith, such that any interpreter could be forgiven for thinking that *salvation in its entirety* 'equates' with justification. Indeed, Gerhard Ebeling suggests just this: 'Justification by faith alone . . . constitutes the whole of Christian faith.'[49]

Such narrow expressions usually have a Lutheran provenance, whereas the Reformed interpretations are slightly broader. However, even within Reformed thinking, the saving work of Christ is heavily oriented around the 'historical' events of the cross and its forensic impact, with Paul's emphasis on the 'centrality' of the cross of Christ as it pertains to ethics / living by virtue of 'union with Christ' (Rom. 6) allegedly occupying a lesser place. In some formulations, the gospel definition is often extracted from Paul's early chapters of Romans, as

Greg Gilbert's summation illustrates: 'Through the first four chapters, Paul explains the good news about Jesus in wonderful detail . . . we'll see that Paul structures his presentation of the gospel around a few critical truths, truths that show up again and again in the apostles' preaching of the gospel.'[50]

Of course, this idea gives the impression that the 'real' gospel focuses on justification, while the other elements of salvation (obviously appearing later in Romans) have a 'soft' connection to the gospel: 'Of course Paul goes on to unfold a universe of other promises God has made to those who are saved in Christ, and many of those promises may very appropriately be identified as "part of the good news" of Christianity, the gospel of Jesus Christ.'[51] It seems then, the gospel is *controlled* by the 'righteousness' agenda with a principal focus on the doctrine of forensic justification, with other 'things' included in a less prominent manner. Consequently, the gospel represents the good news of personal justification with subsidiary benefits; acknowledged as 'part' of the gospel – just not an 'essential' part![52]

However, Paul explicitly gives us the definition we seek in Romans. In defining the gospel, Paul wrote, 'I am not ashamed of the gospel because it is the power of God for the salvation of everyone who believes' (Rom. 1:16). The clause 'power of God for . . . salvation', which does represent the over-arching *imputed content* of this 'gospel news', cannot simply be passed over only to be qualified by a narrow forensic interpretation of the subsequent term 'righteousness'. If this occurs the focus of the gospel can and has become exclusively or primarily legal / moral acquittal, and the ongoing life is deemed a 'secondary or ancillary' concern. Subsequently, the doctrine of sanctification (which also pertains to righteousness) is employed to 'mop up' the moral problems along the road to the final experience of salvation.

While not discounting the immense value of the righteous legal standing of the acquitted sinner, I believe such a constricted referencing of the gospel's purpose limits what Paul is trying to communicate – the comprehensiveness of salvation that the gospel grants. Indeed, such a view hinders the Christian's ability to apprehend the gospel truly and live it out consistently, as it often leads to a practical divorce of faith and obedience. Of course, this approach usually emanates out of the *dark resident fear* lurking in the Protestant anti-Catholic subconscious that a doctrine of works will 'creep' back in:

> If Paul's theology of redemption provides the main structure of his thought, and if his redemptive theology finds its centre in 'justification by faith', and if 'justification by faith' means that one must place no reliance on 'works' in the sense of moral performance, then it is hardly surprising that 'ethics' as a subject has been pushed towards the back of the book. The subject is then hidden in a sanitised compartment to stop its dangerous germs of potential 'works-righteousness' from leaking out to infect the main body of doctrine. *This protestant impulse has regularly tended to cut the connecting cables between faith and obedience.*[53]

Ironically, while striving to prevent or avoid a *justification-by-works gospel*, the downside of the formulations that lead to a practical separation of faith and obedience is that they theoretically place ethics outside of soteriology in a way the New Testament does not. This can actually open the door for a kind of doctrinally disconnected *practice of works-righteousness* where the believer can practise religious disciplines as the means of 'staying right' with God. Or, as is mostly the case, produce a religious faith devoid of submission to Christ's lordship, giving permission for Christians to happily affirm a saving faith in Christ, while living in a manner inconsistent with that very affirmation of Christ; providing a doctrinally legitimated correlate to the courage-suppressing influence of Western culture, previously considered. Indeed, this is partially why many Christians remain unperturbed by their inconsistencies; allowing their consciences to be assuaged by rationally comfortable versions of the gospel that are practically impotent.

However, salvation cannot simply be 'equated' with a forensic definition of righteousness that discounts or ignores practical obedience. In fact, Holy Scripture is replete with references to the contrary: Paul does not hesitate to warn the Corinthians their habitual immorality could jeopardize their *salvation*. The writer of Hebrews is continually exhorting his readers to give attention to their devotion to Christ lest they forfeit their *salvation*. James challenges his readers not to presume that an intellectual form of faith will suffice without the accompaniment of tangible works. John challenges Christians that without genuine love toward brothers and sisters, love toward God, and consequently their standing with God, is null and void. Salvation, then, must encompass a wider scope than simply a 'legal declaration' with an addendum of moralized fringe benefits.

Rather, Paul defined the gospel as 'the power of God for . . . salvation'. But what does that mean? The meaning of the term 'the power of God' will become evident throughout the following chapters. Suffice to say that it pertains to God's powerful initiative, execution and application of salvation, in which the Holy Spirit plays a primary part. With respect to the term 'salvation' (*soteria* Gk.), its emphasis is on deliverance pertaining to the lives of believers (not just their souls),[54] of course with an ultimate focus on eternal deliverance. It may have a past emphasis (Rom. 11:11), a present emphasis (2 Cor. 6:2), and future emphases (Rom. 8:10). It also has a twofold orientation; that which we are saved from and that which we are saved to.[55] Given such a broad and flexible scope, it seems very unnatural to align the gospel of salvation with a 'declaration' of righteousness, alone!

The New Testament's affirmation of the active role of the believer in salvation precludes such a narrow alliance, as the following references imply: 'Continue to work out your salvation with fear and trembling' (Phil. 2:12); 'Godly sorrow brings repentance that leads to salvation and leaves no regret, but worldly sorrow brings death' (2 Cor. 7:10); and 'The hour has come for you to wake up from your slumber, because our salvation is nearer now than when we first believed' (Rom. 13:11). For Paul, then, salvation is a broad concept that encompasses human deliverance from sin from the beginning of salvation to the end – predicated on God's powerful initiative.

Furthermore, Paul's contemplation of the assurance of salvation in Romans 8 highlights this broad scope: 'And those he predestined, he also called; those he called, he also justified; those he justified, he also glorified' (Rom. 8:30). While many in the Protestant tradition insist the elements of this *ordo salutis* are 'separate' acts, Richard Gaffin offers another suggestion: 'If our interpretation is correct, Paul views them not as distinct acts but as distinct aspects of a single act.'[56] Paul uses metaphors to explain the various aspects of salvation, viewing salvation (theologically) as a single act. This makes far better sense, as Michael Allen intimates, 'The Bible is not stingy in its description of God's saving work: justification is a glorious part of this jewel, but it is a many splendid beauty that exceeds God's justifying work alone.'[57]

However, for many Christians whose minds seem 'hard-wired' to filter anything deemed 'gospel' or 'salvation' through the fine grid of a technical / rational view of *forensic righteousness by faith alone*, considering the ongoing Christian life as being an 'essential' component of the gospel of salvation simply fails to compute. One substantive difficulty in comprehending ongoing elements of the Christian life, as encapsulated within the scope of the gospel, is the historical relationship of the concept of law to the concept of gospel. The 'legal' context or frame of soteriology in the history of Christian thought is highly significant to this conversation. In fact, this should be manifestly self-evident given that 'justification' (an intrinsically legal concept) is often central to these systems, which necessarily suggests that the controlling paradigm is legally (law) oriented!

Throughout the history of Western Christian thought, the notion of 'law' is viewed in relation to the gospel. Martin Foord, in his helpful study *The 16th Century Protestant Doctrine of the Gospel in Systematic Theology*, highlights the law / gospel connection. In summarizing medieval scholasticism (e.g. Lombard, Bonaventure, Aquinas and Gabriel Biel), Foord observes, 'Despite the complexity of the tradition there was broad agreement. In the works we have examined, the gospel is fundamentally a "New law". The word "New" relates it to salvation history . . . The word "law" shows that the gospel is the entire administration or arrangement of God's people.'[58] Foord further indicates that every question relating to the gospel revolved around a law / gospel relationship.[59] Of course, 'law' can be interpreted in many different ways, from the entire administration of God's engagement with us, to moral commands. While much more can be said, the precise nature of these particular relationships, or indeed the meaning of the terms, is not critical for our discussion here; what is important, however, is simply the fact that gospel is historically defined with reference to law and often seen as a 'new' law.

With the advent of the Lutheran Reformation, this law / gospel relationship came into sharp focus, in fact antithetical. Law (as a legal concept) now began to control the gospel agenda. Of Luther's view, Foord observes, 'Law focused on what we must do in order to be righteous before God, whereas the Gospel focused on what Christ had done in the place of humans in order for them to be righteous before God.'[60] Melanchthon saw that law and gospel actually provided a framework for understanding the 'whole' of Scripture.[61] Calvin viewed law as both antithetical and complementary vis-à-vis the gospel, in different contexts.

As such, in a tradition where the gospel is framed within, against or with reference to 'law', where the concept of 'law' methodologically shapes the gospel, and especially with the Reformation's narrow emphasis, it is not hard to see why *forensic categories* could be necessarily determinate of Christian interpretations of salvation, specifically leading to a narrow focus on justification (in the Protestant case). Furthermore, when the law (moral commandments) is adopted back into these theological systems as an ethical model, it is not difficult to conceptualize why some modern proponents of this legally framed gospel might want to distinguish, even separate, 'gospel' and 'ethics' in a very rigid manner.

Therefore, with the gospel being defined in relation to law, it is too easy for a Protestant to view any deviation from the idea that the gospel equates to *justification by faith* as erroneous. Such a move from a narrow justification-oriented view of the gospel might even be seen as a default position toward law-based righteousness, leading to justification by works! But what if the gospel, as Paul defined it, was not principally structured with reference to law, but rather to the Spirit?

Reclaiming the Spirit (Romans Introduction)

Is there a more adequate way of viewing the gospel, other than through a legal matrix? It is true that Paul needed to engage with the concept of (Mosaic) Law, given many of his converts were Jews; however, I believe it is the Spirit, rather than the Law, that defines the shape of his theology. Prior to his conversion, Paul used to look at his religious life through the lens of the Jewish Law; however, following his Damascus road experience it all changed. Paul viewed himself and his relationship with God, 'in Christ', through the Spirit. In fact, for the apostle, the Spirit is more than a hermeneutical device to assist in the interpretation and (in his case the inspiration) of Holy Scripture. The Spirit of God influences the way he views all reality: his new life in Christ, the world, the church, his ministry and, of course, the gospel. For Paul, the object of focus is no longer 'his' capacity to fulfil all righteousness through the Law; the object of focus is now Christ: 'I have been crucified with Christ and I no longer live, but Christ lives in me' (Gal. 2:20).

Yes, Paul had a Jewish heritage, but through a revelation from the risen Christ realized that his 'old religion' had been superseded. Rather than simply inventing a new way of defining the gospel vis-à-vis Jewish law, he takes time out to completely reconsider the entire orientation of salvation (Gal. 1:17,18). Paul returns from his reflective sojourn with a new model of 'Christian' soteriology; a soteriology so radically different that many of the Jews can scarcely conceive of it. Paul no longer operates on a law / works paradigm (though he is obliged to interact with it given his 'weak' audience), but a Spirit / grace paradigm, which enables an entirely new way of conceiving of salvation, a way previously unthinkable. Such that the goal of salvation is not 'only' the legal acquittal and the assurance it affords, but an all-encompassing deliverance, that rescues those who exist 'in Christ', not only from the penalty of sin, but its ongoing power, and its presence both provisionally and ultimately. The Spirit changes everything![62]

Coming to terms with the Spirit's role in Pauline soteriology enables us to understand a formulation of the gospel that avoids the problems of associating ethics with soteriology, which tend to divorce faith from obedience, or leave an open door for obedience to have a causal role in salvation. In fact, the Achilles heel of most Christian soteriological systems is their incapacity to 'adequately' address the life between initially embracing the good news and entering into eternity. Whether grace is infused (Catholic) or righteousness imputed (Protestant) the beginning point of justification is relatively easy to conceptualize, as is finally entering into glory with God on the grounds of 'being right' with God. This also is not difficult to conceive of, so long as the believer leaves this life in a 'state of grace' or 'right relationship' with God.

But the real difficulty is conceptualizing how the Christian can be assured of the authenticity of their relationship or standing with / before Christ, while simultaneously navigating the moral perils of the Christian life. How do they avoid the rocks of grievous sin on the left, as well as the sands of self-righteousness to the right? Claims of 'works-righteousness' and counter claims of 'legal fiction' surface as theologians wrestle with the issues of, not only *getting right* with God, but *staying right* with God, and thus *ending right* with God. While I doubt that Paul viewed soteriology in quite this 'threefold' way, it nevertheless appears that addressing this general matter is in the forefront of his mind.

In the opening verses of his Romans epistle he introduces the reader to two value-laden terms: The *Spirit of holiness* and the *obedience of faith*. Could these two concepts form two sides of a key that assists the Christian interpreter unlock a correct understanding of Paul's formulation of the 'gospel of salvation'? Could the Holy Spirit, rightly understood, become as Calvin suggested, 'The key that unlocks for us the treasures of the Kingdom of Heaven?'[63]

In a theoretical endeavour as perilous as the practice of Christian living that it aims to assist, the surest approach is to stay within the bounds of Paul's theological marker-buoys – historically situated texts. Paul had a cohesive understanding of 'Christian' theology, which was practically worked out within the contingencies of the pastoral situation, as Ben Witherington suggests, 'We have what may be called theologizing.'[64] I believe Paul's Romans epistle represents a robust 'theological vessel' well suited for this *pneumatological voyage*.

Why Romans? As Peter Stuhlmacher indicates, Romans has been the text of choice for theologians: 'From Origen through Augustine, Luther, and John Wesley down to Karl Barth, the letter to the Romans has made history both in theology and in the church, and that's because of its contents. Those who wish to know Paul's gospel must study Romans.'[65] Romans is so important to the theological endeavour that Stanley Stowers judges it as the seminal theological text: 'More than any other book, Romans has been the forge of the western psyche . . . I cannot imagine the Augustine we know without Romans, through which he interpreted and shaped the experience of his life.'[66]

However, beyond sentimental value, its effectiveness can be measured in other ways. Paul hadn't visited Rome prior to writing.[67] Consequently, he needed to explain himself in a more perspicuous manner, forcing him to present the gospel of salvation in the most unambiguous way possible. In this regard, Mark Given suggests Paul is prompted to 'Put his best foot forward'.[68] Moreover, writing in letter-essay form, the epistle discloses a carefully set-out presentation of the gospel and bears witness to Paul's fuller comprehension of the theological issues he had developed in the wake of prior doctrinal disputes and pastoral deliberations.[69] Paul is also conscious that this letter will be read and reread publicly, and become the primary text for theological reflection and discussion among the various parties; thus he has to be well ordered.

Moreover, I believe the 'way in' to the Pauline text is to begin by gaining a grasp of the historical setting, social context and the nature of the circumstances of his particular letters. Francis Watson convincingly argues that the Romans epistle presupposes a particular social situation that exists within the Roman church, and that understanding the contents of the letter is determined by understanding the letter's function within that social context: 'The contents of Romans cannot be properly understood without an appreciation of the social realities underlying its apparently theoretical discussions.'[70] Watson believes that Romans represents a diverse community involved in the process of self-definition that is in transition between its Jewish past and its Gentile future, and argues that Paul's 'raw' engagement with the Roman Christian community is most explicit in Romans 14–16.[71] What Watson helpfully highlights is the nature of two groups.

Within these chapters Paul engages two groups defined as the 'weak' and the 'strong'. These groups, broadly speaking, correspond with Jewish-oriented Christians and those who have come to terms with Paul's gospel more readily. The 'weak' position involves a reliance on Jewish law and/or culture (on various levels), and the 'strong' position is in line with Paul's own Gentile-oriented theology. Paul, on the basis of prior knowledge, uses this pastoral problem (differences regarding the consumption of meat and wine, and the observance of days, Rom. 14:2,5,21) to assist gaining favour with those less favourably disposed toward him – the 'weak' (Jewish group). This is evident from Romans 14:1 onwards, where Paul exhorts the 'strong' to be considerate of the 'weak', appealing to Christ: 'For I tell you that Christ has become a servant of the Jews on behalf of God's truth, to confirm the promises made to the patriarchs so that the Gentiles may glorify God for his mercy' (Rom. 15:8–9).

Paul identifies himself as one of the 'strong', and seems quite confident that the 'strong' are on his side theologically; however he appears less confident with regard to the 'weak'.[72] Thus, the 'strong' are exhorted to be considerate like Christ and serve the 'Jews', which offers up the twofold purpose of making the 'Jewish' component more comfortable with Paul, while simultaneously presenting a subtle challenge to the 'weak' to be strengthened in their feeble understanding (cf. Rom. 1:11). Although Watson states Paul's principal aim is unity – 'The purpose of Romans is to encourage Jewish and Gentile Christians in Rome, divided over the question of "the law", to set aside their differences and to worship together'[73] and, as pastorally valuable as it is, Paul's purpose also encompasses both wider and deeper dimensions – missional and theological.

Following Paul's various prior disputes and resultant allegations that Paul was promoting a lawless gospel, Paul declares that he is not ashamed of his 'law-free' gospel of salvation (1:16) a gospel that will be technically expanded upon from Romans 1 – 8.[74] Moreover, this same gospel is the 'power' of God for salvation for 'all'. Thus, this unity 'in the gospel' (14 – 16) is aimed at garnering united support for Paul's ongoing Gentile mission:

> May the God of hope fill you with all joy and peace as you trust in him, so that you may overflow with hope by the power of the Holy Spirit . . . I have written you quite boldly on some points, as if to remind you of them again, because of the grace God gave *me to be a minister of Christ Jesus to the Gentiles with the priestly duty of proclaiming the gospel of God*, so that the Gentiles might become an offering acceptable to God, sanctified by the Holy Spirit. Therefore I glory in Christ Jesus in my service to God. I will not venture to speak of anything except what Christ has accomplished through me in leading the Gentiles to obey God by what I have said and done – by the power of signs and miracles, through the power of the Spirit. *So from Jerusalem all the way around to Illyricum, I have fully proclaimed the gospel of Christ. It has always been my ambition to preach the gospel where Christ was not known.*
> (Rom. 15:13–20, emphasis added)

Undergirding Paul's desire to gain support for this wider missionary endeavour are a number of notable references to the Holy Spirit. In verse 15, Paul seeks that they will be filled with hope *on account of the Holy Spirit* and that this hope might 'overflow', it would seem, toward supporting the Gentile mission, which in promoting the gospel offers hope (v. 12). The goal of that mission is that the Holy Spirit might sanctify the Gentiles. It is *through the power of the Spirit* (signs and miracles) that the Gentiles come to 'obey' God. What is evident at the close of the letter is the significance of the Spirit's power in the administration and execution of the gospel toward the *obedience of faith*.

Significantly, these observations enable us to make clearer sense of the opening verses of the letter, where Paul sets his whole theological agenda for the epistle. It is easy to casually skip over Paul's salutations, dismissing them as a mere formal convention. Yet given Paul is a veritable stranger to his Roman audience, and given that the unity of the church, the success of his future mission, and the theological accuracy of the gospel and its practical relevance are 'on the line', Paul carefully and intentionally tailors, weighs and places every word in this powerful treatise. Very mindful of the Jewish-oriented Christians whom he sought to 'strengthen', Paul's opening salutation to the epistle aims to largely appeal to this contingent.

In Romans 1, Paul describes himself as a servant of Christ called and set apart for the gospel of God; a gospel that was pre-announced through the prophets in the Holy Scriptures (Jewish Scriptures). Moreover, this gospel is not simply Paul's invention, but the gospel that God the Father has appointed him to proclaim: a message of salvation, bearing the *authenticating imprimatur of fulfilled Jewish prophecy*. In describing the subject of the gospel, Jesus Christ, Paul appeals to Jewish sensibilities by reinforcing a natural lineage back to King David – Jesus is the Messiah. Significant to his purposes, Paul wants to establish the divinity and authority of Christ on the grounds of his resurrection from the dead, through the agency of the *Spirit of holiness*.[75]

Highlighting the distinct purpose of his calling in verse 5, Paul relates his ministry of gospel proclamation with the goal of the *obedience of faith*. In concluding the salutation, he reminds the Romans that they are called to belong to Jesus Christ, and by necessary extension *called to be holy*. Thus, Paul establishes his own authority by announcing he is an apostle of the gospel; the gospel grounded in a Jewish heritage, centred on Jesus Christ *the Messiah*, who is marked out *in power* by the *Spirit of holiness*. This gospel then, is to be embraced through faith and to evoke an obedience grounded in faith leading to holiness.[76] Paul is making a clear statement, 'My gospel might be law-free, but it is not law-less', hence the reason for his lack of shame in this context! But in the Jewish mindset, how can a law-free gospel not be lawless? How can a believer be obedient to God without the law? The key of course, as previously suggested, is the wedding of the concepts of *Spirit of holiness* and the *obedience of faith*.

But first, what is the *obedience of faith*? This particular construction appears in Romans 1:5 and 16:26 (esv), representing, as some have argued, a structural parenthesis.[77] Furthermore, 'obedience' vocabulary is more prominent in Romans than other New Testament texts (esv: six of twelve NT occurrences); and faith also features most prominently in this epistle (esv: 21 occurrences). More importantly, however, is their relationship within this construction. Douglas Moo believes *obedience of faith* can be taken three ways.[78] First, it can mean obedience that equates to faith, a view supported by Luther, and used by Paul in Colossians 2:7 and 1 Timothy 3:9.[79] The second option, 'the obedience that comes from faith' – or obedience that is the fruit of faith – is appealing. However, this interpretation unhelpfully frames faith as a logically prior 'intellectual act', making for an 'unnatural' connection. In countering this concern, Glenn Davies translates the construction as a 'genitive of origin', and argues that, taken this way, obedience not only 'flows on' from faith, but also 'flows out' of faith – dependent on it.[80] Davies argues this on the grounds that it is supported by textual evidence (positively in Rom. 1:13; 6:18; 15:18; 16:19 and negatively in 9:32; 14:23).[81] The third option, 'obedience which is faith' is embraced by Ernst Kasemann,[82] who argues that faith and obedience are interchangeable, citing Romans 10:16; 15:18; 16:19.[83] However, of these quotes only 10:16 clearly says what Kasemann wants it to say – to obey the gospel is to believe the gospel. Others still, such as Thomas Schreiner, support a combination view.[84]

However, combined with the *Spirit of holiness*, the concept of *obedience of faith* is perhaps most intelligible. To have faith in Christ is to obey the Spirit-initiated call of the gospel, and this Spirit-generated faith is perpetually authenticated through a Spirit-engendered obedience 'in Christ'. The key to obedience is faith, and the key to this faith-oriented obedience is the presence and power of the *Spirit of holiness*. Moreover, we should be aware that the *Spirit of holiness* phrase exists in a specific context. In Romans 1:3–4, we witness two Greek constructions: *kata sarka* and *kata pneuma* (of holiness); the former normally interpreted as referring to Jesus' personal lineage and the latter ordinarily interpreted as attributing divinity to Jesus.[85] However, the contrast between these two Greek constructions is not unprecedented in Paul's theological logic. In Galatians 4:23, *kata sarka* correlates with the birth process of Ishmael, which in Paul's logic corresponds with 'the law'. He then goes on to contrast in Galatians 4:29 the 'inferior' child of the slave woman, *kata sarka*, with the 'superior' child of the free woman, *kata pneuma*. Furthermore, as we shall later see, Romans 8:3–4 makes a similar contrast.

It is entirely conceivable then, in the context of the Romans epistle and within the text of the opening salutation, that the theological contrast previously set forth in Galatians re-emerges. To his Jewish-biased Roman recipients, Paul seeks to establish the *superior agency* of the Spirit over and against the *inferior agency* of the Law, with respect to understanding, believing and obeying the gospel of salvation. Indeed, the relationship of Law and Spirit is critical. Paul's chief theological antitheses are Grace / Law and Spirit / Law. Combined, this is an antithesis between the Mosaic covenant (controlled by law) and the new covenant (controlled by Spirit / grace). It may also be defined as an antithesis between the holistic sovereign initiative of God 'in Christ through the Spirit', over and against the initiative of human nature (flesh) which relies on the Mosaic Law (or any human system of control) to establish and maintain the Christian's standing before God.

When soteriology is 'framed' in terms of the Spirit, the challenge of *faith* and *obedience* as they are related in the gospel are overcome. Viewing the gospel in this way embraces God's grace by faith 'in Christ', through the power of the Spirit, who initiates, sustains and completes Christian salvation. Ethics (the ongoing Christian life) has a Spirit-oriented provenance, and is worked out though a Spirit-enabled 'union' with Christ. The law has been addressed forensically and subsumed ethically 'in Christ' – in the power of the Spirit. The Spirit of holiness, which powerfully raised Jesus from the dead, is the same Spirit of holiness that powerfully animates the Christian life of obedience; a 'new' life in which the believer is bound to Christ through faith. Perhaps Gordon Fee captures the concept best:

> If Christ is both the content and therefore the source of the gospel, offering 'God's righteousness' freely to all who trust him, then the Spirit, in whose sphere the exalted 'Son of God with power' now resides, is not

simply the Holy Spirit, but the Spirit of Holiness itself – the one who effects the 'righteousness of God' in the lives of the believing community, Jew and Gentile together, in terms of their individual and corporate behaviour.[86]

Conclusion

No religious tradition is immune from time and circumstance. We have considered how the Protestant tradition, relatively effective in its original setting, now finds its theological framework challenged by a new and unprecedented secular reality. The two phenomena of culture and context, working in concert, have acted to limit the effectiveness of its 'gospel' testimony within this new 'secular' dominion; allowing many in this tradition to comfortably embrace (often unwittingly) a private / personal faith without seeing the need to validate it through a practical conformity to the character of Christ. At the heart of this problem is an insufficient understanding of the relationship between faith and obedience.

Seeking a solution requires more than a reaffirmation of traditional maxims; it requires the humility to look anew to God, to rediscover the power of the gospel at its source of empowerment – the Holy Spirit. Reclaiming a powerful testimony of the gospel involves rediscovering the gospel in its most potent form, a gospel that doesn't allow for a comfortable 'doctrinally legitimated' divorce of faith and obedience. However, if we choose to see it, the apostle Paul, in his Romans correspondence, already advocates a holistic soteriology; a system of belief that does not allow for the divorce of faith and obedience. This is not a system undergirded by codified religion (law), but a faith animated by the power of the Spirit; who acts to elicit faith in Christ and empower obedience to the same. Indeed, Paul's formulation operates beyond the limits of law theology – it lives and thrives in the realm of the Spirit.

2

Temple and Spirit: Revealing Unrighteousness

We never truly know our moral shortcomings until we confront the holiness of God. Some in the early Roman church believed their Jewish affiliations excluded them from the ranks of 'ordinary sinners'. However, Paul challenges this line of thought by framing his argument with a powerful religious symbol – the temple. In the Jewish consciousness, the temple represents the supreme representation of the meeting place between God and his people, a symbol that vividly expresses the segregation of the holy from the unholy. No symbol is more effective at exposing the moral gulf that exists between the righteous God and unrighteous people. Nothing exercises more leverage in revealing to the Jewish conscience just how far they have fallen short of God's glory. As the first of Paul's strategically placed metaphors in Romans, the temple highlights the depth and extent of human unrighteousness. In supporting this temple imagery, Paul also draws attention to a significant 'temple-related' custom – circumcision. Jews proudly relied on this 'mark' as proof of God's favour. But Paul will argue that a more profound type of circumcision is required – 'heart' circumcision. In the apostle's estimation, the physical ritual serves to illustrate the need of a deeper reality. If human unrighteousness is to be fully understood, the sin issue *must be seen* as a 'heart' issue, and only the searching gaze of the Holy Spirit can reveal this.

Universals, Particulars and Romans

Before we enter into a discussion on the temple imagery and its relationship to the gospel, it is necessary to address some methodological concerns that might assist us in validating the place of metaphor in Paul's gospel presentation. Up until recently, most Christian scholars in the Protestant tradition have subscribed to Melanchthon's interpretation that Romans is best classified as a *compendium of Christian doctrine*.[1] Yet the source of this method extends further back than the sixteenth century. St Augustine's ubiquitous influence brings to the theological endeavour a certain *individualizing influence*; there is a sense that his theology is 'my' quest for the truth. Augustine was schooled in neo-Platonic rationalism, being influenced by a philosophical tradition that placed the material world in a secondary position to ideas – the realm of the soul. At its root, this philosophical view advocated that the realm of ideas imposed their 'forms' on material reality, thus giving meaning to the material 'things' we perceive.[2]

Applied logically to hermeneutics, this translates as a deductive way of thinking that imposes universals onto texts set within the frame of a wider doctrinal category, assigning value and meaning to them. This mode of thought, in providing for the development of a dogmatic system, often does so at the expense of the particular or concrete context. By extension, this method also has the potential to uncritically import universal theological concerns into the text, that the text might not have any interest in – at least in a primary sense. This form of thinking, albeit in an unconscious manner, can (and often does) force the *'theological' concerns* of the interpreter onto the structure of the text's argument; ignoring, overriding or even dismissing important empirical particulars. (This will be highlighted later in a discussion of Augustine's interpretation of Rom. 7.)

As I have intimated, the full impact of this hermeneutical approach came to the fore during the sixteenth-century Protestant Reformation. The concerns of medieval Christians at the turn of the sixteenth century referred to salvation of the soul, and how the 'individual' Christian gains assurance through justification. Martin Luther, in rejecting the speculative theology of medieval scholasticism, took up an approach more in line with the concerns of the personal religious life – his own! As a young monk, Luther wrestled with his conscience as he strove to live a dutiful religious life, attempting to assuage his moral guilt through works. In bringing *his concerns* to Paul's letters (especially Galatians and Romans), he discovered the solution to his problem in the doctrine of justification by faith alone. Luther effectively brought himself to the foot of the cross, empty of human merit and trusting in Christ for the remission of guilt.[3] Luther finds the answer for 'the' (or his) 'universal problem' not in religious 'good works' but in Paul's explication of the gospel, interpreted principally as justification by faith.

Indeed, Luther found, in Paul, certain circumstances that paralleled his own and extracted 'one' of Paul's emphases making it his primary emphasis (which, given his context, is understandable). However, the 'works' that Luther (and many subsequent Reformation interpretations) counter relate chiefly to Roman Catholic religious duties and only broadly parallel the works of Jewish religion that Paul specifically engages; as Watson suggests, 'Reformation derived readings, in contrast, construe all of "works of law" as embodying a universal human error, *overlook the particular focus* of the Pauline polemic.'[4] Bringing the universal problem of human guilt to the interpretation of Paul, Luther discovers in Romans the 'universal' problem of *the legalism of human works*, a false remedy for countering sin. Similarly, he discovers the 'universal' solution – justification individually appropriated by faith. Paul's specifically Jewish concerns are then homogenized into general human concerns. Although not entirely lacking validity, these universal concerns can become so dominant as to ignore, dismiss or override important particulars.

So against this hermeneutical tradition, considering Romans through the framework of metaphor would seem out of step with this 'traditional' systematic reading of Romans. However, given what is now known about the particulars of the Romans' situation, we can no longer assume this universalizing template is the best means of giving an accurate rendering of Paul's presentation of the gospel. In fact,

Peter Stuhlmacher suggests the exegete can 'no longer' understand the importance of Romans without first coming to terms with *the particulars* of the letter.[5]

The hermeneutical 'turn' toward *the particulars* came to the fore when F.C. Baur instigated a 'bottom-up' view of Paul. This approach minimized individualistic or psychological readings, with their accompanying universal concerns, and delved into historical exigencies. It explored how Paul's gospel accounts for the particular concerns of both Jews and Gentiles in light of God's redemptive purposes.[6] W.D. Davies provides an example of this approach. Davies believes that Paul was deeply proud of his Jewish heritage and never ceased to see himself as a Jew.[7] Davies rejects the notion that Paul's 'conversion' could be framed in terms of Christian conversion, at least as evangelicals might interpret it. Davies believes that Paul's Damascus road experience bears the marks of a prophetic 'call': 'It is clear that Paul's experience falls in line with that of the great prophetic figures of Israel's past . . . he was called by God to be an apostle to the Gentiles from his mother's womb.'[8]

This inductive approach to Pauline studies has significantly impacted theological reflection on Romans, opening new possibilities for getting at the truth of Paul's letter. Stanley Stowers argues that Romans should not be read with an a priori assumption that Gentiles translate as Christians, so as to lose the particularity of Paul's argument.[9] Stowers views Paul's audience in the following categories: empirical readers (those who read the letter), encoded explicit readers (those whom the letter manifestly addresses), and the encoded implicit reader (the ideal competent reader for whom the real message is aimed). Stowers suggests, 'Romans tries to clarify the Gentile followers of Christ in relation to the law, Jews, and Judaism and the current place of both Jews and Gentiles and God's plan through Jesus Christ.'[10] The explicit readers consist of Gentiles, with a concern for moral self-mastery through observance of the Jewish law. The encoded implicit reader is the person for whom the message is aimed; possibly someone proposing the Gentile focus on the law.

Alternatively, Francis Watson approaches Romans sociologically. Against homogenizing and universalizing views of law, Watson seeks to discover the social implications of Paul's discussions of Judaism and Law as it concerns to develop the Gentile church in Rome.[11] For Watson, Moses and Christ are not 'symbols' of Law and grace, but concrete figures related to the ideologies of particular communities: those under the Law of Moses, and those under the gospel of Christ.[12] Christianity in Rome now defines itself as a distinctly Christian 'sect' over and against the Jewish 'reform movement' it began as: 'If the reform movement is able to survive the initial conflict with the traditional authority structures, it is likely it will be gradually transformed into a sect.'[13]

Watson argues this social phenomenon has implications for our understanding of Paul's argument: 'The faith/works antithesis is not an antithesis between faith and morality-in-general, but an antithesis between life as a Christian, with its distinctive beliefs and practices, and life as an observant Jew.'[14] For Watson, Pauline theology is socially grounded in concrete circumstances, and cannot be easily abstracted from them: 'There is the closest possible relationship between Paul's theological reflection and the social reality of Pauline congregations separated and distinct from the communities.'[15] Indeed, Watson understands the purpose of Romans is to overcome the suspicion of Paul by those members of the Jewish-oriented Christian reform community.[16] As we can see, this inductive approach, in providing a closer examination of the historical and cultural particulars, adds depth. It moves beyond Reformation assumptions that the Paul of Romans is simply a sinner 'like us' seeking personal justification.

However, must we consider these two hermeneutical models in such a binary manner? Are they mutually exclusive? Should textual interpretation fall, exclusively, in a deductive direction; bringing one's 'universal' concerns to the text in an attempt to discover the truth for 'us'? Or alternately should it fall toward an inductive explication of the socio-historical concerns, which we might then reapply to our current circumstances? I believe those in the Augustinian tradition were not 'deliberately' disrespectful of Paul's actual circumstances (as far as they understood them) in bringing their concerns to the study of Romans. Indeed, modern New Testament scholars who approach Paul inductively do not approach the text from a value-neutral position either, and unwittingly bring their own prejudices and biases to the text, as well.

To be realistic, a *consciously synthetic approach* to understanding the gospel, as presented in Romans, is more hermeneutically honest. In such a case, interpreters of Paul come to the text of Romans with a conscious awareness of their own theological concerns, within their own historical context (which, after all, 'is' the nature of the theological endeavour). However, the same interpreters must keep a keen eye on the particular concerns of Paul's historical, cultural and theological factors. They must grasp the nuances of the first century to make fully informed decisions about meaning. Such a synthetic approach serves the aim of theological interpretation best, recognizing Paul and his own time, and doing justice to the Spirit-guided work of theology in the present-day situation. It is through the grid of this method, chiefly aided by the Spirit's guiding discernment, that I approach Paul's use of the metaphor within the text, and its powerful influence in shaping the meaning of Romans.

The gospel, the centre and the metaphor

The previous discussion regarding *universals* 'necessitates' we discuss the correlative issue of the 'centre' of Paul's theology. Under the *compendium of Christian doctrine* ideology, Paul's approach is characterized as the systematic formulation of *doctrine*. Among many modern Protestants, as if under the spell of some kind of Copernican logic, it has become the accepted norm that one doctrine must be 'central' to his overall schema. For the Protestant Reformers, given the particular nature of their theological concerns, the central focus of Paul was the doctrine of *justification by faith*. Yet with the rising awareness of the socio-historical particulars of the Pauline context, a more religio-practical dimension of Paul has emerged which challenges this 'purely' dogmatic appraisal. With the possibility of a more 'realistic' Paul, other than the guilty individual seeking personal justification, a more complex understanding of the apostle, his audience and their particular concerns has emerged.

For example, a representation has emerged of Paul the 'mystic [spiritual]'.[17] Because of Albert Schweitzer's contributions, this 'mystic' interpretation and its correlate emphasis on the doctrine of 'union with Christ' offered a solid challenge to traditionally held 'centrality' of the Protestant theory of justification by faith.[18] Schweitzer argues that Paul connects liberation from the law with the forgiveness of sins and that this is made possible through the mystical doctrine of 'being-in-Christ'.[19] Forgiveness is not 'directly' accomplished by faith, but by being freed from sin through union with Christ's dying and rising: '[It] takes place in the believer from the moment he goes through the dying and rising again with Christ.'[20]

Schweitzer admits this is hard for the modern mind to grasp: 'We do not easily reconcile ourselves to seeing a quasi-physical process take the place of an inward appropriation.'[21] Paul presents forgiveness as a consequence of the atoning death of Christ and union with the death and resurrection of Christ; out of which the believer emerges 'sinless' in the eyes of God.[22] Forgiveness and freedom from the law are linked in the notion of union with Christ. Righteousness by faith is secondary, as Schweitzer argues, 'The doctrine of righteousness by faith is, therefore, a subsidiary crater, which has formed within the rim of the main crater – the mystical doctrine of redemption through the being-in-Christ.'[23] Schweitzer declares that Paul's use of *righteousness by faith* serves the purpose as a polemic against Judaism. He suggests that those who consider this doctrine as central have found themselves unable to consistently adumbrate Christian ethics.

If nothing else, Schweitzer's contributions made it clear that the 'centre' of Paul's theology and his understanding of the gospel cannot simply be assumed. So, must there be *one concentrated and narrow centre* to Pauline theology? Christiaan Beker rightly intimates that this quest for a doctrinal centre cannot adequately account for the whole of the gospel: 'Today it is more widely recognized that Paul's thought cannot be grasped in terms of a systematic doctrinal core.'[24] Beker doesn't deny a coherent core to Paul's thought but argues for a method that enables an understanding of this *so-called centre* more clearly: 'Paul's centre is not a theoretical proposition that is subsequently applied to sociological contingencies . . . Indeed, the gospel is not a legal structure or a finished product of thought that permits a pyramid of propositional deductions.'[25]

Beker believes that Paul locates the coherency of the gospel in the apocalyptic interpretation of the Christ-event and not 'simply' the event itself. The Christ-event discloses the proleptic triumph of God in history embraced by faith and the power of the Spirit, foreshadowing its manifestation in glory.[26] This centre is viewed as a symbolic structure brought into language (the apocalyptic language of Judaism) by Paul's expression of his experience of Christ. Beker distinguishes between primary and secondary levels of language within this symbolic structure: 'primary' refers to the Christ-event in its meaning for the apocalyptic consummation of history, and 'secondary' represents the contingent application of the *triumph of God* into particular situations. Beker contends that arguments that set doctrines against one another (such as justification against participation) are overcome in such a formulation.[27] However, I believe the 'real' value of Beker's approach is not his apocalyptic interpretation, but how he orientates particular doctrines with reference to the whole.

If there is such a thing as a centre or a principal focus of Paul's theology, it is not the specific doctrines that describe the nature of the relationship with Christ, but I want to contend that it is Jesus Christ himself! To the Philippians, Paul wrote, 'I consider everything a loss compared to the surpassing greatness of knowing Christ Jesus . . . I consider them rubbish, that I may gain Christ and be found in him . . . I want to know Christ and the power of his resurrection . . . becoming like him in his death' (Phil. 3:8–10). As you can see, Paul was captivated by Christ and possessed with a desire to embrace 'him', to know 'him' and to become like 'him'. As such, to embrace Christ cannot be seen as synonymous with embracing 'merely' one doctrine about him; as Beker indicates, embracing 'the centre' does not necessarily imply 'solely' embracing one secondary 'symbol' (e.g. justification) as the sole means of explaining the Christ-event. Paul does not describe knowing Christ through justification or participation or adoption 'exclusively'. Rather, he contingently employs these varying concepts to emphasize the nature of the believer's engagement with Christ; who 'is' the primary focus of saving faith.

These doctrinally loaded 'symbols' approach the same subject of 'knowing Christ' from quite different perspectives. Herman Bavinck promoted a similar multidimensional approach in his reflections on Christ's death: 'The Scriptures continually view the suffering and death of Christ from a different perspective and in each case illumine another aspect of it. Like the person, the work of Christ is so multifaceted that it cannot be captured in a single word nor summarized in a single formula.'[28] Indeed, making provision for such a multifaceted understanding in the theological endeavour allows for so-called competing theologies to coexist, without competing: 'In theology, various "theories" occur side by side, and in the preaching of the church, now one and now another aspect of the work of Christ is in the limelight.'[29] Therefore, a multidimensional framing of Paul's gospel renders arguments about a central or a controlling 'doctrine' redundant.

In light of this, it is my contention that Paul's understanding of the gospel must be considered only with a prior acknowledgement of *Jesus Christ as the principal focus* of his theology, and not simply through one 'central' doctrine or theme that defines his work in relation to humans.

I would contend that Paul employs various 'devices' to describe this primary truth about Jesus from different perspectives. We might say that Christ is a precious 'multifaceted' jewel; the various doctrines, themes or symbols Paul employs represent the facets. They give form to his representations of connecting with, embracing and growing in Christ, and are simply employed to highlight different qualities of that jewel (or our relationship to it). Moreover, these facets should not be set against each other, as if 'only' one should occupy the centre or exclusive focus. Each theologically significant symbol adds a special emphasis within the contingencies of Paul's explication of the gospel. These symbols sequentially come together to form a holistic soteriology, leading the reader into a deeper faith-based devotion to Christ and admiration for his beauty.

Further to this multidimensional understanding of Paul's theology, the actual 'manner' in which those particular 'doctrines' come to us is supremely important. Paul does not favour the use of abstract theoretical propositions, but consistent with his Jewish heritage employs the powerful and effective device of the metaphor to his argument. Metaphors are integral to human communication. In fact, David Williams believes the metaphor lies at the root of all human language, with all written language symbols beginning as a picture: 'It is probably true to say that most of our words started out as figures of speech that we use, and moved from the category of conscious metaphor into the ranks of ordinary words.'[30] If this is true of human language, in general, this is evident in Scripture with its abundant use of word-pictures. While the metaphor might be common to human language, this is a device employed by the Holy Spirit (directly or indirectly within the text of Scripture) to powerfully engage the imaginations of those in need of hearing God's truth, e.g. Agabus binding Paul (Acts 21:11).

But how does the metaphor function? Generally speaking, a metaphor may be described as a figure of speech whereby we speak about one thing in terms of what we understand about another thing – a thing that we are more familiar with.[31] The metaphor is a highly effective aid to the communication and perception of truth. Williams describes it this way, 'It helps us to get a handle on the truth, but does not necessarily furnish an explanation, certainly not a complete explanation of the truth in question.'[32] However, the brilliance of the metaphor is that it does far more than engage the rationalistic mind. The metaphor carries the meaning of the concept by also engaging the imagination, which in turn excites other faculties such as the emotions, thus bringing together a representation to the reader's or listener's mind, such that the truth is not merely reduced to a formula or proposition, but framed in terms of a rich picture which can convey truth in a way that is more readily and powerfully grasped.

For example, Paul, in speaking of breaking down the 'dividing wall of hostility' in Ephesians 2:14, almost certainly was referring to the literal temple wall that marked out a racial and religious divide. For the Gentile, this may have conjured up emotions such as shame, resentment, even sadness; for the Jew the emotions might have been connected with pride, security and privilege. The 'bringing down of the wall' metaphor carries into the discussion between those Jews and Gentiles who have now encountered Christ all the emotions that were involved in the hostility between them in the first place. Because of this emotive connection, the metaphor is able to 'more powerfully' engage the imagination and more effectively convey truth than mere abstract propositions.

Yet, whenever the imagination is spoken of regarding truth claims, there are often strong reservations among the more rationally minded. In theological formulation, people with a rational disposition are often suspicious of the imagination, and withdraw to propositions as the means of apprehending truth. Paul Avis suggests in this regard, 'This is how the majority of Christians today – especially Bible-loving conservative evangelicals – see the scriptures: they tend to view them as a system of factual, descriptive propositions, bearing divine authority, to be taken at face value and as literally as possible.'[33] Avis believes those who interpret Scripture in this manner struggle to accept that the Bible communicates truth in an indirect and oblique manner, often constrained by historical and cultural particulars. For this constituency, placing too much weight on the metaphor in the act of interpretation is to base the endeavour on the 'shifting sands' of human subjectivity.[34]

But Avis argues that Scripture should be viewed quite differently: 'My starting point is that divine revelation is given about all (though certainly not exclusively) in modes that are expressed to the human imagination, rather than any other faculty (such as analytical reason or the moral conscience).'[35] In support of this view, the Scriptures clearly reveal that theological truths are most powerfully, accurately and relevantly communicated in picture-form. This form is designed to use the imagination in the process of analogically conveying the unfamiliar. One has to go no further than the Old Testament prophets or Jesus' use of the parable! Theology can and does operate most effectively within the realm of symbolic analogy.

Rather than viewing the imagination in engagement with metaphor as a pretext for subjective speculation, the metaphor brings to bear on the theological endeavour of a concrete realism – a 'grounded' truth. The temple, the courtroom, the slave market, the family are all 'real' things and the imagination brings those things to bear analogically on the divine truths of God. Metaphor and imagination do far more to ground the truth solidly; they actually do it in a concrete setting, free from dizzy heights of abstract speculation, which incidentally pure rationalism is even more predisposed toward! Indeed, when the pages of the Bible are examined, it becomes clear that biblical faith is largely bolstered by powerful symbols, and these symbols serve to effectively 'gather up' and intensify the truth of the revelation of Jesus Christ, e.g. the 'I am' statements in John's Gospel.[36]

Coming to and having faith in Christ is not simply a rational decision, but a holistic 'spiritual' endeavour that employs all the faculties. 'Faith is the act of the whole person and has as its object a personal god . . . provided we remember this; we may speak of the role of various faculties introducing faith: reason, conscience, and imagination.'[37] Paul's gospel engaged the human believer holistically and expected a holistic response. The metaphor represents one of the powerful tools that Paul employed for communicating an all-embracing gospel, and should be given credence in this capacity. By using metaphors, the apostle engages with the powerful agency of the human imagination, connecting familiar symbols with unfamiliar divine truths, thus providing a way back to a concrete application of the newly grasped truth, within the domain of real life. In communicating the gospel thus, Paul capitalizes on the analogical correspondence between ancient metaphor and contemporary situation, making the gospel relevant and effective.

The gospel is not a philosophical proposition; it is a robust life-transforming truth, and Paul's use of the metaphor powerfully brings this fact to life. The metaphor reaches beyond rational speculation and spiritual enlightenment, to ground understanding practically. However, Paul does not merely conjure up metaphors to communicate truth, but sensibly draws on symbols that are readily available to the Roman Christians in their own cultural context and symbols recognizable to readers cognizant of the Jewish Scriptures. In alluding to and quoting from Holy Scripture in his theological explications, Paul not only appeals to divine authority, but draws on a written tradition saturated with powerful images; as Richard Hays argues, 'He finds in Scripture a rich source of image and metaphor that enables him to declare with power what God is doing in the world in his own time.'[38]

The Temple and the 'Real' Problem (Romans 1:18 – 2:24)

After a prolonged, though quite necessary, methodological introduction, we shall now proceed with Paul's argument based on a latent temple metaphor. In introducing his argument regarding the universality of sin, Paul enters the imagination of his readers at an important intersection of concepts: the intersection between the divine and the human, between Jew and Gentile, between sin and holiness, between law and grace, and between ignominy and glory. For exposing the 'relative' depth of sin, no metaphor has more potency than the temple, with its symbolic capacity to highlight both divine holiness and human sinfulness. The temple concept has relevance to both Gentiles and Jews, but in the Romans context, especially Jews who were over-confident in their religious credentials.

In a similar use of this metaphor in his letter to the Ephesians, Paul frames the gospel and its relational implications with temple imagery, exposing the Gentile plight under the wrath of God. He then goes on to explain that through the gospel, the Gentiles now enter the same privileged position as the Jews. In this case, the gospel not only gives Gentiles access to God, it also breaks down the prejudicial and segregating 'dividing wall' of hostility between Jew and Gentile. Together now, these forgiven sinners have access to God's presence through the Spirit (v. 18). With all prior privileges and limitations abolished 'in

Christ', Jew and Gentile come together forming a metaphorical 'new temple' of God's presence, manifested as the church: 'And in him you too are being built together to become a dwelling in which God lives by his Spirit' (Eph. 2:19–22). In the Ephesians account, the temple metaphor serves the Gentile-oriented perspective, but in Romans the same concept, though more subtly alluded to, serves to develop an appreciation of the depth of the human plight from a Jewish-oriented perspective.

While not immediately obvious, the temple concept is quite significant to Paul. Paula Fredrickson identifies the temple as a prominent theme in Paul's letters: 'The Temple remains absolutely central, driving all of Paul's messy metaphors for Jesus' death as a sacrifice. No less importantly, it also supplies the chief terms by which Paul conceptualises the incorporation of his pagans – Christ into Israel's redemption.'[39] However, most Protestant readers are so conditioned to read Romans through a forensic (legal) lens that other equally important metaphors and images are often lost to their perception. Of course, the connection between the legal metaphor and justification and reconciliation in Romans 3 – 5 may appear quite obvious to them. This is so, because Reformation thinking has geared the interpreter's mind to mesh with these legal concepts. As such, in viewing the gospel through a forensic lens, there is a natural tendency to look only for the metaphorical markers (legal language, etc.).

Yet for those conditioned by this tradition, the temple metaphor in Romans 1 – 2 is not so immediately obvious; simply because they aren't looking for its 'markers'. However, once we understand the markers, this metaphor becomes much more obvious to the interpreter. The key markers for identifying the temple metaphor are: the glory / creation theme, and the Jew / Gentile distinction.

Creation and glory are temple-related ideas. In Romans 1:18 Paul stresses that God's wrath against sinful humanity is obvious because the divine order of things, in which the created order 'should' direct glory to God, has been inverted. God's invisible qualities (eternal power and divine nature) have been clearly seen through what has 'been made' (Rom. 1:20), which should naturally result in humanity's worship of God – his glorification. But it does not. Within the 'temple of creation' the distorted sinful heart no longer seeks the glory of God. Rather it has exchanged God's glory for the worship of material images – embracing idolatry (Rom. 1:21–5). John Walton argues that the creation narrative of Genesis 1 implies that God establishes the earth as his temple; a space where humanity and the created order bring him glory. He suggests that the design of the Jewish temple reflects this: the outer courtyard representing the cosmic spheres beyond the earth, the antechamber holding the representations of light (menorah) and food (bread of the presence). Moreover, the veil represents the separation of the heavens and the earth, dividing God's dwelling place from the abode of humanity.[40] The temple reminds fallen humanity that sin has hindered worship.

In Romans 1 the themes of creation, worship and glory are integrated. In Romans 1:19–23 Paul reveals how the created order, designed to instigate divine worship, itself became the object of worship, subverting God's glory. In the Old Testament we see a pre-emptive justification for this. In Psalms the themes of creation, worship and glory come together: 'Praise be to his glorious name for ever; may the whole earth be filled with his glory' (Ps. 72:19), and again 'Be exalted, O God, above the heavens, and let your glory be over all the earth' (Ps. 108:5). Furthermore, the glory of the Lord is judged to fill the temple; the one place in this fallen world where the Jews worship God: 'The glory of the Lord entered the temple through the gate facing east. Then the Spirit lifted me up and brought me into the inner court, and the glory of the Lord filled the temple' (Ezek. 43:4–5). The temple becomes a microcosm of the created order, as it should have been, a space where humanity worships and glorifies God.[41] It is notable, that in the new heavens and earth, the temple is entirely absent. God is the temple, and in the 'new' creation where God intimately dwells with his people, the light provided by the created elements of sun and moon is replaced by God's glory (Rev. 21:22–3). The language of glory, creation, and worship signal that we are dealing with a temple-oriented metaphor.

The other key temple 'marker' is the Jew / Gentile distinction. This is more obvious in Ephesians 2; however the division between Gentile sinners and privileged Jews is also in focus in Romans 1:18 – 2:29, particularly the Jewish attitude toward it. As Paul writes these opening chapters, it is not difficult to imagine him reflecting on the events recorded in Acts 21:25–30. Visiting the temple, Paul finds himself amid a conflict centring on the acceptance of Gentiles, being accused of (among other things) teaching against 'this place' [the temple]. At the heart of this dissention, Paul has brought Gentiles into the temple area and defiled the holy place (v. 28). However, Paul was clearly making a statement that Gentiles were now acceptable to God 'in Christ', yet the Jews, zealous for their law and traditions, strongly resisted. Although Paul gave a defence of this event in Acts 24:12,18, 25:8 before Felix and Festus, it was simply a legal defence. Now in Romans 1 – 2, Paul has a chance to make a defence on behalf of the Gentile sinners, through his Jewish-biased interlocutor (Rom. 2:1). Both Jew and Gentile are on equal terms before God – equally unrighteous!

Of course Jew / Gentile relations had to be treated tenderly by Paul, as he engages his diverse Roman audience. Paul's prior conflict within the Galatian churches had taken its toll on his reputation.[42] Paul knew the Romans were aware of his interaction with the Galatians by means of transiting visitors from Ephesus and Corinth.[43] Consequently, Paul's approach to the Jew / Gentile relationship had to be diplomatically presented to avoid misunderstanding and potential rejection of his message.

This is especially true since the Roman church probably emerged out of the Jewish communities. It was by ad 49 that internal issues in the Jewish communities led to a wholesale expulsion of the Jews from the Rome – among who were Priscilla and Aquila (Acts 18:2). The Roman commentator Suetonius noted, '[Claudius] expelled from Rome Jews who were constantly making disturbances at the instigation of Chrestus [commonly held to be a reference to Christ].'[44] Now, Tacitus' record of Nero's persecution makes no mention at all of the Christians being a Jewish sect, indicating the Christians had established an independent identity from the Jews.

When Paul wrote to the Romans, around ad 57, he was writing to predominately Gentile churches,[45] which had more than likely broken away from the (now defunct) Jewish communities around eight years earlier. However, Thomas Tobin believes it was a widely accepted fact that the Jewish laws and customs were held in high esteem within the collective Roman (Gentile) mind.[46] Therefore, given the 'positive' acceptance of *Jewish laws and ethics* by the wider Gentile population – coupled with the lack of personal influence from Paul – it was most likely that the largely Gentile church approved and practised the Jewish law-ethic, while some within (the weak) were relying heavily on 'the law' to give them an understanding of religious life and definable moral boundaries.[47]

In light of this, Paul's concern for the Romans was that they understand the 'whole' truth of the gospel clearly. He desires they understand the faith that rectifies one before God compels obedience; not an obedience that 'relies' on the Jewish law, but an obedience that 'trusts' in Christ and God's *new way* of the Spirit; to work itself out in ethical conformity to God's will – the 'obedience of faith'. In all this, Paul has the rather difficult task of challenging deeply held Jewish beliefs while not offending their immature (weak) religious sensibilities. He boldly wants to make a shameless statement of his gospel, while gently challenging those with Jewish loyalties to see things his way: 'I am not ashamed of the gospel, because it is the power of God for the salvation of everyone who believes: first for the Jew, then for the Gentile' (Rom. 1:16).

In engaging with the problem of unrighteousness, Paul considers the 'sins' of Gentiles and Jews separately. The temple metaphor perfectly fits this approach. First he deals with those in the metaphorical 'outer court', the Gentile sinners. It is worth noting, while the context largely suggests that Gentiles are in view in Romans 1:18–32, although Gentiles are not specifically mentioned: 'The wrath of God is being revealed from heaven against all the godlessness and wickedness *of men* who suppress the truth by their wickedness' (Rom. 1:18, emphasis added). Paul mentions the wickedness of people. William Campbell believes there is a general agreement that Paul describes the typical sins of the Gentiles as seen from a Jewish perspective. He represents how Jews would think of and describe Gentile sinners (Gal. 2.14).[48] Besides this, Paul is also setting a rhetorical trap for his Jewish-oriented interlocutor, as revealed in Romans 2:1; the one who thinks his religious privilege places him above Gentiles.[49]

The apostle wants to make it patently clear that all people, including the Gentiles, are hopelessly lost and in desperate need of the salvation offered in the gospel. We have already touched on the noetic effects of sin, and from Romans 1:19–22 see how the pagan mind became futile in its thinking and suppressed the truth presented to it. However, the problem the gospel seeks to address is not merely mental lack; it is a moral problem that denies God his glory, and denigrates their own human status: 'Paul does not say here that human beings fail to know God because they are intellectually unfit or because they fail to reason properly. Rather, they fail to respond fittingly to the God they know.'[50]

Sin is like a cancer, and the moral contamination migrates from the darkened mind to an even darker lifestyle; a lifestyle that dishonours God. The first practical step toward moral depravity is to abandon the true God and create substitute gods; gods that can be used to fulfil selfish human desires and ambitions (Rom. 1:25). In abandoning knowledge of the true God, and by extension true worship, God delivers these heathens over to the results of their abandonment: exponentially quickening moral depravity, most clearly manifest as malevolent sexual conduct. Such moral deviation would have evoked in the Jewish consciousness visions of Sodom and Gomorrah – the supreme historical representation of human depravity.

Paul catalogues, not just the depth of pagan depravity, but now also its breadth: 'They are full of envy, murder, strife, deceit and malice. They are gossips, slanderers, God-haters, insolent, arrogant and boastful; they invent ways of doing evil; they disobey their parents; they are senseless, faithless, heartless, ruthless' (Rom. 1:29–31). The manifestation of these sins makes it clear (at least to the Jewish consciousness) that God's wrath (as with the city of Sodom) is clearly hanging over these Gentile sinners.

Yet, for all this, it is not the Gentile sinners that Paul 'really' has in his sights here. Brendan Byrne argues that Paul is trying to beguile the interlocutor with conventional Jewish anti-Gentile polemic, to get the implicit reader to sit back and proudly boast, 'That's the Gentile world we all know.'[51] Yes, the Gentiles are sinners; yes, the wrath of God hangs over them; and yes, this is obvious! But as Byrne observes, there is more to it: 'The principal target from the start is the Jewish [oriented] audience, seen as sitting in habitual judgment upon the behaviour of the surrounding Gentile world.'[52] Obviously, the Gentiles in the metaphorical 'outer court' of the temple are defiled, under the wrath of God and weighed down with immovable sinful burdens. But what of the Jews (or those who call themselves Jews) in the temple's 'inner court', with their privileges of election, covenant and law; will they escape the divine indictment?

Paul makes the allusion that the temple's 'inner court' is no place to hide from God's wrath, as he now engages those who would find comfort in Judaism and the alleged benefits it brings. Paul's argument runs like this: You, who are confident with the Jewish system and look down on the Gentiles across the 'dividing wall'; have a careful look at yourself (2:1)! You imagine yourself to be privileged, elected, called, circumcised and knowledgeable in the law; don't get too smug, because that same law will condemn you! Yes, God's standard of judgement against the Gentiles exposes their sin and reveals they are under wrath, but are 'you', Jew, any better (2:3)? God's wrath might be quite obvious concerning Gentile behaviour, but your sophisticated religious practices with their secret sins are known to God. Indeed in ignoring these sins, you are storing up the wrath of God for the last day – when each person Jew or Gentile will be seen for what they are (2:5–6).

God values good works, but only authentic good works that emanate of a genuine faith, not mere superficial religion (2:7,13). Those who are self-seeking (no matter who they are) will receive wrath, and the privileged religious person will be judged more harshly in this regard. Let it be known that God shows no favouritism, even to those in the 'inner court' (2:11). In fact, a Gentile who follows his innate moral compass will be in a better position than a self-righteous Jew who tries to keep the Law. Now, if you *call yourself* a Jew (2:17) who promotes the law, do you break it (2:17–20)? For example, you publicly detest idolatry and pagan temples, but do you rob God of his glory in his 'temple' by focusing on your own righteousness, instead of humbly walking by faith and sincerely worshipping him (2:22)? The fact is, your religion dishonours God, even while you blindly pursue it in the name of God (2:24)!

The notion that the 'you' or 'mere human' that Paul directs his admonition toward in Romans 2:1 is commonly understood as a [imaginary] Jew and should not be taken for granted. This is no self-righteous Pharisee, resolute in the ways of human tradition. But, as our previous discussion has outlined, this interlocutor is most probably a naive Gentile or ex-Jew allied with the 'weak' camp, with a strong predisposition to rely on Jewish law-based morality. Frank Matera believes this person is confident with their Jewish religion and ethics, which appears superior to any other ethical 'system'. However, they are now confronted by Paul's sobering challenge that it is not simply possessing the law that matters, but its careful observance.[53] For Paul, the 'just' will live out their salvation by faith; faith that is manifested in genuine Spirit-formed obedience. In pointing out the superficial obedience of his implied reader, Paul is seeking to show that even the most pious Jewish person, who thinks that their Jewish privileges will be enough to secure favour with God, is sorely mistaken. Works of the Jewish law do not hide deep-seated human unrighteousness, and they cannot amend it either.

Therefore, when considered with reference to the temple concept, a more nuanced assessment of the unrighteousness problem emerges. The *real* problem is not simply a generic issue that *all* people are sinners who need their souls saved! Human unrighteousness is exposed as being so deep that no one can claim to be excluded from the divine indictment against it. Those smug in their orthodox beliefs (in this case Jewish beliefs), who believe their doctrinal privileges – election, the law and their covenant status – will grant them an advantage with God, should not assume their perceived benefits will enable them to transcend the divine indictment against 'all' humanity (Rom 1:18–32). The fact is, even those who have access to the *inner court* are still out! Although looking back at the Gentile 'sinners' with a sense of superiority, they might assume confidence in the Jewish religion, looking forward to God's perfect presence in the holy of holies and the perfection needed for entry, the true state of these self-confident and self-righteous sinners is exposed; they are guilty – all are guilty before a holy God. For Paul, then, employing a temple metaphor represented an indirect and non-confrontational way of engaging this diverse group, allowing them to draw their own conclusions as they came under the Spirit's conviction about their personal moral status before God.

The Spirit, Sin and the 'Heart' of the Gospel (Romans 2:25–9)

Bringing into sharp relief the holiness of God and the sinfulness of humanity, the image of temple serves as a stark reminder that religion and religious works cannot be presumed upon to gain favour with God. But surely the 'true' Jew who has received 'the sign' of divine ownership could be in a more advantageous position? Surely only the uninitiated Gentile would be excluded? Is that not written in the Scriptures? 'Any uncircumcised male, who has not been circumcised in the flesh, will be cut off from his people; he has broken my covenant' (Gen. 17:14). For the devout Jew, this distinguishing sign of covenant membership represented the tangible mark of membership, as Hans-Christoph Hahn indicates, 'Circumcision is the sign that Israel belongs to the covenant with God . . . It is a guarantee of the blessing promised in the covenant.'[54]

This was such a powerful symbol within the Jewish psyche, that apostasy of a Jew was related as having the foreskin surgically sewn back on.[55] This symbol effectively represented a belief that membership was permanent – 'once and for all'. However, such a belief was intrinsically predicated on the understanding that its recipients would manifest covenant obedience: 'For both Jew and Jewish-Christian it was axiomatic that acceptance of circumcision involves the obligation to keep the law.'[56] No doubt, a percentage of Paul's readers had thought they had faithfully accomplished this. Nevertheless, having already attacked the credibility of the implicit audience; those who 'brag about the law' (Rom. 12:23), Paul seeks to further undermine their religious pride, by tearing down their confidence in one of the 'temple-related' foundational pillars of Judaism – circumcision.

The Jew might boast in this most sacred of symbols, but Paul has a challenge for those who are confident in the value of their circumcision: 'Circumcision has value if you observe the law, but if you break the law, you have become as though you had not been circumcised' (Rom. 2:25). Circumcision is not independent of the law, and cannot be appealed to in the vain hope that moral misdemeanours might be overlooked. On the contrary, circumcision commits the Jew to the obligation of a life of keeping the law. Even from an old covenant perspective, law-keeping is not simply a matter of superficial observance (Deut. 10:16; 30:6; Jer. 4:4). God calls his people to prove their covenant membership through obedience, an obedience that comes from the 'secret places' of the heart.

Yet, Paul is doing more here than reiterating that which has already been stated in the Old Testament. He is now setting circumcision and its law-keeping correlative of moral rule-keeping aside, in favour of something 'entirely' new. Thus, having already called into question their law-keeping credentials, and linking the value of circumcision with these credentials, he now destroys their confidence in circumcision as well. In so doing, Paul has now reduced the boastful Jewish sympathizer to the level of the previously outlined Gentile 'sinner'.[57] In taking this bold step, the apostle is not just destroying Jewish religious confidence in the previous law-based administration; he is actually setting up a scenario that calls for a 'new way' of being allied to God; a new way of finding confidence to enter and remain within God's favoured presence – beyond the law.

In setting forth this 'new way', Paul establishes a base-line that *righteousness* (initial or ongoing) does not and cannot come from religious allegiance to the Mosaic Law: 'If those who are not circumcised keep the law's requirements, will they not be regarded as though they were circumcised? The one who is not circumcised physically and yet obeys the law will condemn you who, even though you have the written code and circumcision, are a law-breaker' (Rom. 2:26–7). Hypothetically then, if a Gentile kept the law he would surpass the Jew who did not and, since Paul has already argued that the Jews don't 'really' keep the law, this potentially places them behind the Gentiles.

However, we should not be too quick to assume that Paul is proposing the possibility that Gentiles could *actually* keep the requirements of the law. Rather, he is establishing that the righteousness that God requires transcends religious privilege, which is a matter of something more substantial than human striving. Having broken down the metaphorical 'dividing wall' and placed the Gentile sinner and the privileged Jew in the same moral position, in the 'outer court' of the temple, Paul settles the issue lying in the forefront of the mind of his interlocutor (the representative of his implicit audience), laying aside all doubt that the insurmountable human problem is inexcusable unrighteousness. This now opens the way to discuss the manner in which righteousness might be gained.

If the Gentiles have futile minds and wayward morals, and self-righteous Jews are lacking an authentic awareness of their moral inadequacy, then only the power of God can expose their sin. Only the Spirit can expose the futility of the Gentiles and the pride of the Jews, breaking down any 'dividing wall' that distinguishes and divides their 'alleged' moral differences. At bottom they are all humans with sinful hearts. Therefore, ultimately, the heart of the problem is the problem of the 'heart'. Only the secret work of God can address this issue, only an inward work of the Spirit can truly expose this insurmountable obstacle to a restored fellowship with God. Indeed, the solution must 'only' lie beyond the Law as Paul indicates, 'A man is not a Jew if he is only one outwardly, nor is circumcision merely outward and physical. No, a man is a Jew if he is one inwardly; and circumcision is circumcision of the heart, by the Spirit, not by the written code' (Rom. 2:28–9a).

The 'true Jew', or more precisely the person who finds favour in the eyes of God, does not find this favour by virtue of manifest religious actions or symbols: law-keeping or circumcision. Circumcision (namely membership among God's chosen covenant people) is on the grounds of something else now – a transforming action on the human heart under the divine agency of the Spirit. Outward or manifested *religious symbols* under the 'new' administration have no value, as Paul notes elsewhere: 'Neither circumcision nor uncircumcision means anything; what counts is a new creation' (Gal. 6:15), and also he writes, 'For it is we who are the circumcision, we who worship by the Spirit of God, who glory in Christ Jesus, and who put no confidence in the flesh' (Phil. 3:3). The true Jew or favoured one of God enters into and remains in God's fellowship by virtue of God's supernatural action through the Spirit.

As he concludes his argument at the end of Romans 2, Paul is thinking about something more than an authentic internalization of the law by virtue of Spirit. In fact, as we have already seen, this notion has a clear precedent in the Old Testament, within the orbit of the Law.[58] John Calvin has interpreted Paul's statement in Romans 2:28 along the lines alluded to in the Old Testament, and not fully appreciated the 'newness' of Paul's understanding of the Spirit's work in the gospel: 'And the reason for this mode of speaking is this – where the voice of God sounds, all that he commands, except it be received by men's insincerity of heart, will remain in the letter, that is, in the dead writing; but when it penetrates into the heart, it is in a manner transformed into spirit.'[59] For Calvin, the outward rite without piety represents the 'letter', whereas the spiritual design of the rite equates to the 'spirit'. It is not difficult to see how Calvin could arrive at this position, given his understanding of the Old Testament concept and indeed Paul's 'positive' appraisal of the law with respect to the Gentiles in verse 26.

While it might be true to say that the Spirit plays a prominent role in ongoing Christian morality, it is not simply by means of augmenting the literal law commands. In fact, Paul wants to firmly establish that righteousness cannot in any way be derivative of human merit, either in an initial or ongoing sense. This role belongs to the initiative of the Holy Spirit. On this matter, Thomas Schreiner's assessment that Paul is considering the letter / spirit antithesis in terms of God's actions within distinct epochs of salvation's history makes good sense: 'The grammar does not refer to a particular way of interpreting Scripture. Instead, the contrast between the letter and spirit is a salvation and historical one.'[60]

Further to this, David Lincicum suggests that the simple 'inward / outward' duality with which Paul describes the true Jew obscures the apocalyptic background of these terms with their roots in Deuteronomy 29:28, which is only six verses prior to the Deuteronomy 30:6 passage on 'heart circumcision', and believes Paul is drawing from these sources. Lincicum argues that Paul does have a language for 'inwardness', but the allusion in Romans 2:29 is more toward 'hiddenness'. This means for Paul the inner reality of heart circumcision as an instantiation of eschatologically 'hidden' mysteries that God reveals in his time – salvation history time!

Thus Lincicum concludes, 'Paul, therefore, fuses Deuteronomy's "circumcision of the heart" with other prophetic visions . . . and interprets this to have come about now for uncircumcised Gentiles as well as the Jews – a new state of affairs that was previously hidden but has now come about through the revelatory action of God in Christ.'[61] Paul's references to heart circumcision and the Spirit argue for the Spirit's agency within a new epoch where eschatological promises have been fulfilled, and a new modus operandi has come into being.[62]

We might then say that Paul's language here is the language of transfer and fulfilment, as Brendan Byrne elucidates; 'Paul sees in the transfer from the field of *letter* to that of *spirit* the fulfilment of the biblical pledge to renew Israel and, with more immediate reference to the present context, the eschatological re-definition of the "real Jew" and "true circumcision".'[63]

Therefore, Paul's new covenant soteriology transcends old covenant religion. It does not embrace spiritualized law-keeping, as if the law in its old covenant manifestation had some 'literal' continuing power. Paul, in encapsulating his argument within a latent temple metaphor, has highlighted the fact that no matter who seeks to be right with God – Jew or Gentile, pagan or privileged – everyone stands on the 'outer court'. All the privileges of Judaism and the stringent and diligent execution of them (whether they are outward symbols or moral laws) count for nothing in God's *new economy of the Spirit*. God desires to create for himself a new 'people of God' who will stand in his presence and walk in his ways, not on the basis of the 'letter' but in the mode of the Spirit.

For the implicit reader, who places confidence in the Jewish law as the means of establishing or sustaining their relationship with God, Paul has comprehensively stripped away all the confidence, and left them without an excuse. The apostle has now established a firm 'baseline': law has no effective relationship to the establishment or maintenance of a right standing with God. In fact, his argument suggests that righteousness comes only through faith 'in Christ', through the Spirit, as Gordon Fee observes, 'One is no longer a part of the people of God by adhering to the boundary markers of Jewishness; one is part of the people of God on the basis of Christ and the Spirit alone.'[64]

In Paul's world, the Jewish-oriented believer was tempted to find their approval by outward signs, and observance of laws. But, according to God's *new economy of the Spirit*, acceptance and approval with God is not on the grounds of these distinguishing marks. Rather it is on the basis of the unseen, a sign of approval secretly imprinted on the human by the Holy Spirit's powerful working. The Spirit initiates and enables 'in Christ' that which the law desires to fulfil but is unable to achieve – the approval of God. The removal of the value of the tangible, in this instance, reveals the approval of God by other means; human merit can lay no claim to the administration of God's grace in Christ through the Spirit. But how does it lay hold of the benefits of this heart circumcision? It is not enough to highlight the problem, for the problem invites a solution foreshadowing an answer, suggesting that another facet of Paul's salvation message needs to be investigated.

Conclusion

In this chapter, we acknowledged that Paul's *principal focus* in the gospel is Jesus Christ *simpliciter*; and not merely one aspect of his work, dogmatically defined. How Paul expanded on the primary value of Christ in the gospel was determined by various perspectives on the gospel's truth, set forth via relevant metaphors – in the case of Romans 1 – 2, the temple metaphor. For Paul, the temple represents a powerful image that the Jewish-oriented imagination simply could not ignore, and a potent symbol from which their religiously oriented conscience could not escape. Although a religiously confident Jew might find some comfort in religious privilege, as they consider their own position relative to God's holiness they are clearly reminded just how far they fall short of God's glory. The temple sets sin and the unwitting sinner squarely in their place. Moreover, Paul also expands on the temple metaphor by drawing his readers' attention to the temple-related symbol of circumcision. In appealing to this 'most sacred' symbol of Jewish privilege, pointing out its inadequacy if the law is violated in the smallest way, Paul not only emphasizes the futility of human works, but also stresses that God is looking for a deeper mark of membership – a circumcised heart. Invariably, gaining favour with God requires more than embracing religious rituals; it demands the inner faith-producing work of the Spirit to elicit a genuine heart transformation.

3

Law Court and Spirit: Acquitting Sin's Penalty

If one is to be just, right or holy before God, an encounter with law cannot be avoided. In Paul's explication of divine rectification, no metaphor more forcefully carries the argument of acquitting sin's penalty to his legally oriented audience than the law court, and no symbol is better suited to explaining his pivotal legal concepts of justification and reconciliation. To the modern mind, 'legal' has an impersonal tone, but for Paul, God's rectifying work encompasses more than a remote legal pronouncement of sin's acquittal; it also embraces a concomitant erasing and cleansing of existential guilt. Christ's rectifying work is personal, and therefore engages 'real' people, reconciling them to a 'real' God, and must address 'real' guilt. Through the Spirit's endowment of faith and the believer's receiving Christ on the grounds of this same faith, the 'legal' conditions for justification are met; correspondingly, this same Spirit-endowment removes the existential burden of guilt. We might then say, on the grounds of the gospel, whosoever enters this metaphorical courtroom under the legal condemnation of the law is also able to leave that same courtroom fully exonerated through Christ's complete Spirit-applied work, having secured a new *status of being*. Moreover, in granting Christ's benefits to the penitent sinner, the Holy Spirit simultaneously endows the forgiven sinner with the peace of reconciliation, establishing a new *state of being*.

Courtroom and Condemnation (Romans 3:1–20)

As a practical theologian, Paul did not develop his soteriology as one 'coolly' detached from tangible realities of everyday life. C.J. Den Heyer suggests the 'stock and trade' of Paul's theological approach extended beyond the propositional: 'His letters inspired and irritated people because he did not argue in the abstract but contextually. His thought had a practical bent.'[1] For Paul, the metaphor is a far more realistic and powerful tool than pure reason, for it grasps his readers' hearts, souls and minds in disclosing his gospel of salvation. In this regard, no metaphor more powerfully evinces the senses than the law court. In considering the subject of one's standing before God in the legal setting, Paul engages his readers with a sense of fearful expectation that the truth expounded might evoke a 'real' response.

In the courtroom, a person's life hangs in the balance: acquittal means freedom, and condemnation translates as real imprisonment – both are 'actually' significant. Of course, the apostle Paul is no stranger to the courtroom and the consequences attending it. In the book of Acts there are numerous accounts of Paul's imprisonments. In 2 Corinthians 11:23 he indicates he has been in prison more often than other 'servants' of Christ. While in some instances he may have been imprisoned without a trial (Acts 16:37), this would certainly not have been the case in all instances (Acts 23 – 27). While Paul's court / trial appearances were not on the grounds of personal lawlessness, the experience of such events more than adequately equipped him to understand the gravity of the process. These experiences, doubled with his knowledge of God's future judgement (Rom. 14:10), embedded the legal metaphor powerfully within his own consciousness.

Of course, we must never forget that Paul had a Jewish heritage and deep appreciation for law. Raymond Collins believes the notion of the 'mercy seat' (God's judgement seat symbolized by the ark's cover), as a symbol of God's graciousness in the face of sinful condemnation, could not have escaped Paul and his Jewish-oriented audience. Such people would imagine themselves before the temple (as if it was God's courtroom) on the Day of Atonement, as the high priest enters to make an offering on their behalf: 'The image of the sinner standing speechless before the divine tribunal in the language of accountability brings the reader into the courtroom.'[2] Collins also argues that the imaginative scenario evoked by Paul's judicial imagery is further enhanced by his discourse on God's law.

In writing about the judicial process in Romans 3:21–31 Paul mentions the law no less than seven times; and indeed speaks of the law in Romans some 66 times between Romans 1 and 8.[3] Indeed, moral law and cultic practice are interconnected in Jewish thought. The sinner under the just condemnation of the law comes before God's 'mercy seat' seeking atonement. However, in the case of the old covenant Jew its 'real efficacy' was merely symbolic (Heb. 9:8–9); only the atoning work of a perfect sacrifice could 'actually' acquit the beleaguered sinner (Heb. 9:11–12). Thus, knowledge of the divine law within the Jewish religious system provided a solid basis from which Paul could metaphorically lead his readers into the divine court and prosecute his case for the gospel.

Paul was also writing into a culture for which the law court had significant social meaning. A.A. Rupprecht believes that in order to understand Paul's encounter with the law (i.e. Roman law) it is necessary to have a clear picture of a provincial administration in the Roman world. The legal process was relatively straightforward: 'Most basic to Roman law was the concept the cases will be heard by an individual, usually a Praetor, who would render a decision binding on both parties.'[4] In almost all cases, the decision rendered was final, and only those with special privilege might appeal to the higher court of the emperor. Jill Harries argues that the events recorded in Acts, while not accurate in every detail, are largely consistent with Roman legal processes.[5]

Furthermore, the relationship between Jewish law and Roman law may not be as distant as one might naturally assume. In the provinces, the rabbis were both interpreters of religious and civil law and often presided over legal courts.[6] The evolution of rabbinic tradition was influenced by parallel social structures that incidentally applied to Roman law. Roman law, conversely, took up religious ideals, as Harries argues, 'Although fundamentally different from Jewish law, Roman law in itself was founded on early "sacred law" traditions, established under the Kings, sometimes with a ledger of divine guidance . . . The earliest Roman law code, the Twelve Tables, contain both religious and civil law.'[7] Given this, Paul's Roman readers (even with no Jewish background) would have had some social basis to conceptualize the legal metaphor within the religious context.

Against this background, we approach Paul's exposition of the gospel in the third chapter of Romans. We find that Paul initially takes the opportunity to restore some dignity to his Jewish-oriented readers, after the potential offence to their religious sensibilities in Romans 2. He has already stated in Romans 1:16 that the gospel is the power of God for salvation, 'first' for the Jew and then for the Gentile! Now in Romans 3:1–2 he reiterates the Jewish advantage with respect to hearing the gospel. Of course the Jews have a historical and cultural advantage over the Gentiles; they have been entrusted with the Holy Scriptures, the 'very' words of God!

Yet, the apostle's respite is only brief, as he quickly returns to the argument in line with Romans 2; that this advantage has not also been taken up as it should and thus failed to translate into faith in God (v. 3). He makes it clear; the unfaithfulness of some Jews has not nullified God's faithfulness or his rightful place as judge of the whole world. So, after setting aside any arguments that might auger toward self-vindication, Paul (as a prosecuting lawyer) returns to his previous conclusion that none are righteous, making *special reference* to the privileged Jews. Yes, the Jews may have an advantage, but this does not make them inherently better! Gentile and Jew alike stand condemned under God's righteous law on account of their common sinful nature. God the judge of the world presides over the divine law court and Paul is now about to read out charges, extracted from the 'very' words of God.

Paul begins his indictment in Romans 3:10–12 with a reference to Psalm 14. The full-text reads, 'They are corrupt, their deeds are vile; there is no-one who does good. The Lord looks down from heaven on the sons of men to see if there are any who understand, any who seek God. All have turned aside, they have together become corrupt; there is no-one who does good, not even one' (Ps. 14:1–3). This is a reference to the 'fool' who says in his heart there is no God, but Paul sees it fitting the implied Jewish audience (even the most righteous), those with knowledge of God who fail to understand what God wants. Of course this psalm is not the only reference, such indictments are replete and similar quotes can be located in Exodus 32:8; Ecclesiastes 7:20,29; Isaiah 53:6; 59:8; 64:6 and Jeremiah 2:13.

Indeed, the apostle offers no respite now and continues to address the sins pertaining to speech in Romans 3:13–14, sins that are readily enacted but quickly forgotten by the religious person. The condemnation of the same can be quickly cross-referenced in Psalms 5:9; 12:3–4; 36:3; 52:2 and 57:4. As if that were not enough, Paul, the prosecutor continues in Romans 3:15–18 to outline the ungodly conduct of Jewish sinners. He addresses those who wreck destruction along the path to self-gratification (citing passages such as Isa. 59:7–8), and hold no fear of God before them (Rom. 3:18), as if to state by such an indictment, 'You are not even aware that God holds you guilty; this is just how sinful and deluded you really are!'

We have already learned that sin has a moral / relational dimension (obvious by the scriptural content quoted), and the degree of that catalogued sin is actually quantifiable. Paul makes it clear that sin is determinable by direct reference to God's word, drawn from the principles of God's divine law. These are the charges before the court, and those with a Jewish heritage cannot say they were without knowledge of these charges because they have been 'entrusted' with the Scriptures (v. 2) that have been exposing their guilt for millennia past. With the use of Holy Scripture (law), God, through Paul, has effectively set forth the divine indictment tangibly exposing the true moral status of all humans; especially the privileged Jews, forcing them to soberly reflect on their moral standing against a measurable and credible standard.

Paul writes, 'Now we know that whatever the law says, it says to those who are under the law, so that every mouth may be silenced and the whole world held accountable to God' (Rom. 3:19). His purpose is clear: those who think they are without sin must clearly see the gravity of their moral deficiency and acknowledge their need for another way to escape the 'inescapable' condemnation of the law. Furthermore, defining sin in this manner, existential aspects come into play, namely guilt; something Paul was personally familiar with: 'I would not have known what coveting really was if the law had not said, "Do not covet"' (Rom. 7:7b). In Romans 3 Paul has shown the self-righteous Jew or Jew sympathizer the 'legal' and by extension 'existential' extent of the problem: they are law-breakers, they are guilty, there are just grounds for a penalty, and they need to make amends. But how is a solution sought, and where is the answer to be found? By returning to the law?

In building this argument toward a conclusion, within the space of a few lines the apostle simultaneously outlines both; the effectiveness and ineffectiveness of the law within his soteriological scheme. First he speaks of the value and effectiveness of the law in exposing sin and assigning guilt. For those who are under the jurisdiction of the law (i.e. the Jews), the law pronounces the verdict, leaving them without an excuse or escape from the situation of 'silent' guilt in the courtroom of God.[8] Calvin offers a summation of the 'mouth being silenced' by the law: 'It is a metaphor taken from courts of law, where the accused, if he has anything to plead as a lawful defence, demands leave to speak, that he might clear himself from the things laid to his charge; but if he is convicted by his own conscience, he is silent, and without saying a word waits for his condemnation.'[9] For the 'privileged' Jew, the privilege to speak has been silenced by the very words of the law they had so proudly claimed as a grounds for privilege. The law, in exposing sin, of even the most righteous Jew, exposes the source of their false confidence – human pride. In so doing, the law fulfils its principal function, as Luther states, 'that proud men do know their sins and be humbled'.[10] In this regard, the law is totally effective.

But how can God hold the 'whole world' accountable if the law only speaks with authority to those who are under the law (the Jews)?

We need to realize that Paul has already effectively shown that the Gentiles are under the wrath of God, and is simply applying an *a fortiori* argument. That is to say, if the Jews (those with a greater status of privilege within God's economy) cannot be excluded from the condemnation of sinfulness, surely it's a given that everyone else (the whole world), falls within the classification of guilty.[11] Remember, it is on those with Jewish sympathies that Paul has his sights here.

With this final argument he ensures that the Jews are the 'last domino' to fall. Their silencing within the dock by the law guarantees that all humanity, whether they are in this particular court room or not, have been silenced – no one has any grounds for a plea bargain. At this point the metaphor is most powerful; the sinner is guilty as charged, condemned by the law, condemned by their own conscience, and condemned by the very things that might have acted as their defence. With fear and trembling they must now await the dreaded verdict of the divine judge.

However, regarding the ineffectiveness of the law, the final verse of the section: 'Therefore no-one will be declared righteous in his sight by observing the law' (Rom. 3:20), clarifies the apostle's argument. If the defendant is seeking exoneration before the bar of God, then in Paul's mind, it can *never* come via works of the Law. In this regard, 'the law' is completely ineffective. Paul wants to make it clear that justification (rectification with God) cannot be on the grounds of works of the law. Why? Because the law invariably condemns works, as C.K. Barrett argues, 'As long, therefore, as God's righteousness is manifested and understood in terms of the law it must spell wrath. The only hope is that God should find some other means, beyond the law and religion, of manifesting his righteousness.'[12]

We must be clear; Paul is not simply saying law cannot justify us, but has an indispensable value as an ethical system in the Christian life; that we might return to the law as a means of 'preserving' this right standing – most certainly not! Significantly, 'law' in this context is not a synonym for human 'good works', but specifically works related to the Jewish religion; cultic, social or moral. So, being justified by faith and then returning to the Jewish law system (in any form) is anomalous to Paul's salvation logic and contrary to his gospel. The apostle is now offering a new paradigm for soteriology that involves: a new basis – grace; a new atonement – Christ; a new means – faith; and a new power – the Spirit. For Paul, any continuing relationship between the gospel and the 'system' of Mosaic Law is antithetical.[13]

Righteousness, Faith and the Law (Romans 3:21ff.)

In approaching the section of Romans that many consider the 'heart' of the gospel, it is important to understand the nature of the argument Paul lays out in Romans 3:21–6. This discussion must be considered with a view to the *larger context* of his dealings with Law-oriented theology. When Paul wrote his letter to the Galatian Christians, his intent was to persuade them not to incorporate the beliefs and practices of traditional Judaism into their newfound Christian faith. Having begun with the Spirit, Paul sees a potential reversion to the Mosaic Law (at any stage of the Christian endeavour) as an abandonment of the gospel (Gal. 3:1–3). Of course, Galatians is an epistle charged with polemic intensity, and seeks more than the rejection of law-based theology; it also seeks to convince the genuine believers to reject the teachers proclaiming it. As such, the intensity of Paul's argument could leave any Jew, distanced from yet aware of these specific events (i.e. those in Rome), concluding that Paul considers 'any' Jew illegitimate – having no legitimate connection to Abraham (because the Law makes them offspring of the 'slave woman', Gal. 4:30)!

Given that Galatians precedes Romans, it's conceivable the Roman Christians, in processing the Galatian scenario, might justifiably expect Paul to be hostile to 'all things' Jewish, as Tobin signals, 'None of this would have endeared Paul either to his fellow Jews or, more to the point, to the most Roman Christians, who saw their own beliefs in close continuity with both the Jewish scriptures and the Jewish people. All this will significantly affect, as we shall see, the way Paul argues in Romans 3:21 – 4:25.'[14] Therefore, Paul has to carefully navigate his gospel explication through suspicious and 'potentially hostile' territory!

Until this point Paul has focused on exposing human inability and revealing its proclivity toward self-attainment of righteousness. Having cleared the ground, he now presents his valid alternative: *righteousness by faith in Christ – apart from the Law*. Aware of the Galatian fall-out in Rome, Paul carefully seeks to present a new way of 'being set right' with God that doesn't demolish all Jewish sensibilities relating to the Law's authority, but carefully distances itself from it, by breaking new ground. Paul is not seeking to ruthlessly demolish and subsequently renovate law-soteriology in the presence of his 'weak' readers. Rather than presenting an argument of brutal 'destruction / reconstruction', he advocates an argument for 'new construction', challenging them to 'move out' of the old and 'move in' to the new.

However, with such a radical move away from law, how can moral righteousness be conceptualized, especially given that the Jewish mindset requires 'law' as a heuristic to frame justification? In response, Paul advances an alternative form of justification that needs no 'law framework' to prop it up. *It is a justification founded on grace offered through the redemptive work of Christ and held together by faith; faith which, itself, is a gracious gift of the Spirit.* For a correct understanding of justification, the Spirit's role is absolutely essential, as N.T. Wright confirms, 'The Holy Spirit is, in fact, the usually forgotten element in justification, and I am convinced that only when we come to the doctrine from this angle . . . we can gain the full Pauline picture.'[15] While Paul only presupposes it at this stage in Romans, it is the Spirit that enables such a soteriological structure to take shape, allowing his 'new way' of justification to actually stand. This 'new way' of being justified introduces righteousness from God that, although directly avoiding a reliance on and engagement with the *Law system,* is ironically validated by it!

What then is the nature of this righteousness offered? Some have argued that it relates to God's covenant faithfulness, as Wright puts it, 'God's faithful justice, his determination to put the world to rights through putting humans to rights.'[16] Others in the Reformation tradition consider this righteousness as a 'thing' that is passively credited or imputed to the account of believers on the grounds of faith – an 'alien' righteousness.[17] Yet both of these perspectives tend to objectify the righteousness of God, to the point of considering God's actions on behalf of humanity as an abstract transaction. However, there is a richer dimension to the righteousness that is endowed by God, richer than the notion of 'rightness' or 'rectitude' actively imputed.[18]

Righteousness in the Old Testament is very much considered from a relational point of view – a covenant concept. Over and against the Greco-Roman concept of righteousness as an 'ideal' concept, it pertains to the moral quality of God's relationship with his people. James Dunn observes, 'Righteousness is not something which an individual has on his or her own, independently of anyone else . . . People are righteous when they meet the claims which others have on them by virtue of their relationship.'[19] When Paul talks about the righteousness of God, he is considering it relationally. In the gospel, those who are unrighteous enter into a right 'relational' legal standing with God, on the grounds of his gracious actions in Christ, apprehended by a *relational trusting faith*. But this is not simply a matter of legal 'rectitude' alone; this right relationship necessarily translates into consequential 'right' relationship(s) – with God and by implication others. Don Garlington observes, 'Thus, there is more at stake than a changed status; those who had been dead are now alive; they are new creatures in a new creation. In this light, Paul's statement becomes an exhortation for Christians to live as those who are washed, sanctified and justified.'[20]

Yes, in apprehending the righteousness of God by faith, believers are apprehending a forensic (legal) status. However, this status consequentially demands 'actual' moral conformity to God (Rom. 10:3). When God reveals that righteousness that comes through Christ, this is more than the technical imputation of a 'thing'; it is a relational engagement that demands a response. The believer, on the grounds of faith in Christ, enters into a right relational standing with God. This relationship subsequently and necessarily *flows onto* a right moral relationship with God and by extension others (cf. 1 John). In concert with Paul's prior argument, this righteousness 'engagement' can never be grounded on human merit or draw upon human morality in any *causal sense*, because it comes 'apart from' works of the Law! Significantly then, such a 'non-law / works' engagement is only possible by virtue of the initiative and 'relational presence and power' of God's Spirit, whose key role is the endowment of saving faith.

The righteousness comes by way of the Spirit's gift of faith.[21] How then are we to interpret the Greek word *pistis* (ordinarily interpreted as faith)? The first way of interpreting *pistis* may be defined as 'anthropocentric'. That is to say, Christ is the object of the faith, and this faith then, is the faith of the believing person. In this view, justification by faith is perceived as the individual finding personal acquittal before God the judge, on the grounds of personally trusting Christ, much like the 'individual' Abraham.[22] Despite attempts to discredit this position by caricaturing this reading of faith as either 'individualistic' or even 'introspective', it is very difficult to avoid that this objective sense of 'faith in Christ' is the best, most straightforward and natural reading here.

In fact, when Paul says no 'one' will be declared righteous by observing the law, and then goes on to indicate that 'now' a righteousness is from God through faith to 'all' who believe (Rom. 3:20–22), there is no doubt that the 'actual' faith of believing persons is in view. Francis Watson also suggests, 'The emphasis on "faith" indicates, for Paul, the divine saving action would be incomplete if it failed to secure human participation, in the form of its own acknowledgement and the communal and individual life based on that acknowledgement.'[23] There is no avoiding the fact that personal faith must be involved in any relationship with Christ. (However, this will be discussed in greater depth in a following chapter.)

Another interpretation of *pistis,* often set over and against the former view, may be considered the 'theocentric' position. In favour of a theocentric thrust through Romans, Stanley Stowers argues, 'Romans sets up the discussion so as to focus on God's righteousness and how God, not Gentile ethics, Jewish work with Gentiles, nor human activity, makes Gentiles righteous.'²⁴ Advocates of this theocentric view place the emphasis on God's saving action, leading to *pistis* being rendered, the 'faith / faithfulness of Christ'. While this position endeavours to 'avoid' faith being anthropologically located, that it might not become a human work, it can lead to the opposite position. This is illustrated in Stowers' rendering: 'Thus God "justifies the one who lives on the basis of Jesus' faithfulness"',²⁵ which appears to open the door for human religious merit to become the basis of God's justifying work, albeit connected with Jesus' faithfulness! Of course, the gospel is predicated on the saving initiative and the faithfulness of Christ the Messiah. However, it seems to me that Paul's focus here is more on the instrumentality of appropriating this righteousness. In this regard, there are only two options: law or faith! Paul simply establishes that redemption comes through Christ, and Christ is on the side of faith; even if the application of faith is potentially ambiguous, as again Francis Watson helpfully clarifies, 'But the *pistis Christou* phraseology in itself refers simply to the faith that pertains to Christ, without further specifying the nature of that pertinence.'²⁶

The final rendering of *pistis* under consideration is what I have deemed the 'sociocentric' position. By this term, I am referring to an orientation of *pistis* that sees its application toward ecclesiology. This should not be simplistically construed, as some suppose, as meaning that a person is 'saved' by being in the community of faith. Rather, it emphasizes that *faith* is the defining characteristic of God's church – God's new covenant people. N.T. Wright likens it to a 'badge' worn by the Messiah's community: 'that it is the faithful death of Jesus that reconstitutes the people of God, and it is the faith of believers which therefore appropriately marks them out as members of that people'.²⁷

Such a view does not dispense with the necessity of personal faith, but sees that such a saving faith is essentially located within God's *faith matrix* – the church. While strange to the modern mind, in the first-century world of 'social divides' this would have been significant. Belonging to a community of Law, or a community of faith, determined truth. True doctrine was nurtured in the true community – the faith community (cf. 1 John). This is especially relevant in Rome, where the 'weak 'and 'strong' believers were separated by their position on faith as Watson argues, 'Common to both parties within the Roman Christian community is a simple fact of "believing," and allegiance to Jesus Christ as Lord. When this faith becomes the basis for unity rather than an occasion of division, then the blessings of joy, peace, and hope that follow from faith will finally be realized, in the power of the Holy Spirit.'[28]

However, what is without contention here is that *the righteousness of God* that is established in the gospel is by 'faith not Law'.[29] Understood thus, how *pistis* (faith) is nuanced may not be as critical to Paul's particular argument as previously thought. Whether *pistis* is conceptualized in terms of *God's faithfulness* in establishing the new covenant 'faith regime' orientated in Christ in which personal answering faith is exercised; whether this is viewed as an identifier for the *community that held to the faith* in Christ soteriology; or whether this applied to the individual who simply put their personal *trust in Christ*; this is not of ultimate importance to the particular argument Paul is making in this context. What is most important to Paul, I believe, is that the gospel of salvation vis-à-vis righteousness is on *the side of faith*, not *the side of works of the Law*.

Moreover, introducing the Holy Spirit into this 'faith' discussion enables a richer, if not clearer understanding of the issues at stake. The Spirit enables the adoption of a multifarious view of faith (in relation to righteousness). The Spirit establishes the divine frame in which justification by faith is established (new covenant). The Spirit engenders the faith by which the individual believer can trust in Christ (regeneration). The Spirit establishes the community of faith, which is the vehicle of God's redemptive actions in the world (body of Christ) in which individual faith life is nurtured. The Spirit subsequently empowers a faith-derived ethical righteousness that validates the faith-based righteous status in Christ. Therefore, Spirit-endowed faith is the modus operandi of gaining and maintaining this new status of righteousness in Christ – apart from the law.

Furthermore, this *right standing* before God is available to 'all' (in a qualitative sense) who have faith; Jew or Gentile – it matters not. But faith in 'faith' does not justify. In Romans 3:24, Paul states that justification is possible by God's gracious provision of Christ's redemptive work; in this regard Christ and his redemptive work is the focus of this saving faith. The object of the justifying faith, more precisely, is the atoning sacrificial death of Christ.

However, Stowers believes this 'traditional' sacrificial view of atonement is less than adequate, arguing that traditional interpretations have ignored the ongoing validity of the Jewish temple cult: 'When the historian permits Jewish practices of the second temple to stand on their own right, in their own cultural and historical context, the similarities with Christian ideas melt away.'[30] He also believes the temple system was not premised on 'essential' broken divine / human relationships, and deduces that forgiveness came on the basis of repentance and reparation.[31] This view is predicated on the notion that Paul's Jewish sympathies predisposed him to endorse contemporaneous Jewish practices; that he saw both religions legitimately operating side by side. Yet when we examine Paul's New Testament letters, Paul is clear that Christianity does 'in fact' supersede Judaism (2 Cor. 3; Rom. 7:6; Col. 2:17; Heb. 10:1) and furthermore, the thrust of Paul's discussion in Romans 3 that justification is 'apart from' the law (including the Jewish temple, past or present) would confirm this.

In point of fact, Paul finds no shame in supporting Christ's atonement in terms of Christ's propitiating blood sacrifice. In Romans 3:25 he plainly mentions 'faith in his blood' as the basis of demonstrating his justice against previously unpunished sin, so as to be consistently just, as the divine judge, as well as the gracious justifier. Moreover, this 'blood' language is not isolated. It appears in Romans 5:9, which speaks of being justified by his blood with a view to being saved from God's wrath. In his discussions on the Lord's Supper in 1 Corinthians the blood of Christ is a central theme. Again, in Ephesians 1:7 and 2:13 Christ's redemption is related to his blood sacrifice, which also appears in Colossians 1:20, where peace with God is only enabled by Christ's blood on the cross. Furthermore, if we attribute the authorship of Hebrews to Paul, then all notions of Paul supporting the ongoing Jewish cult and 'bloodless' forms of atonement simply dissipate: 'Without the shedding of blood there is no forgiveness' (Heb. 9:22).

In Paul's mind (in this context) faith's object is quite clearly Christ's penal / sacrificial atonement. As offensive as such a notion might be to the sensibilities of some, we must acknowledge that accepting this 'brutal' truth is only possible via the faith-producing power of the Spirit of God. The Spirit enables us to overcome the offence of the cross and empowers the believer to embrace the redemption offered therein. Paul writes in 1 Corinthians that Christ 'crucified' is a stumbling block to Jews and foolishness to Gentiles. How, then are these obstacles overcome? Faith in Christ through the power of the Spirit – nothing less! In 1 Corinthians 2:4 Paul asserts it was not 'wise or persuasive' words that have won them over, but the Spirit's power. The wisdom of this age rejects Christ crucified, but through the Spirit's enabling it becomes the wisdom of God: 'The man without the Spirit does not accept the things that come from the Spirit of God, for they are foolishness to him, and he cannot understand them, because they are spiritually discerned' (1 Cor. 2:14).

Paul's confidence in this new soteriology is solid. If the justification of God through faith in Christ's redemptive work is embraced in the faith-enabling power of the Spirit, it necessarily follows that human boasting must be nullified (Rom. 3:27), not simply reduced or lessened as Calvin suggests, 'For he treats not of the lessening or the modifying of merit, but Paul leaves not a particle behind'.[32] The boasting that might be embraced by the privileged Jew (sympathizer) has been extinguished. This is not on account of the law being fulfilled in some way, but on the basis of God's gracious bestowal of faith; the faith to embrace the redemptive work of Christ. We know that the very nature of boasting is to look to 'oneself' as the source of confidence; faith (in Christ) on the other hand is essentially a negation of self-confidence and a grasping of an alien confidence.

Confidence in 'the flesh' which finds its religious expression in law-keeping is abandoned, as the object of confidence is now located outside the believer's 'natural' consciousness – in Christ. Such an utter abandonment of self-confidence and the embracing of the unseen (in faith) can only be derivative of a supernatural working – the working of the Spirit. Paul writes in Ephesians 2:8 that the Christian has been saved by grace, through means of faith, which is a 'gift' of God. This gift is animated by the Spirit, with the resultant faith extending beyond rational assent being actualized as 'real' confidence: 'But *by faith* we eagerly await *through the Spirit* the righteousness for which we hope' (Gal. 5:5, emphasis added).

Justification is attained by faith, over and against works of the Jewish law. God does not discriminate: Jew, Gentile, circumcision and uncircumcision are all categories that have no substantive value under the 'new' faith regime. Yet having vehemently stressed the virtue of faith over and against the law, why then does Paul seem to positively affirm the law (Rom. 3:31)?

Paul's positive appraisal of law should not be interpreted abstractly; a view that treats the concept of law homogeneously, dismissing the empirical nuance in Paul's situation. Paul is dealing with 'weak' believers, sympathetic to Jewish laws and customs, those with whom he needs to affirm the values of the law within God's grand redemptive scheme. He is not merely affirming the Law on account of: its divine derivation; its inclusion within the corpus of Scripture; its value as a 'schoolmaster' leading the sinner to Christ; or even its capacity to rebuke the lawless (1 Tim. 1:8). Rather, Paul is affirming it because the Law as an integral component of 'Holy Scripture' is foundational in predicting, establishing, verifying and validating this 'new way' of salvation (Rom. 3:21). Paul affirms that the gospel does not nullify law as God's prophetic word, with its 'gospel-validating' authority. But, with respect to its ongoing practical validity within soteriology, his discussion in Romans 6 – 8 will dispense with any notion that validates its continuing efficacy.

Abraham and Crediting Righteousness (Romans 4:1–25)

At the conclusion of the previous section Paul affirmed the Law (Holy Scripture) in its gospel-validating capacity. In Romans 4, Paul puts that principle to work, by showing that 'faith righteousness' is not only confirmed by the Law, but by Abraham, the quintessential Jew. In maintaining that faith and not works of the law seizes righteousness, Paul convinces his readers (from Scripture) that a *faith-oriented soteriology* has a solid Jewish heritage. Prior to this, in his Galatians correspondence, Paul set Abraham over and against the Law and its adherents. In this particular context, he shows that the Law affirms Abraham as the father of Jews and Gentiles 'alike'; the father of all who embrace this new faith-based righteousness.

While not supporting the Law as the means of Christian living, Paul nevertheless shows that it has value in establishing this new inclusive way of relating to God – the way of faith. He wants to send a clear message to the Jewish sympathizers (those who are potentially wary of his 'alleged' anti-law / Jew theology) that Abraham is on their side, the side of faith; indeed the Law validates this faith! The inclusion of Abraham is more than a random example of faith-based righteousness, but establishes that faith-based righteousness is deeply rooted in Jewish tradition (Rom. 4:1); a tradition founded on the promises of God by 'our' forefather Abraham – the father of 'all' who believe.

As a more tangible expression in support of his case, Paul sets forth an anecdote from Abraham's life (Rom. 4:17–22). Paul not only wants to confirm that faith can be the grounds of righteousness, but also wants to show that faith righteousness is no 'fictional hope'. God, who validates the 'new' faith theology, will honour it by fulfilling his promises, as he did with Abraham. Paul reminds his readers of the story of Abraham's calling and faith-challenge to leave his original homeland and seek the land God promised to give him.

Following God's covenant promises, Abraham (despite his childless wife and old age) trusted God to find a way to accomplish that which was promised. Ultimately the execution of the promises was contingent upon God's faithfulness, however the experience of them was contingent on the trusting faith of Abraham. This story is designed to evince a powerful response from his Jewish-oriented readers, as Tobin states, 'All of this heightens in Paul's Roman Christian audience a sense of the depth of Abraham's faith, that was credited as righteous, as well as a sense of the power of the God who keeps the promise made to Abraham.'[33] Paul's purpose is clear: he establishes that righteousness is the benefit accrued to those who trust God, which is exemplified by, though not exclusive to, Abraham. It is granted to all who whole-heartedly trust the ultimate object of God's promises – Christ.

Because Abraham was *an individual* who 'actually' received this righteousness, this section of Scripture has to be given more than a passing mention. In Romans 4:3, Paul argues that Abraham is 'credited' with righteousness on the grounds of faith. Consequently, the inquiring Christian must ask the inevitable question: What is the nature of this crediting? In other words, how is this righteousness or right standing *actually* appropriated? In quoting from Genesis 15:6, Paul affirms that Abraham was 'credited' with righteousness on account of his believing / trusting in God. Therefore, righteousness is not transferred on the basis of human merit, but on the grounds of a faith response where the object of trust is God and not the human subject.

However, with respect to the actual nature of the transfer, this concept of 'crediting' is based on the interpretation of the Greek word *logizomai*. Among other uses, *logizomai* had a legal / commercial sense in ancient Greek usage, and was related to the logical attributing of a value.[34] Although having a non-religious origin, within the LXX the term took on a personal slant, with the notion of objective quantitative reckoning giving way to a qualitative heartfelt reckoning, within the context of a personal engagement with God. This is evident where matters such as guilt, righteousness and purification are discussed (Gen. 15:6; 2 Sam. 19:19; Ps. 32:2).[35] And while Paul uses the term here, within his 'legal' metaphor, in its technical and/or legal sense (Rom. 4:4), he also applies it in a relational manner as well (Rom. 4:6–9).

Now given the significance of imputation for Protestantism, we shall briefly digress to discuss its relationship to our discussion here. Medieval Catholicism advocated grace could be *infused* and therefore righteousness *imparted* to the Christian, implying that gaining this righteousness could be interpreted as partially derivative of human cooperation. Because of this, Protestants consider the matter of righteousness 'transfer' of supreme importance. Given the nature of their opposition, the Reformers' understanding of justification manifested a rigid distinction between what God does 'for us' and what he does 'in us'. Justification was a divine declaration of righteousness 'imputed'; sanctification spoke of the subsequent work of the Spirit within the believer producing a resultant righteousness (holiness). The doctrine of the 'imputation' meant that the righteousness transferred (Christ's) was of an external or 'alien' nature.[36]

This imputation theory of an alien righteousness received significant treatment from Luther's successors. Alister McGrath argues that in Melanchthon's writing subsequent to the Augsburg Confession of 1530, there is a greater emphasis on an alien righteousness imputed, with the use of terms such as: pronouncement, acceptation and forensic, etc.[37] Making assertions that righteousness could be bestowed as an *alien value* doesn't really address the issue of the *manner* of the transfer 'fully', as Michael Bird points out, 'Yet "to credit righteousness" is not communicating the mechanism of how justification occurs as much as it is stating in biblical terms that justification does occur.'[38] This being the case, it is no surprise that Roman Catholics levelled claims of 'legal fiction' at the Protestants!

As the Reformation tradition developed, the distinction, in some cases, the separation, of what God does 'for us' in Christ (justification) and what he does 'in us' (sanctification), became reified in the Protestant consciousness. An expression of this is clearly seen in the theology of the nineteenth-century theologian, Charles Hodge: 'Imputation never changes the inward, subjective state of the person to whom the imputation is made . . . So when righteousness is imputed to the believer, he does not thereby become subjectively righteous.'[39] Although these rationally conceived and logically efficient ways of stating things may have served to clearly set the Protestant position apart from the perceived errors of Catholicism, unfortunately they created theological problems downstream.

A most basic example of this is the granting of a false confidence in an abstract faith, which doesn't concomitantly necessitate existential transformation. It gives rise to the 'faith without works is dead' syndrome, as Bird effectively illustrates, 'By stressing the forensic nature of justification, Reformed theology has always has a propensity to bruise the nerve that connects faith with obedience.'[40] Yet as we have already considered in the opening chapter, to people like Martin Luther such a transaction could never be conceived in such a rationalistic or abstract manner. For Luther righteousness is apprehended by faith, but *the manner of the righteousness by faith transaction* is not simply a remote rational action. For the German Reformer, faith manifested as personal 'heart devotion': 'Faith taketh hold of Christ, and hath him present, and holdeth him enclosed, as a ring does the precious stone. And whosoever shall be found having this confidence in Christ apprehended in the heart, him God will account for righteous.'[41]

Indeed, Luther affirms the source of righteousness is Christ's 'alien' righteousness, but the bestowal of such righteousness was never abstracted by rational categorization. That is why he speaks of confidence in Christ being 'apprehended in the heart'. This can only be based on a 'prior' working of the Spirit 'in' the heart to produce faith, which in turn apprehends the righteousness granted *extra nos*. No person can apprehend the righteousness of Christ, if they were not first subject to the intimate prevenient work of God's Spirit, in awakening it! Of course, the justification of the sinner takes place in the justifying work of God through Christ's atonement, which is an event external to human influence and control, but the *experimental appropriation* of this justifying work takes place in the transformed heart by the agency of the Spirit, who secretly echoes the eternal efficacy of the historical event within this existential state of faith.

Luther's organic concept of imputation transcends the mechanical operation that is Hodge's interpretation, as Mark Seifrid suggests, '"Justification" is no mere transaction to be applied to my account.'[42] Luther's notion of imputation is not the means of a false 'rationalist' confidence in the *doctrine of justification* at the expense of Christian experience. Rather it is 'relationally' integrated to become the basis of true confidence for those seeking to address the practical exigencies of life: 'And this acceptation, or imputation, is very necessary: first, because we are not yet perfectly righteous, and while we remain in this life . . . we are sometimes left of the Holy Ghost, and fall into sins, as did Peter, David, and other holy men.'[43] For such as Luther, the bestowing of righteousness, while legally conceived in terms of imputing value, can never be divorced from a relational context.

In returning to the argument in Romans, in Romans 4:20 Paul gives us a glimpse of the nature of Abraham's 'saving' faith. It was actually an 'empowered' faith, directed toward God and his glory; a faith that was 'persuaded' to trust in the saving power of God. Paul notes that faith like this is the kind with which God credits the 'believer' as righteous. Surely such faith cannot be generated from Abraham himself, thus being derivative of human power? What then is the provenance of such faith that makes it efficacious toward God's favour? The passive voice of the verbs 'empowered' and 'persuaded' indicates that something outside of Abraham's influence was acting on him to produce such a 'sure' faith. Surely this influence could be nothing more than God himself – through the Spirit.

In Galatians 3:5 Paul connects the Spirit with belief, and then appeals to the example of Abraham, indicating that he received the gospel in advance with the injunction: 'All nations will be blessed through you', and was credited with righteousness because of his faith. Through the blessing given to Abraham, the Gentiles through faith in Christ received the promise of the Spirit (Gal. 3:14). Could then the Spirit connected with the faith of the Gentiles be the source of Abraham's faith, by which he was *persuaded and empowered*? Although the Scriptures don't explicitly link the faith of Abraham with the Spirit, if the Holy Spirit resided in kings and prophets under the old covenant (Ps. 51; Acts 28:25), then surely Abraham would not be exempt from such a dispensation of God's empowering presence, as he became the pre-eminent example for those under the new administration of the Spirit? Faith such as Abraham's can only be of a supernatural derivation.

Consequently, the saving faith of Abraham becomes the quintessential model for those who seek a right standing on the grounds of faith, apart from the Law. If circumcision and law-keeping played no part in Abraham's 'right standing' then neither should they for those under the new covenant who seek the same favour with God; the Romans – and of course, us (Rom. 4:23–4)! If Abraham's faith was based on a supernatural working of God then the faith of those under the new dispensation must also be derivative of the Spirit's enabling. This, then, is the circumcision of the heart that Paul had previously alluded to (Rom. 2:29)!

In the New Testament narratives, the work of the Spirit is mostly deemed as subsequent to faith. However, it would be unwise, even dangerous, to assume that human faith must reach up to God under the power of the 'flesh' in order that the Spirit might reach down and engage us. An unbeliever 'dead' in their trespasses and sins (Eph. 2:1) has no capacity to 'reach up', for without the quickening Spirit it is impossible (1 Cor. 2:14). Therefore, this saving faith is a gift (Eph. 2:8), a gratuitous dispensation of God's grace that sets the sinner's heart free to believe in and adhere to God. And it is the Spirit's empowering that seals the bond of our faith: 'We have not received the spirit of the world, but the Spirit who is from God, that we may understand what God has freely given us' (1 Cor. 2:12).

In seeking to understand the 'manner' in which righteousness is credited to our account, John Calvin recognizes the answer lies beyond human wisdom. In fact, it must necessarily lead the interpreter to seek why this is the case, and subsequently conclude that reason prompts us to 'climb higher' [than itself] and examine the secret energy of the Spirit.[44] Calvin, rightly, affirms that without this secret working of the Spirit the righteousness that we seek in the gospel cannot be appropriated by human effort: 'By his secret watering the Spirit makes us fruitful to bring forth the buds of righteousness.'[45] In fact, Calvin is not so ready to divorce what *God does* 'for us' from what *God does* 'with / in us' either. Why? Because it is all God's sovereign work! Although Calvin may distinguish these two things for polemic purposes, to 'realistically' appropriate the gospel truth, a separation of the two is 'practically' impossible, as he suggests, 'No one can duly know him without at the same time apprehending the sanctification of the Spirit. Or, if anyone desires some plain statement, faith rests upon the knowledge of Christ. And Christ cannot be known apart from the sanctification of his Spirit. It follows that faith can in no way be separated from a devout disposition.'[46] Thus the justification that God bestows on us by virtue of Christ's work through the Spirit's ministry has a necessary 'existential' dimension, and it is to this element we now turn our attention.

The Spirit and 'Real' Justification (Romans 5)

Locating Romans 5 within Paul's overall argument is not easy. Does it belong with Romans 1–4? Does it belong with Romans 6 – 8? Is it a 'bridging' chapter? Some argue that linguistically the prevalence of 'righteousness' terminology ties this chapter to earlier chapters.[47] Supporting this rearward connection, John Murray argues, 'We may not forget that the apostle is still dealing with his grand theme, justification by faith.'[48] On the other side of the debate, some argue for a connection with the later chapters, on the grounds that Paul's argument addresses the 'result' or 'consequence' of justification.[49] Brendan Byrne suggests that Paul now speaks from 'within' the community of the believing: 'Now the focus shifts from faith to hope.'[50] It should come as no surprise that others still might opt for a 'bridging' designation for this pivotal chapter.

In Romans 5:1, Paul introduces his readers to the concept of 'peace'. He does so, not merely to establish believers' legal status, but to establish a concomitant 'state of being' that is theirs 'in Christ'. Those who possess Christ 'possess' peace in its fullness. In verse 2, the believer has gained access (a temple inference) into a 'state of grace', in which they perpetually stand. In fact, Howard Marshall relates it as God's presence: 'In the Christian context, peace is associated with God's presence and is an ongoing consequence of that presence.'[51] In such a state, there is no law-engendered guilt existentially lingering to draw the justified Christian back to a campaign of law-ethics. On the contrary, the Spirit engenders freedom.

The proof of 'legal' peace with God is existential peace with God. This is further validated as the Spirit works out the commensurate reality of joy (v. 2) in the believer's life. Joy orients the believer's focus in a forward direction, as Christoph Schwöbel suggests, 'It is the Spirit that authenticates the message of reconciliation to us as God's grace and truth for our lives and so gives our life an orientation that is no longer determined by the past but is oriented towards the future consummation of God's communion with creation.'[52] Yet the presence of the Spirit does a greater work. The Spirit projects the future, or more accurately the eternal perfection back into the present, empowering the believer to gain a comprehensive victory over the ubiquitous 'power' of sin. Colin Gunton puts it beautifully in this regard, 'The victory of Jesus stands behind; its final revelation lies ahead. It is the gift of the Spirit to enable anticipations of the final victory to take place in our time.'[53]

The presence of the Spirit issues an indefatigable hope to those who trust Christ. The hope that Paul speaks of from verses 2 to 5 is not a sanguine wish, as if to say, 'Oh yes, we have this notion of justification that speaks of legal acquittal, yet somehow we hope and pray that God will actually come through with it!' This is not how it is at all. Stating that 'we' rejoice in the hope of the glory of God in verse 2, Paul goes on in verses 3 to 5 to practically adumbrate the very 'substantive' nature of that same hope; he writes, 'Not only so, but we also rejoice in our sufferings, because we know that suffering produces perseverance; perseverance, character; and character, hope' (Rom. 5:3–4).

The nature of hope is 'real'. It enables justified believers to do more than endure suffering – it enables them to rejoice in it. This kind of authentic suffering, embraced 'in Christ', produces the trait of perseverance, which then develops Christian character, and further draws out an even stronger hope. For Paul, the 'status' of justification through Christ, in the Spirit, genuinely alters our 'state of being': despair becomes hope, hope works through the process of character development, and then produces a more abundant hope. Such a substantive hope does not disappoint, simply because of its divine derivation – sealed with the Holy Spirit, whom 'he' has given. The Spirit that produces the gift of faith, then the blessing of hope, also validates justification by the presence of love 'poured out' in the heart. This Spirit-generated love[54] for God and others[55] therefore seals our salvation,[56] ensuring that this justification is certainly no 'legal fiction', but is existentially experienced through a sure and certain hope of its final realization.

Paul continues to assure Roman readers in verses 6 to 11, reiterating the existential side of God's justifying work through Christ, through the theme of reconciliation. In fact, reconciliation should not be sharply distinguished from justification, as Marshall argues, 'Justification and reconciliation are used side-by-side, as alternative ways of expressing the same reality; both are the present experiences that guarantee future salvation.'[57] With this concept of reconciliation, Paul is able to back up what has already been discussed regarding forensic justification. While justification is based on a past event present as 'legal' assurance, reconciliation, although based on the same 'past' event, speaks of an ongoing, present, relational assurance (vv. 9–10).

The love of God 'poured out' in the hearts is realized relationally. Paul explains that Christ did not die for friends, but enemies; reconciling them to himself – now as friends. The argument goes, 'If Christ did this for enemies, then how much more that we are now friends; will "actual" salvation be ours?' The apostle affirms that believers can rejoice in this truth of reconciliation, as it undergirds their assurance and hope of final salvation. Marshall, who sees 'reconciliation' as central in Paul's thought, sums it up this way, 'The intended readers of the letter have thus been reconciled to God, and they are now destined for final salvation. It might be claimed that here reconciliation is brought in . . . to back up what has been said about the primary concept of justification; but one might equally well say that reconciliation is the climax of the section.'[58] Either way, assurance of the atoning work of Christ is affirmed.

In Romans 5:12–21 Paul appears to be offering up a condensed theological summation of his entire argument up until this point; setting it out as a series of contrasts. The contrast of those in Adam with those in Christ; the contrast of the trespass that brought sin into the world with the gift of God's grace in the Christ event; the contrast of judgement with justification; and finally the contrast of Law's condemnation with God's super-abounding gift of grace. Having already established that there is no difference between Jew and Gentile, with respect to privilege, he now demarcates 'all' humanity along different lines – federal headship. First, there are those under the headship of Adam (which corresponds with all humanity in their natural state) and second, there are those under the headship of Christ (justified believers). Sin entered the world through Adam, but was not held into account until the Law of Moses exposed it; nevertheless, death, the *consequent companion* of law-breaking, reigned, proving all humanity as sinful (despite the absence of Mosaic Law to expose it).

In Romans 5:15 Paul introduces the concept of 'gift'. This can be easily seen as a synonym for God's grace; however Orrey McFarland sees it as somewhat more significant, believing that Paul carefully chooses words to emphasize the excessive and incongruous nature of the gift of Christ and its implications.[59] This gift of God, through Christ, is contrasted with the trespass that brought death, through Adam. Most interpreters of verse 15 take it to mean 'But the gift is not like the trespass'. However, C.C. Caragounis, considering the statement rhetorically, argues for an opposite interpretation: 'But is not the gift like the trespass?' Given the presence of the Greek particle (*ou*)[60] and the resident typology, this is entirely conceivable. Yes, on the one hand the 'content' of the 'gift' of God's grace in Christ is not like the trespass, yet methodologically (in a representative sense) it is; the trespass brought death to the 'many' (all humanity), correspondingly, the gift brought life to the 'many' (all 'in Christ').

Furthermore, there are two 'gift' words at play here: *charis* and *dorea*. Is their appearance simply to amplify the nature of grace? I think not. Paul wants to concretize the 'gift' concept. Out of the abundant grace of God flows the specific gift of righteousness (v. 17) through Christ; a gift that brings justification (v. 16) – the righteousness that overflowed to many. Despite the recipients' lack of merit, the gift is still given: 'Excess is primarily a result of incongruity, a lack of fit between Giver, gift, and recipient; the gift abounds because a righteous God gives to sinful humanity what it does not deserve.'[61] Paul stresses the ubiquity of death through the 'one' act of sin and then the efficacy of the life-solution through 'one' act of grace – the gift of Christ. He wants to drive home that 'this is real'!

However, there is something more to this gift phenomenon! Paul touches on obedience as it relates to the 'one man' in verse 19. He then goes on to point out that no matter how much the law 'increased', the gift of grace super-abounded to bring about eternal life through Christ. It seems he is building toward a new discussion. The super-abundance of grace has nullified the condemnation of the Law. But what of obedience in the Christian life; how does this law-free gospel address that? Without the Law as the primary moral guide, is the believer simply cut free to live how they wish? Indeed, Paul's use of the concept of 'gift' has something to add in this regard. While God's 'gift' of righteousness through Christ is not contingent on any human precondition, Paul did not view it as entirely 'unconditional' either!

It seems that Paul's conceptualization of 'gift' is *not* a no-strings-attached notion that releases the acquitted sinner to live as they want! McFarland believes Paul's idea of gift actually trades on the antique concept of gift-giving that carried with it an (apparently paradoxical) notion of freedom and obligation.[62] Grace begets grace, and generosity begets generosity: 'This is the simple shape of all gift-giving relationships in antiquity: all gift giving contains this tension, the non-legal obligation that arises and exists within prior relationships.'[63] Indeed, in Romans 8:12, Paul speaks of an 'obligation' not to live according to the sinful nature. In 1 Corinthian 6, he exhorts the believers (as the temple of the Holy Spirit) that they are not their own but should honour God with their bodies. In Romans 15 he speaks of the spiritual blessings the Gentiles have received from the Jews, therefore they 'owe' it to support them materially (note that in all instances the Spirit plays a role). It seems, the 'gift' of righteousness in Christ is not simply embracing the 'indicative' only to ignore the 'imperative'. The gift of God carries with it a condition that is without precondition.

How this unfolds, as a component part of Paul's gospel, will be seen as we move onto Paul's critical explication of the unique idea of 'union' with Christ in Romans 6.

Consequently, in Romans 5 the presence of justification language and the fresh emphasis on existential hope should not be necessarily seen as antithetical. Taken from an overarching metaphorical perspective, the subject matter is not that difficult to process. Paul relates how the justified believer might reflect on the existential dimension of their justified status. In Romans 5 the believer is still located within the legal context; indeed this justified person is still at the courthouse, but they are now there in a different capacity. The language of Romans 5 suggests that the law-court metaphor is still controlling the argument. Terms such as justification, reconciliation, trespass, law, command, condemnation and disobedience validate this. Yet the more positive tone might be accounted for through an understanding that we are now looking at the same reality from the other side of this 'justification coin'. We flip the coin from Romans 4 to Romans 5 and discover reconciliation – the existential side of forensic justification. Conversely, we can flip back from Romans 5 to Romans 4 to reveal forensic justification – the legal side of experiential reconciliation.

The implication is that, taken from an existential perspective, the person who trusts in Christ for their justification cannot be legally right with God without being existentially or relationally at peace with God, and vice versa. Although we may adumbrate the legal and existential as distinct concepts in any polemic context, they can never be 'temporally' divorced. God does not allow the justified sinner to leave the courtroom as one that simply rationally comprehends that they have been legally acquitted, while still carrying the existential burden of unforgiveness and the weight of its guilt. Paul wants to declare that justification before God is something more than a notional concept, a 'legal fiction'; he wants to affirm that the justified sinner can now leave the 'the court' rejoicing in the reality of what it 'actually' means to be justified!

If we are to avoid locating justification as a mere intellectual construct, then coming to terms with justification's existential dimension is important. In fact, it is important for two reasons. First, abstract constructions create in the 'believing' subject a false confidence that salvation resides in mere 'knowledge' of doctrine. As such, practical expressions of faith are seen as optional; the danger of which should be patently obvious (what James deems as a 'devil's faith'). Second, it can lead to the opposite problem, where having grasped 'knowledge' of justification, the assurance-deficient 'believer' can remain plagued by unremitting guilt. As a consequence, a programme of practical justification by works may 'secretly' ensue, predicated on this unresolved guilt. In this case, the Christian life is animated by a subtle works regime, grasping assurance from tangible religious piety, becoming a form of godliness that lacks power (2 Tim. 3:5).

However, when an appreciation of the Spirit's prevenient agency – in forming the faith that apprehends the 'alien' righteousness of Christ – is grasped, the *lurking threat of human merit* that drives people to fearfully cling to the intellectualist formulations dissipates. Rather, through the Spirit, the Christian embraces a double-sided grace. Christ's atoning action is complete, for the believer, when it is holistically appreciated: the 'position' of our status of guilt has been removed, as has the existential 'condition' of guilt associated with it. The Spirit enables the Christian believer, metaphorically speaking, to stand on the steps of the courthouse following the acquittal and look out with confidence; freed from legal condemnation, emancipated from inner guilt – at peace with God in both respects.

Therefore, Paul's presentation of the existential dimension of justification has great value. The believer attains 'actual' assurance, which as Michael Weinrich affirms, also 'guards against isolating the doctrine of justification and treating it in abstraction'.[64] This, of course, has been a legacy in some rationalist versions of Protestantism. However, of interest in this regard, is the Regensburg Colloquy (1541), which represented a valiant attempt to reconcile the juristic with the existential, at the time deemed as corresponding to the Protestant and Roman Catholic concepts of justification.

On the Protestant side, the stress was on the 'alien' (imputed) righteousness, gained by faith; on the Roman Catholic side justification was linked to God's initiative through the Holy Spirit's infusion at conversion or baptism (inherent righteousness).[65] Anthony Lane argues that Regensburg emphasized that at conversion the believer receives both *inherent* and *imputed* righteousness.[66] Therefore, sanctification is not set out as something sequentially consequential, but as an inseparable gift to imputed justification. While the goal of the colloquy failed due to irreconcilable differences, it is interesting that the position advocated was subsequently affirmed and adopted by one of Regensburg's more influential attendees, John Calvin, in his views on 'double' grace.[67]

Not only at Regensburg, but one of the ongoing obstacles to comprehending an appreciation of this double-sided grace among Protestants is a resistance to the Roman Catholic notion that the Spirit ontologically 'infuses' grace. Volker Rabens astutely identifies the problem: '[In this view] Paul appears to understand the Spirit "as a heavenly substance that transforms the human being substantially", and that such an ontic transformation of humanity produces ethical life as its result (Wrede).'[68] However, in proposing a better alternative that might overcome the limitations of this 'infusional' model, Rabens suggests a 'relational' engagement between the believer and the Spirit is more in line with Paul's thinking. He argues that Paul's theology is relational in nature and, for Paul, intimate and loving relationships are necessarily empowering to those within them.[69]

In justifying his position, Rabens appeals to Pauline texts such as 2 Corinthians 3:18. He suggests that Paul in this text (in contrasting Moses' veiled face) portrays the believer as beholding the Lord and being transformed; a transformation that is attributed to the Lord, who is the Spirit: 'On the basis of this Spirit-created intimate relationship to God in Christ, believers are transformed "into the same image", that is, their lives portray more of the characteristics of Christ.'[70] Although Raben's focus is ethics, the idea is readily transferrable to the existential side of justification (which arguably enters the realms of 'union with Christ', the basis for Pauline ethics). Therefore, through a relational / existential (not ontological) engagement with the Spirit, the believer 'relationally' embraces Christ and his entire work, being simultaneously justified, sanctified and transformed!

Conclusion

In offering God's solution to the problem of human unrighteousness, Paul is mindful of his 'weak' audience. Even though he knows the law is ineffectual, Paul carefully delivers an argument that upholds the authority of the law, while affirming its insufficiency and incapacity to address the problem of sin. Using a legal metaphor to frame his argument, the apostle powerfully convinces readers of the law's inadequacies and then, by way of contrast, sets forth a new way of being 'set right' with God – faith in Christ. Not only is the content of this 'new' soteriology non-legal, but so is its methodology; the Spirit of God providing the administrative structure for this new system.

Having exposed the root problem, the Spirit enables justification by endowing the faith to adhere to Christ. Moreover, because of the Spirit's personal ministry, justification is more than an abstract 'legal fiction', lacking existential validation. The Spirit that grants the faith to embrace this justified status also simultaneously enables 'real' reconciliation with God – relational peace. This peace is existentially validated, as the love of God is 'shed abroad' in the believer's heart through the Spirit's abiding presence. Therefore, being set right with God is not simply a legal declaration to be notionally appropriated by a rationally conditioned 'faith', but a relational experience to be existentially appropriated in genuine saving trust – enabled and empowered by the Holy Spirit.

4

Slavery and Spirit: Emancipating from Sin's Power

The gospel has introduced a new dominion of God's rule. The old dominion of law, sin and death has been overthrown by the new dominion of Spirit, righteousness and life – Christ's death has vanquished the penalty of sin within this reality. But what of the lingering influence of the human 'flesh', the faculty that generates sin; can the gospel counter this too? Given the New Testament injunctions to actively embrace a lifestyle of holiness as a commensurate aspect of our saved state, the idea of sin's lingering power animated by the 'flesh' cannot simply be ignored, or even partitioned off as a by-product of salvation.[1] It seems inevitable that countering this lingering power must also fall within the gospel's compass. Yet, communicating the 'existential' deliverance from the power of sin, flesh and law offered a significant challenge to Paul, given his Jewish-oriented readers' proclivity to embrace law ethics as the ordinary means of overcoming sin's power. Despite this challenge, Paul introduces a radical 'new' ethical system that serves to uphold the moral imperatives at the heart of the Mosaic Law, even as it simultaneously supersedes the process of its historical administration. But, how is this possible? Paul introduces his readers to the 'new way' of the Spirit, a 'way' that represents a powerful ethical system, which has at its heart the concept of identification or spiritual union with Christ. To explain the necessity, plausibility and possibility of this new Spirit-empowered way of life, Paul structures his wider argument in Romans 6:1 – 8:13 primarily around the metaphor of slavery.

Union and Slavery (Romans 6)

Paul's prior exposition of justification by faith created as many questions as it supplied answers. Does God's grace negate moral necessity? Does justification by faith imply that the ongoing moral life is no longer a concern? What role does the law now play? Despite the challenge, Paul does not back down on unmerited grace, nor does he water down his emphasis on moral necessity. In fact, rather than negating the moral imperative, he suggests that the message of grace inexorably demands moral obedience: 'We died to sin; how can we live in it any longer?' (Rom. 6:2). The nature of the ongoing Christian life is clearly a subject rife with the potential for confusion and misunderstanding. In this regard, misinterpretations generally fall in two directions: first, an emphasis on law morality with bias toward legalism and, second, an emphasis on antinomianism with its bias toward moral licentiousness. Paul had to contend with both.

On the one hand, there are those who believed duty to the law was necessary to remain in God's favour. For these, Paul's purely 'grace-oriented' gospel seems scandalous, as Richard Hays suggests, 'The argument is shocking, not only because it seems to deny the privileged status of Israel as God's elect people but also because it threatens to undercut all motivation for seeking to live in obedience to God.'[2] Yet it was Paul's desire, that these pro-law Jewish / Gentile readers might not reject the gospel because they saw it as 'antinomian'. On the other hand, he also contended with those who negated the need for a moral framework in the light of grace, those who seized upon the 'spiritual' gospel as a licence for gratuitous moral neglect, as Eric Osborn suggests: 'There were those who imagined that, because they had received the Spirit of God, they were free from all obligations or any limitation upon the inclinations.'[3] In fact, Paul encountered in Corinth those who saw the endowment of the Spirit as precluding moral necessity in the ongoing Christian life; Osborn again: 'The Corinthian enthusiasts believe that they had already within themselves all the righteousness of God, the blessings of the last day, as a spirit filled them and enable them to speak the words of God.'[4] It seems then, that Paul is confronted with a doctrinal 'Gordian knot'. How does the gospel of grace 'untie' the continuing power of sin without approving works of the law, while simultaneously upholding moral necessity?

Logic suggests that the capacity of the moral subject be elevated to gain mastery over the power of sin, or conversely downgrade the gravity of sin, such that immorality is no longer a problem. Significantly, Paul opts for neither. In fact, his solution is so radical it could have been scarcely imagined. Rather than downgrading sin, or upgrading the sinner, he actually removes the sinner (sinful 'self') from the moral equation entirely (Rom. 6:6)! But how does he achieve that? For Paul, it is the death and resurrection of Christ that is the key to his new ethical paradigm.[5]

Paul argues the case, from within the grace paradigm, that the Christian person is intimately connected to the particular *transformative event* of Christ's death and resurrection. By their faith-based *solidarity with Christ*, they share in Christ's death and resurrection; and by association, the corresponding status accompanying them. Through this *identification* with Christ, sinners are disengaged from the powerful reign of sin, as Watchman Nee explains, 'God sets us free from the dominion of sin, not by strengthening the old man, but by crucifying him . . . by removing him from the scene of the action.'[6] Thus, by 'mysteriously' linking the Christian person's status to Christ and his death, effectively crucifying the 'old self', Paul can confidently proclaim the fact of a 'new' Christian status: 'Therefore, if anyone is in Christ, he is a new creation; the old has gone, the new has come!' (2 Cor. 5:17). In Christ, the sinner is effectively 'dead' to sin.

Of course, the key to understanding this status is the 'in Christ' phenomenon. Paul speaks in terms that indicate that believers are realistically united with Christ, so as to imply that when Jesus Christ died the Christian believer 'realistically' died with him. Subsequently, as Christ was raised, also the believer is raised to a newness of life, free from the dominion of sin. Yes, Christ's representative death made atonement for *sins*, but the believer's 'participation' with Christ in this event also establishes a new state of affairs in which the *sin nature* has been crucified as well. In this way, association with Christ breaks the power of sin, *the flesh*. Of course, this has profound ethical implications: 'In the same way, count yourselves dead to sin but alive to God in Christ Jesus. Therefore do not let sin reign in your mortal body so that you obey its evil desires' (Rom. 6:11–12). So, through 'union' with Christ, the ethical obligation remains, as Constantine Campbell rightly suggests, 'The objective nature of believers' death with Christ entails the subjective obligation to live out death to sin, as it were.'[7]

But given the concrete historicity of the crucifixion / resurrection event, how is this kind of solidarity with Christ *actually* possible? To make sense of the conceptual connection between believers' present status and the Christ events, Paul reminds his readers of the analogical value of Christian baptism (Rom. 6:3–5). Robert Tannehill views Paul's use of baptism as a 'natural' common denominator in this regard: 'It is likely that Paul refers to baptism in Rom. 6 because he believes the idea of dying with Christ in baptism is known and accepted by the Roman Christians, so that through it, they can be led to understand Paul's conception of the relation of the believer to sin.'[8] Yet, there is more to this than simply a 'notional' connection between physical baptism and the historical death of Christ. Given the ethical context, and discussions in Paul's other epistles, it would seem the Spirit is actively involved here as well. Presumably, the Spirit's role is to engender the faith that lays hold of Christ: 'Having been buried with him in baptism and raised with him through your faith in the power of God' (Col. 2:12). The Spirit's role is simply taken for granted in this context.

In implying the Spirit's role in 'binding' this faith union, Paul was drawing on the early church's practical awareness and indeed his own experience of a close connection between baptism and the Holy Spirit (Acts 2:38; 8:12–16; 9:18; 10:47; 19:5). Whatever Paul or his readers 'might' have been thinking, we do know that being 'in Christ' and 'in the Spirit' are related ideas, as Campbell points out, 'Paul is capable of using the language "in the spirit" alongside "in Christ."'[9] Paul speaks of a 'spiritual' union with Christ, when addressing an ethical issue with the Corinthians: 'But he who unites himself with the Lord, is one with him in spirit' (1 Cor. 6:17); given that the Holy Spirit is referred to in verse 19 'spirit' cannot simply be reduced to a synonym for 'mind'. Furthermore, Paul sees the Lord [Jesus] as the Spirit: 'Now the Lord is the Spirit, and where the Spirit of the Lord is, there is freedom' (2 Cor. 3:17). For Christians their transformative freedom from the law is a direct consequence of the Lord, who is present as the Spirit. This 'union' with Christ, even if it entails other elements, is principally a union 'through' the Spirit.

However, understanding the concept of 'union' is not without its problems. The ancient world of Christian thought was not immune from the influences of Platonic ontology. Plato advocated a dualism between body and soul, between the physical and spiritual, and a movement toward one was a movement away from the other. Through a process of education the 'enlightened' soul could progress to a higher state, toward *the One*. With respect to the Platonic quest for 'union', Rebecca Lyman observes, 'For a Platonist, therefore, union with God was ultimately possible, but extremely difficult; for the disciplined few, the mind could be trained for strenuous contemplation of the One.'[10] In this Platonic scheme, union with the divine represented an abstraction away from the material, achieved through intellectual contemplation. Ultimately, this could be imagined as a unity with the divine substance.

Bruce McCormack argues that an uncritical adoption of certain Greek ontologies into Christian thought has served to shape certain 'participationist' views; even that of the seminal Reformed thinker, John Calvin.[11] McCormack believes viewing 'union' with Christ from a participationist perspective potentially jeopardizes the primacy of justification.[12] Participation in God's substance is viewed as by-passing the need to accept his atoning work. McCormack posits as an alternative to participation 'with Christ' a 'covenant ontology' model of correspondence: 'We are what we are through correspondence . . . unity of Christ takes its rise through a unity of wills, not through a unity of substances.'[13] However, this mind-oriented 'unity of wills' appears 'practically' not that dissimilar to the Platonic unity with 'the One'![14] Do you see the problem here? When conceived through the lens of, or in reaction to, philosophically oriented Greek ontology, union with Christ must be considered as a fusion of substances, or something abstracted and separate, which we can only 'correspond' with.

However, is 'participation' with Christ really as suspect as claimed? Calvin strenuously advocates the Holy Spirit's engagement in this regard, 'But he unites himself to us by the Spirit alone. By the grace and power of the same Spirit, we are made his members, to keep us under himself and in turn to possess him.'[15] Calvin was very aware of the dangers of 'fusing' substances or natures. When confronted by Osiander's notion of 'essential righteousness' he responds, 'He says we are one with Christ. We agree. But we deny that Christ's essence is mixed with our own.'[16] Nevertheless, it is not difficult to see how Calvin could be perceived as uniting substances, as Todd Billings intimates, 'In clarifying what he means by "participation in Christ", Calvin says that participation is not a "mere imitation" of Christ, but a real or "substantial" participation.'[17] In attempting to clarify Calvin's position, Seng-Kong Tan offers a possible explanation, 'Hence to be partakers of the divine nature, means a participation not of essence but of quality; thus it is not substantial, but nonetheless, it is still ontological as participation in the nature which involves a sharing in the properties of the essence.'[18]

Yet, whenever 'union with Christ' is logically defined, little *practical* headway is gained. While reflection on this matter may be intellectually stimulating, a preoccupation with ontological speculation only serves to derail Paul's actual intent in his Romans correspondence, which is not abstract reflection on the nature of 'being'. Paul, rather, is more concerned to provide a reasoned explanation for what he 'actually' had experienced in the Spirit – victory over the sinful nature. Indeed, Paul himself had experienced the emancipation from sin's power as a consequence of a real 'spiritual' union with Christ. That it is 'real' is certain for the apostle; 'how' it is 'actually real' remains a divine mystery of the Spirit's working. For Paul it is the relational, rather than the ontological dimension of 'union' that is most pertinent; that is why he frames his discussion based on the metaphor of slavery.

Slavery was integral to Roman society, with as many as two-thirds of the empire's population being designated slaves.[19] The Roman Empire owed much of its prosperity to the conquest of the surrounding nations. As the economic cost of conquest was usually quite high, the empire required a return on its investment. Part of that economic return was realized through the acquisition of foreign lands with their material resources and taxable population, and part was realized through the acquisition of human capital – slaves. As with previous empires, slaves represented a valuable resource and an inexpensive means of expanding Rome's borders and building its vital infrastructure. For the meagre price of human subsistence, slaves were employed in various ways, depending on the need. They were little more than expendable chattels. It was an undeniable reality that burgeoning ancient societies such as Rome simply could not efficiently function without human slavery.[20]

In fact, the cultural apparatus of the Roman 'urbanized' state was predicated on the idea that the luxurious provision of the minority elite must come at the expense of the majority slave populous.[21] As such, there was a strong sense of class distinction. The municipal aristocracy stood at the top of a 'steep' social pyramid, with impoverished poor, usually consisting of a good number of slaves, forming its base. The middle section was usually composed of artisans, tradesmen, merchants and other skilled workers. In this vertically stratified society, as Abraham Malherbe states, 'The sense of high and low pressed heavily on people.'[22] It was into this urban social context the Christian gospel first came. In fact, Malherbe argues the setting of early Christianity was principally urban, because 'there was a greater openness and a willingness to give a hearing to preachers of new religions'.[23]

In this setting, the Christian church grew, but unlike its pagan counterparts grew 'differently'. What set Christianity apart was its 'inclusive' approach. Unlike the Roman *societies*, which were fiercely homogeneous and exclusive, Christianity welcomed all classes of people. Thus, in an unprecedented way the social elite were exposed to an intimate engagement with the enslaved.[24] The mixture of all the social aspects of Roman society shaped the Christian church and its understanding; as Wayne Meeks remarks, 'The Christians whose moral formation we are trying to understand, lived in the world of the early Roman Empire, and that world also lived in them: in their thinking, in their language, in their relationships.'[25] In short, every Christian had an intimate understanding of slavery and its implications.

Paul considered all humanity a 'slave' to sin, and the gospel of Christ the means of emancipation from it. He used the metaphor of slavery as a means of communicating the influence and effect Christ and gospel brings. From Paul's letters, we can see that he was personally familiar with slavery, describing himself as a 'slave' of Christ (Rom. 1:1; Titus 1:1). He also saw in the work of Christ a form of slavery (Phil. 2:7). Furthermore, his entire letter to Philemon centred on a discussion about a slave, Onesimus. Other letters, too, feature the theme of slavery on a pastoral level (Eph. 6; Col. 3; and 1 Cor. 7). Paul then uses these practical ideas of slavery to relate to deeper religious truths.

In his discussions on the moral freedom that Christ brings (discussions set against the slavery of the law and the flesh), Paul's greatest theological use of the *slavery metaphor* is seen. The apostle uses the slavery metaphor in Galatians 4 to point out to the Christians that loyalty to Christ precludes 'slavery' to the law. No longer is the 'yoke' of the law a burden (Gal. 5:18). These believers should not despair at the former mastery of the 'flesh' (human nature) either, because Christ's empowering presence, through the Spirit, has addressed that 'power' too! For Paul, then, emancipation from the 'slavery' of sin (in its various forms) ultimately comes through the Spirit: 'So I say, live by the Spirit, and you will not gratify the desires of the sinful nature' (Gal. 5:16).

Of course, this is evident in Romans as well. Here, Paul employs the metaphor of slavery to explain that the Spirit sets the beleaguered sinner free, not only from the penalty of 'sins' but from the power of the 'sinful nature' that generates them. Having conceptually established the believer's 'union' with Christ through the idea of baptism (Rom. 6:3–4), Paul seeks to establish the real value of this 'union'.

He speaks with a kind of certainty that conveys the true effectiveness of this union and its resultant benefits. Paul contends that the 'old self', previously under the bondage of sin, has been crucified with Christ – it is dead. The net effect of this new 'state of being' is that sin nature has no capacity to exercise power by animating sinful acts, 'because anyone who has died has been freed from sin' (Rom. 6:7). The bond of slavery to the 'old self' has been broken because that 'self' is actually dead!

Commensurately, by virtue of Christ's resurrection, this person has been raised to newness of life, where sin and its effectual partner, death, have no dominion at all. The believer's life is no longer enslaved to the mastery of sin, but subject to the new mastery of God: 'But the life he lives he lives to God' (Rom. 6:10). As this is the new reality vis-à-vis sin, believers are compelled to make this reality 'personal', reckoning themselves dead to sin and alive to God. Indeed, Paul exhorts them not to yield the members of their body for the service of unrighteousness. Rather they are to surrender themselves to God (the new master). Having surrendered their will to his mastery, they are to yield their members as instruments for God's righteous service (Rom. 6:13). Of course, this is only possible through the 'in Christ' phenomenon, in which they have transferred realms; from the burdensome realm of slavery to sin, to a free realm of slavery to righteousness.

In Romans 6:15 Paul reiterates the rhetorical question of v. 1 regarding ethical conduct in the light of grace. This time, he clearly sets it in contrast with the law. Indeed, the antithesis between law and grace is really an antithesis between two 'domains' of power, as Tannehill argues, 'This setting is the contrast of two dominions and their lords.'[26] This is clear in verse 16, where Paul alludes to slaves offering themselves to someone in service. In this case the alternatives are: on the one hand, sin and its correlate death, and on the other, obedience and its correlate righteousness (leading to holiness and life, v. 22). Obeying the gospel (v. 17), the Christian is set free from the old domain of law, sin and death. Through a Spirit-engendered 'faith union' with Christ they have been transferred into the new dominion of grace, Spirit and life. Therefore, the ethical implications for a 'slave' of Christ are profound. There must be no compulsion to render service to the 'old master'; Tannehill again: 'It is a key part of the theological basis of Paul's ethics. The Christian cannot lead a life of sin while under grace just because the new master, like the old, has a complete claim to his service and holds him in his power. In this aeon, as well as the old, he stands under a master who commands him and acts through him.'[27]

Paul is clear about Christian conduct in view of the gospel's emancipating power. Because of the advent of the realm of grace through the gospel, there is no ethical 'opt-out' clause, allowing the Christian 'slave' to ignore or dismiss morality within this new realm. The distorted notion of having Jesus as a Saviour while considering his lordship as optional – divorcing faith and obedience to logically prevent works 'seeping' into justification – is simply nonsensical. Those who have been transferred into the new dominion of grace are now 'bonded' to Christ 'in the Spirit', and as such are servants of Christ, slaves of righteousness. These *slaves of Christ* are bound to a life of faith-based, Spirit-enabled obedience to the Lord. The gospel doesn't negate the ethical imperative on account of God's grace; rather it affirms and incorporates it. To be justified by Christ is to be incorporated into Christ, to be incorporated into Christ is to be transformed into an entirely new person. God, in the power of the Spirit, as Richard Hays puts it, 'grasps us and remakes us'.[28] Having been grasped and remade by the Spirit, the Christian person can no longer return to a reliance on the law or an associated duty-driven works as the means of upholding or augmenting this new state – that existence is now dead.

Law and the Christian State-of-Being (Romans 7)

Having laid the foundation for moral necessity commensurate with God's grace, Paul moves on to the issue of process. The discussion about morality within the context of salvation, set out in Romans

6 – 8, cannot refer to salvation from a forensic 'causal' perspective. In fact, Paul's preceding argument and discussion on human inadequacy (Rom. 1 – 2) and the all-sufficiency of Christ (Rom. 3 – 4) has dispelled any notion that human merit contributes anything toward 'gaining' or indeed 'maintaining' the benefits of salvation. The apostle's discussion on justification has already settled salvation in terms of the 'penalty' of sin and the believer's legal standing before God. What is now under consideration is the gospel's role in delivering the believer from sin's lingering 'power'; thus salvation is being considered from a present 'existential' perspective.

If we have understood Paul's previous discussion on solidarity with Christ in Romans 6 rightly, then to be justified by faith implies incorporation 'in Christ', which itself implies a 'necessary' imperative to walk in the manner of Christ. Consequently, walking in the manner of Christ necessarily implies 'not' being controlled by the power of the flesh. At stake here, then, is the means by which this malevolent power might be overcome. The *matter* of sin's lingering power and necessity for it to be overcome in the believer's moral life has been the primary subject of consideration in Romans 6, but now in Romans 7 – 8 the *manner* in which sin's power, vis-à-vis *the flesh*, respectively 'cannot' and 'can' be overcome, is clearly in view.

Without question, Romans 7 is among the most theologically contested passages in Holy Scripture. The principal contest in this debate usually relates to the identity of the 'person' being described in the text. Is Paul describing a Christian or pre-Christian experience? Is this the struggle of an unbeliever under the law, or the wrestling of a believer under grace? At the fountainhead of this debate is the seminal contribution of St Augustine. Augustine always understood the nature of the discussion in Romans 7 as 'experiential' in nature, describing Paul's struggles with passion and law.[29] However, was Paul describing himself prior to conversion, as one 'under law' or as a Christian 'under grace'?

Augustine began believing the person being described here is 'under the law' and 'prior to grace', possibly Paul in his unconverted Jewish state.[30] Taken this way the person described is within the realm of sin, and cannot perform what the law commands; thus they are driven to grace and repentance. However, this position was modified in ad 397, such that grace was assumed to initiate the move toward repentance. This deepened Augustine's understanding, as Eugene TeSelle indicates, 'He still seems to assume that the struggle is prior to conversion, not after it. But there is an intensified interest in the inward dynamics of the human self, and it is not surprising that Augustine wrote his confessions at the same time.'[31] However, by ad 411 Augustine became convinced that the person being described must be fully 'regenerate' because, according to his reasoning, who could delight in the law except a righteous believer? This later position is clearly seen in Augustine's comparison of the 'righteous' patriarch Job with the person in Romans 7: 'But the language in which the Lord commends Job might also be applied to him who "delights in the law of God after the inner man, while he sees another law in his members warring against the law of his mind".'[32]

But what had instigated the radical change in Augustine's mind? Certainly, the controversy with the Pelagians contributed in no small part. Pelagius himself argued that the person in Romans 7:7ff. is 'under the law': 'From here on he speaks in the person of one who accepts the law, that is, who first comes to know God's commandments while he is still in the habit of breaking them.'[33] Pelagius argues that because Paul was 'set free' by grace, the person he describes was not someone in his present state: 'This shows that [the apostle] is speaking in the person of someone else, [not in his own person].'[34] Over against Pelagius, and the Pelagian denial of sin's continuing influence and the need for grace, Augustine took his new stance. In his writings *Against Two Letters of the Pelagians* and in *Against Julian*, as well as his *Retractions*, the church father repudiates his early position on Romans 7.[35] Yet Augustine's argumentation owes more to dogmatic principle than exegesis. Indeed, Augustine and even Pelagius uncritically filtered the particulars of the text (and the wider context for that matter) through their dogmatic categories out of polemic concern, largely in ignorance of Paul's particular concerns.

Highlighting the consistency of Augustine's dogmatic soteriological construct (*ordo salutis*) despite his complete exegetical back-flip on Romans 7, Christopher Bound's analysis brings into sharp relief the strong imposition of Augustine's dogmatic method on his exegesis.[36] He outlines Augustine's system (*ordo salutis*) as follows: 'prior to law' – ignorant sinners; 'under the law' – awakened conscience by law, anxiety over guilt and aware of need for salvation; 'under grace' – infusion of grace toward conversion and a desire to delight in God's law, though fleshly desires are in conflict with the Spirit; and 'in peace' – the heavenly state after death. Bounds suggests that Augustine's larger system remained completely unchanged, despite his polemically motivated exegetical shift.[37] In the more mature position Augustine broadly interprets Romans 7 as Paul's personal Christian experience, and by extension the 'normal' experience of every Christian 'under grace'. Taken this way, the law serves to initially drive a person to seek grace; thus Romans 7:7–13 is the person 'under law', where the law makes sin more sinful.

However, in Romans 7:14–23 the categories change, representing Paul's (and the Christian's) present testimony 'under grace'. Why? Because in Augustine's logic, only a person 'under grace' could delight in God's law through the Spirit![38] As further proof of his dogmatically dominant method, TeSelle highlights that, despite Augustine's sermons (151–6) running sequentially through Romans 7–8, Augustine leaps ahead in sermon 152 to Romans 8:3–4, because he sees Romans 8 as the 'the key' to Romans 7, thus reading the Christian 'Spirit' experience back into Romans 7.[39] That said, such a reflexive reading is not altogether wrong, as Paul did not write his letter with chapter divisions. Yet unlike Augustine's final position that 7:12–25 represents a Christian's day-to-day life, Paul is clear in 8:2 that the authority / power (law) of the Spirit sets him free from the authority / power (law) of sin and death, that he said in 7:23–4 held him captive. In fact, Augustine's early position – that Romans 7 represents someone not yet following Christ – is a more consistent rendering of the text (although not entirely right), and despite achieving what many perceive as a 'realistic' dogmatic construct of the Christian life, it seems that Augustine's polemic concerns allow his dogmatic system to override the more natural exegetical meaning of Paul.[40]

Augustine's interpretive 'method' also influenced subsequent interpreters. John Calvin is in lock-step with Augustine in this regard: 'But Paul, as I have said already, does not here set before us simply the natural man, but in his own person describes what the weakness of the faithful is, and how great it is. Augustine was for a time involved in the common error; but . . . retracted what he had falsely taught.'[41] R. Ward Holder observes of Calvin's interpretative method with respect to Romans 7, 'Calvin had to abandon the medieval tradition that accepted Romans 7 as a description of life under the law, and Calvin was not an interpreter who lightly discarded the church's exegetical traditions.'[42] In turning away from his favoured exegete, Chrysostom,[43] Calvin chose to side with the doctrinally orthodox interpretation of Augustine. Thus, Holder contends, in a contest between principles (in Calvin's case the supremacy of Augustine's orthodoxy) and exegetical rules, the former clearly wins: 'Finally, theologians in general and Calvin, in particular, allow hermeneutic principles to overwhelm exegetical rules in cases of this agreement.'[44]

Calvin, like the influential Augustine before him, carried on the tradition of allowing 'orthodox' dogmatic universals to gain ascendency over the particular exegetical nuances of the text. In the process of maintaining what is believed to be 'sound' theology, he then forced onto the text a meaning that made 'good' theological sense, but missed Paul's thrust! Such an influential interpretation has transferred to posterity a certain orientation and meaning of Paul's argument that fails to grasp the nuance of what Paul is actually arguing for. In fact, the primary meaning of the text is not 'centred' around the identity of the 'self' and its moral struggle. Of course, a moral struggle is discussed, but more importantly, Paul's argument is oriented around the inadequacy of the law. It is focused on the futility of embracing law as the means of existentially overcoming the power of sin (the flesh) – the subject under consideration.

In fact, in Romans 7, Paul is not concerned with describing the 'normal' Christian struggle. On the contrary, the apostle is outlining the 'insufficient' moral life under the law. He seeks to connect with his readers by highlighting the anxiety and futility of addressing the power of sin by means of the law. That the law is the subject under examination is clearly seen by his opening verse: 'Do you not know, brothers – for I am speaking to men who know the law' (Rom. 7:1). To be consistent with all that has gone before, those 'who know the law' must be none other than ex-Jews or pro-law Gentiles within the Roman church who viewed the law favourably as the means of expressing their Christian faith. These believers, as Watson suggests, 'are to choose life within the reign of grace rather than death within the realm of the law'.[45]

Paul wants to encourage them to no longer look to the law as the means of overcoming sin's power, but ultimately to the Spirit. As Paul approaches this vital subject, he does so on the basis of the previously establishing notion of the ethical life through a non-nomistic 'union with Christ'. He is actually seeking to present life under the law as a negative foil against which to reveal a more adequate way that originates 'in Christ' and comes via the Spirit.[46] If the grounds for union with Christ is the believer's death with Christ, it is fitting that having established the subject matter of the law (7:1a), Paul should now state that 'the law has authority over a man only as long as he lives' (Rom. 7:1b).

Romans 7:1–6 is a synopsis of Paul's greater exposition in Romans 7 – 8. True to form he uses a metaphor to establish the termination of the believer's relationship with the law – the metaphor of marriage. Marriage is a relationship bound by law, and it is perpetually binding as long as both parties are alive. If one of the parties should die, then the contractual relationship ceases. Thus the woman (in Paul's illustration) is released from an obligation to the binding law and is free to marry again. If, however, the woman in question seeks a marriage while the previous legal arrangement is valid, she is an adulteress. But in this case, the husband has died and, as such, the 'new bond' cannot be deemed sinful. In this, Paul seeks to assuage the fears that these believers might have believed that abandoning the law is tantamount to 'religious adultery'.

Of course, no simile is logically tight, but Paul's point is clear, 'So, my brothers, you also died to the law through the body of Christ, that you might belong to another' (Rom. 7:4). By virtue of their 'union with Christ' they have died to that former relationship with the law, and are now 'married' to Christ. They are now in a relationship that enables the 'bearing fruit to God', or a righteous life. Under the previous 'marriage' with the law, the law did nothing but arouse the sinful passions and the outcome was not righteousness but sin; the fruit of which was death.

By dying to the law that once bound them through their 'death with Christ', believers have been released from that previous legal arrangement and are free to express devotion to God in a new manner: the way of the Spirit. An entirely new way of relating to and serving God has come into being! As Brendan Byrne suggests, Paul sets forth a rhetorical argument: 'Setting positive over against negative, a new situation over against the past, he [Paul] highlights a superiority of the new to reinforce the hope it contains.'[47] Once we see that Paul has in view a critique of the law, with the specific intent of exposing its inadequacy for addressing the power of sin (especially to the pro-law constituency), the identity of the 'self' being discussed in Romans 7 is far easier to ascertain.

Careful not to come across as anti-Semitic, Paul wants to reveal the law's ineffectiveness without denigrating the law per se (for it is still God's law). Paul elects to accomplish this with a first-person discourse. This is specifically designed to provide a mirror against which his pro-law readers, through reflective self-examination, may see the validity of his argument. The crux of the argument is that the law is ineffective. Luke Timothy Johnson convincingly argues that Paul brings to bear a 'speech-in-character' method, where he adopts a certain position as his own: 'Such personification enables an author to bring a logical position vibrantly to life, by "performing" it. The ancient rhetorical designation for such "speech in character" was *prosopopoiia* ("making a mask"), and it fits what Paul is doing here very well.'[48]

The fact that Paul can do this so convincingly and with such conviction, indicates that he may be relating his own struggles as a law-oriented believer wrestling with his 'new' faith; an 'immature' believer, who had to come to terms with the inefficacy of the law in relation to the 'new' life in Christ. This non-threatening 'empathetic' discourse provides the perfect platform for his argument. The argument is that law is an invalid means of suppressing the power of sin and enabling the ethical outworking of the righteous status in Christ.

Thus, in taking the 'weak' position, Paul seeks to draw his 'weak' readers to embrace the 'strong' position. Showing that the believer is 'not' to serve in the old way of the written code, and being aware of his readers' sensibilities, Paul (in v. 7) establishes that the law (command) *simpliciter* is not inherently sinful. The law is the very thing that exposes sin, and not only exposes it but actually incites the human nature (the flesh) to be more sinful: 'But sin, seizing the opportunity afforded by the commandment, produced in me every kind of covetous desire' (Rom. 7:8). Paul indicates that without the law (commandment) there was no conscious awareness of sin, but with an awareness of the commandment the reality of sin sprang to life. And with sin coming to life, the reality of death became evident. Thus, Paul establishes the principal function of law is to reveal sin, exposing it as sinful!

Moreover, in appealing to the commandment relating to covetousness, the apostle draws his readers into a similar context that Adam and Eve faced in Eden.[49] The law given by God to Adam and Eve was designed to give life. However, it incited within them covetous desires, and they were deceived by sinful desire. The commandment that was designed to save them actually ended up condemning them! Not wishing to denigrate God's divine law, Paul points out that despite its inherently good and holy disposition, the law is ineffectual in securing the righteousness desired (a point made explicit in Rom. 8:3).

Although the law places the religious adherent in a hopeless predicament, Paul sees good in this (Rom. 7:13). Through the goodness of the commandment, the sinfulness of sin is exposed for what it really was, sinful beyond measure – a harbinger of death (v. 13). Ironically, this dreadful condemnation is for a good purpose; just as the night is coldest before dawn, so the darkest awareness of sin opens up a new sense of self-awareness – an awareness of abject slavery to sin and the desperate need of emancipation from its power.

Given that Paul frames this whole section principally with the metaphor of slavery, he appropriately reintroduces the concept here to further highlight the hopeless plight of the person employing law as the means of moral conquest. Although a person may acknowledge the goodness, the spiritual derivation and spiritual purpose of the law, they cannot escape the 'unspiritual' state that holds them captive to the malevolent forces of sin (v. 14). Although the well-meaning religious person might employ the law to inform their moral consciousness of what is right, the sinful nature (the flesh) will not allow them to fulfil its demands; on the contrary, the law condemns them (vv. 17–21)! Though this person might acknowledge what is right and good, and consciously desire it, the capacity to enact the good is 'mysteriously' hindered by sin's malevolent power; a power generated by the 'unspiritual' flesh. Thus, on account of their law-oriented moral methodology, they incorrigibly lack the capacity to manifest their desire for righteous obedience (vv. 22–3).

Furthermore, in Paul's mind, works of the Jewish law are no longer a legitimate expression of devotion to God. In fact, to continue in the once valid old covenant 'system' of religion is to deny God's new way 'in Christ' – the way of the Spirit. Under the 'old' regime, a Jew was incorporated into God's people, as a privileged birth rite or by being a converted proselyte. The works of the law (circumcision, moral law-code-keeping, ceremonies, sacrifices, etc.) represented the legitimate expression of showing one belonged to God's people. Although such works are not an attempt to 'earn' salvation, they are a valid and necessary expression of covenant obedience.

However, given that this (previously legitimate) system is now 'defunct' (by virtue of the new covenant and Christ's work in establishing it), works of the law, as an expression of obedience, are also defunct, being replaced by the 'new way' of the Spirit. A maintenance of, or reversion to, the 'old way' of the letter (Rom. 7:6) effectively says to God, 'I don't feel secure in this new way; I want to trust the old way of expressing obedience.' By adopting this position, a person stops trusting God ('in Christ') and they start relying on their own 'comfortable' way of expressing obedience – works of the law. By extension, works 'of the law' manifestly represent a faith-denying expression of obedience. Consequently, this person remains a perpetual slave to their quest for existential righteousness; trapped by a practical endeavour of self-justification through the law, even while they may 'claim' to follow Christ.

While these religious adherents might be set on grace and the commensurate hope of moral freedom, an enduring reliance on law holds them captive, enslaving them to their natural state, condemned by the very law they put their hope in.[50] As Paul indicates, such a life is a morally engendered 'existential hell'; eagerly desiring the good but lacking the capacity to attain it: 'What a wretched man I am! Who will rescue me from this body of death?' (Rom. 7:24). A slave in the ancient world lived in a 'body of death'; it was usually not a matter of 'if' they died in an untimely way, but when. Whether they laboured in the mines, fought as a gladiator or served in a household where they could fall out of favour on a whim – they potentially lived under a continual death sentence. Paul identifies such a metaphorical 'wretched' state of moral slavery when he considers the plight of the religious person trying to walk in conformity with God through adherence to the law. They too, exist as the 'living dead', bonded to the law. For Paul the only answer is Christ: 'Thanks be to God – through Jesus Christ our Lord!' (Rom. 7:25).

Indeed, this problem is not solved by simply appealing to Christ's justifying actions on the cross every time law-engendered pangs of sin overwhelm. This approach is akin to adopting the 'rational' equivalent of personally crucifying Christ over and over again, denying the sufficiency of Christ's 'once-for-all' death. The solution to sin's *power* is not guilt-driven consolation through rational reflection on the historical forensic work of Christ. Rather, the solution is the believer's Spirit-engendered reckoning of 'union' with Christ (Rom. 6:11). Jesus is the crucified and risen Saviour, with whom the old sinful nature died. Through Jesus, the redeemed 'self' is raised to serve in newness of life – life in the power of the Spirit. In breaking the bonds from the power of sin through union with Christ, the gospel empowers deliverance 'from' *the flesh*, and the old system of law that enslaved the self-nature. The gospel emancipates believers from the law's domain of influence, condemning power and legal method. That is why the apostle can so heartily exclaim: 'Thanks be to God!'

Paul concludes his argument: 'So then, I myself in my mind am a slave to God's law, but in the sinful nature a slave to the law of sin' (Rom. 7:25). Like a substance addict that hates the nature of their condition but lacks the power to break the addiction that binds their mind and wrecks their body, the person under the law is in a hopeless predicament – a slave to both body and mind. It seems, then, that not only are human works incapable of paying the sin's *penalty*; they are equally impotent in mitigating sin's *power*. Yet as strong as the power or sin is, as debilitating as the weakness of the flesh is, and reviling as the condemning voice of the law is, the Holy Spirit's power is greater still.

Spirit, Power and Life (Romans 8:1–13)

Against the hopelessness emanating from law religion, the gospel finally uncovers the majesty of the Spirit, shedding abroad the hope of freedom to those once wretched souls. In the text of Romans 8 we hear echoes of Zechariah's prophetic words: '"Not by might, nor by power, but by my Spirit," says the Lord Almighty' (Zech. 4:6). Through the agency of the Spirit, the gospel 'in Christ' is able to counter the *power* of sin. The necessity of the righteous life that Paul held out in Romans 6, impossible under the law as argued in Romans 7, is now set out in Romans 8 as possible for those truly 'in Christ'. This is no 'fictional' hope; 'this power' has been previously validated, as Klaus Haacker states, 'It is the Holy Spirit as life-giving power, revealed as such in Christ's resurrection, who is able to perform the miracle of changing the hearts and minds of believers so that the ethical essence of the law begins to shape their lives.'[51]

That Paul would powerfully represent the Christian plight under the law in terms of a slave under a sentence of death indicates the actual futility of this law predicament. Yet such a predicament provides the perfect foil against which to state the 'good news'. It is with no small amount of elation that Paul proclaims good news for those who escape the futility of the Christian life under the law. Now, rather than speaking in terms of a stylized life of 'I' under the law, Paul plainly speaks of the present reality of 'you' (pl.) 'in Christ'. This movement marks a clear turning point from the previous argument, as Ben Witherington indicates, 'It is clear enough that we have turned a corner when we reach Romans 8. There is no more diatribe and no more impersonation.'[52]

Now, against the dark background of wrestling with sin under the slavery of the flesh and condemnation of the law, hope rises as this new and present spirit-reality of liberation 'in Christ' is heralded.[53] The negation of condemnation adumbrated by Paul here cannot be attributable to a rational appreciation of the forensic work of Christ.[54] The argument commenced in Romans 6:1, enshrouded by the metaphor of slavery, now arrives at its principal application of 'no condemnation'. The focus must be the *existential reality* of the Christian experience 'in Christ'. Freed by the power of the Spirit, the believer escapes both the power of the sin and the power of the law to condemn the sinner. This particular good news is just as much 'gospel' news as Jesus' death forensically addressing sin's penalty.

That the Spirit is deemed the agent of this emancipation is clearly set out: 'Because through Christ Jesus the law of the Spirit of life set me free from the law of sin and death' (Rom. 8:2). Thomas Schreiner interprets law here as the Mosaic Law: 'According to this construction, the Mosaic Law is in the realm either of the Holy Spirit or of the powers of sin and death. If the law is appropriated in the realm of the Spirit and by faith, then one is liberated from using the Mosaic Law in such a way that it leads to sin and death.'[55] Taken this way, it assumes that the law is the agent that sets one free. However, if this is the case, it seems to contradict Paul's argument that sets the law as the agent of enslavement and instrument of death (Rom. 6:15; 7:1,4,9,11,25), and specifically the stark contrast of the two in Romans 7:6. Alternatively, Witherington suggests that 'law' in Romans 8:2 should be interpreted 'rule' or 'principle';[56] while this makes more sense, it still doesn't capture Paul's intent.

Given the action of 'setting free' is in view, 'law' seems to be freighted with the meaning of *power or authority*. Interpreted this way, the morally 'enabling' power or authority of Spirit is able to break the morally 'binding' power or authority of sin and death (validated by law). Given Paul's portrayal of law as an authority working in concert with the sinful nature leading to death (Rom. 7:1–5), this seems more plausible.[57] What is communicated is a contest of powers. In this context, the Spirit comes to dominate over sin, as Byrne suggests, 'From lack of righteousness (sin) has been removed because a new moral force (the Spirit), available in Christ Jesus, has brought release from the ethical "impossibility" created by the dominance of sin.'[58] Taken this way, through our union with Jesus Christ, in which the old self died and was raised anew to life by the power of the Spirit, we have been freed from the authority of sin and death. The essential point is that it is the Spirit's power that emancipates from the 'enslaving power' of sin and death, making way for authentic moral conformity, not through the law; but in spite of it – through the Spirit. There is now a new power animating morality, a power that operates outside the law, yet fulfils the intent of the law in a way previously unimaginable.

Moreover, that 'law' connotes the notion of power is strengthened by Paul's reference to its negation: 'The law was powerless' (Rom. 8:3). Given, as previously discussed, that Romans 7:1–6 forms the synopsis of the entire section, the spirit / law antithesis of Romans 7:6 is again being played out here. Consistent with his previous argument about the law's 'essential' goodness, Paul states that the source of the powerlessness regarding the law is actually the human nature corrupted by sin (the flesh). Rather than simply contrasting the 'weak' power of the law with the 'strong' power of the Spirit, Paul is careful not to present the Spirit's power as taking a separate route to the work of Christ and the Father. In highlighting the Trinitarian operation of breaking sin's power, Paul reveals that God (the Father) sent 'his own' son in the likeness of a sinful man to be a sin offering. Reintroducing juristic categories, Paul speaks of substitutionary atonement. The son, as a representative of sinful humanity, is presented as the atoning sacrifice; as a human, Jesus represents sinful humanity, the Father's condemnation of the human Jesus (the representative of sinful humanity) effectively condemns sin on behalf of sinful humans.

It is the 'actual' effectuating work of Christ in his atonement that addresses sin's *penalty* and, coterminous with it, in disempowering the 'sin nature' is effective in breaking sin's *power*; the benefits of which the believer appropriates through being 'in Christ', by faith through the Spirit. As John Murray helpfully intimates, 'There can be no release from this bondage, contemplated in its judicial character until sin as power receives this judicial condemnation in the cross of Christ and until the effectual application to us takes effect.'[59] Thus it is impossible to divorce juristic and participatory / moral benefits regarding Christ's work and its application to the believer. Recognition of both Christ dying for us and us dying with Christ are necessary for the complete addressing of the sin *problem.*

This 'dual' working of Christ becomes the 'real' basis of the Christian life as having the potential to live consistently with God's will. The breaking of sin's power is purposeful, and the purpose pertains directly to the 'big' argument of the whole section: the emancipation from sin's power and the capacity to live in a manner that pleases God, or to 'fulfil' what the Law requires.[60] Those who see this section as referring to Christ's atoning sacrifice fulfilling the law's 'legal' or 'juristic' demands, that we might no longer be under *sin's penalty*, and then subsequently see morality as unimportant or disconnected, plainly ignore the context and thrust of the argument in Romans 6 – 8. And those that might assume that the Spirit empowers 'law-keeping' and that the law might be fulfilled have not understood the argument of Romans 7 and its clear statement about the inefficacy of law-keeping!

Yet, the Christian's relationship to the fulfilment of the law is not a subject without contention. Calvin argues that an understanding of those 'renewed' by the Spirit as being able to fulfil the law introduce an 'alien gloss' to Paul: 'For the faithful . . . never make such a proficiency, as that the justification of the law becomes full or complete.'[61] Calvin posits that this must then refer to forgiveness, for when the obedience of Christ is accepted on our behalf the law is satisfied. However, given Calvin's negative appraisal of the Christian life in Romans 7, such an interpretation of 8:4 is a foregone conclusion for him. Of course, Calvin's analysis is theologically true; it's just not the subject under discussion in 8:4. Moo in concert with Calvin speaks of the law being fulfilled through believers' incorporation into Christ and the believers' faith in Christ (who accomplished the law).[62]

However, in relation to Christian behaviour, 'walking' in the Spirit is connected with the law's fulfilment, a point that Moo acknowledges as a necessary mark in those for whom Christ's fulfilment applies, but doesn't adequately answer.[63] However, limiting the discussion to forensic or juristic categories ignores the wider context of sin's power. This is explicated by the metaphor of slavery as a whole, and is especially evident in the positive thrust of Romans 8 regarding the emancipation from sin's power, as set over and against Romans 7. Indeed, Schreiner's assessment is much more correct here: 'The judicial work of Christ is the basis of the transformed life of His people. The forensic and transformative works of Christ should not be wrenched apart . . . The work of Christ on the cross freed believers from both the penalty and power of sin.'[64]

Furthermore, Schreiner correctly asserts, 'There are good reasons for saying that Paul has in the mind the actual obedience of Christians'.[65] Because Paul does not argue for the believers keeping the law in their own strength, which is precisely the argument of 8:3, rather it is believer's obedience that is exclusively animated by the Spirit; only the Spirit fulfils the law. Thus, with the power of sin 'broken' being the centre of the argument, the plain reading of the text renders the following meaning: The law is powerless to enable its fulfilment because the flesh is weak; Christ's redemptive work destroyed the power of sin; for the purpose of enabling 'us' to keep the law's requirements who walk / live (not according to the flesh) but according to the 'new way' of the Spirit.

The power of sin prevents believers from living according to God's will. However, Christ has destroyed that power. Now the believer has appropriated Christ through the Spirit; that Spirit of Christ lives out the Christ-life in accord with God's will (previously designated as law). Yes, the believer is able to fulfil the *law's demands*, which is not the same as saying the believer is able to exactly keep all the *law's commands*. Such a fulfilment can only be attributable to the Spirit's power and any suggestion that human merit or effort may be credited with such fulfilment misrepresents Paul's argument for the Spirit's supremacy vis-à-vis sin's power!

For some who equate the gospel exclusively with justification, any suggestion of human obedience in relation to law fulfilment seems repugnant – a potential 'open door' to works righteousness. However, such narrow formulations come up against the problem of how to 'attach' ethics to soteriology in a manner that does not lead to the previously mentioned problems of either legalism or licentiousness – a problem that Albert Schweitzer clearly identified when he challenged the 'centrality' of justification to Paul's overall thought. Schweitzer argues that, in such formulations, soteriology and ethics are precariously divided, and thus become uncomfortable counterparts:

> In the doctrine of justification by faith, redemption and ethics are like two roads, one of which leads up to one side of a ravine, and the other leads onwards from the opposite side – but there is no bridge by which to pass from one side to the other. But Paul is here in the favourable position, as compared with the Reformers, of not having to make desperate efforts to procure the unprocurable material necessary to build this bridge. For in the mystical being-in-Christ he possesses a concept of redemption from which ethics directly results as a *natural function of the redeemed state*. In this concept, there is a logical foundation for the paradox that the man before redemption was incapable of good works, but afterward not only can but must bring them forth; since it is Christ who brings them forth in him.[66]

For Schweitzer, Paul's doctrine of union with Christ solves the legal / ethical conundrum: 'This being-in-Christ is the prime enigma of the Pauline teaching; once grasped it gives the clue to the whole.'[67] When a Christian grasps what it is to be 'in Christ', when they 'know' the commensurate power of the Spirit that attends such a union, the fact cannot be avoided that natural human agency is impotent in empowering the moral life.

Rather, the potential to overcome sin's power is only actualized when Christians 'deny' the power of self and by faith in Christ enter into a domain of grace that enables 'relational' conformity with God's will – by the Spirit. Paul presents the solution to the 'what' of 8:3, as the Spirit. The Holy Spirit that endowed, enabled and empowered Christ toward the completion of his redemptive work through his death and resurrection (providing the basis of our capacity to live in conformity with God's will), is the same Spirit that Christians now 'live by'. L. Ann Jervis speaks of the Spirit creating a 'territory' or an 'environment' which enables the believer to live consistently.[68] This created space corresponds with the domain of grace, in which the Christian is free from slavery; it is the freedom that gives the ex-slave space to move and live; a space which also corresponds to the present manifestation of God's kingdom: 'For the kingdom of God is [a matter of] . . . righteousness, peace and joy in the Holy Spirit, because anyone who serves Christ in this way is pleasing to God' (Rom. 14:17–18).

Living by the Spirit encapsulates more than a new 'space' without law. Living by the Spirit represents an empowered life, a way of living within that space, in which the 'essential' requirements of the law can be kept as pleasing to God; as Jervis adds, 'Those who walk "according to the Spirit" fulfil the law's just requirement (8:4). That is, the Spirit guides and empowers living, as God wants humans to live. If people accept the guidance of the Spirit, the Spirit shapes their values and intentions and desires.'[69] Within such a domain, obedience is 'demonstratively' revealed as loving devotion toward fellow believers and neighbours: 'He who loves his fellow-man has fulfilled the law' (Rom. 13:8).

Such an 'unnatural' life of love loudly testifies to the gospel's emancipating Spirit-power, negating any claims of human merit regarding law fulfilment. Such a life is not burdensome but joyful; if it is otherwise then the quality of one's relationship with Christ should be investigated. The Christian under the Spirit's influence does not live as a 'law-keeper'. This Christian unconsciously lives out God's will in joy, for within the 'new' realm of the Spirit, there is no need to keep 'literal' laws. The very source of truth that empowers the moral life, the Holy Spirit, actually indwells the believer (1 John 5:6).

To be 'in the Spirit' is to be removed from the realm of 'power' of the flesh. As Paul progresses from the previous discussion onto Romans 8:5–8, the two alternatives for living are set out clearly as 'according to the flesh' *kata sarka*, or 'according to the Spirit' *kata pneuma*; alternatives we have already pre-emptively encountered in Romans 1. However, now, the direction of the discussion takes an empirical turn, as Paul wants to provide a kind of 'practical test' to validate his prior reasoning. Paul challenges his readers to examine their actual lives as evidence of the 'inner' power that animates their outward actions, providing a similar contrast as he presented in Galatians 5:19–23. Those who live according to the flesh prove that their minds are set on the desires of the flesh. They have not grasped the gospel in its fullness. On the contrary, those who live in accordance with the Spirit (those that reveal the fruit of the Spirit) show that the Spirit is the animating force behind their lives; their desires correlate with the Spirit's desires, revealing they have grasped the gospel.

With such a revelation, Paul issues a warning (Rom. 8:6–8), that the mind of the sinful person leads to death; such a mind is hostile to God, as it will not submit to the intentions of God's law, in fact, is unable to. As such, the person who is without the Spirit and lives according to the flesh, albeit with a tacit acknowledgement of the law, will be tormented by the reality of being unable to please God, with all the attending consequences that flow on from that. On the contrary, those who are controlled by the Spirit beget the reality of life and peace; existentially, as well as prospectively. The point is now clear; the only way to escape the power of sin and live in a manner that pleases God is through the Spirit (vv. 8–9)!

The apostle extends the logic of his empirically orientated argument into the eschatological domain. Paul wants to make it clear that not only do those who *live by the Spirit* please God, but the same Spirit of God also guarantees 'actual' victory over those potent powers of sin and death – validated and guaranteed by the resurrection of Christ. So, even though the material body suffers under the 'effects' of sin, leading toward bodily death, the Spirit guarantees life beyond this current state.[70] Thus, for those in whom the spirit of God dwells, in whom righteousness is revealed as the Spirit's influence, their righteousness validates they belong to Christ.

So indispensable is the connection between the Spirit and Christ that those without the Spirit of Christ are deemed to not belong to Christ (v. 10). Despite claiming to 'have' Christ, those who deny the Spirit's primary moral presence effectively deny Christ. Those who have Christ indwelling, through the Spirit's indwelling, are assured that their spirit (inner self) is 'alive' toward God, manifested by virtue of the righteousness that is evident in their lives. Paul, as Johnson suggests, ties it together here: 'The present passage brings home once again the extraordinarily close connection Paul draws between the resurrection of Jesus, the gift of the Spirit, the transformation of the human spirit, and the resurrection of humans to eternal life; all of this being "the gift of God in Christ Jesus".'[71] If a person manifests righteousness as a product of the indwelling Spirit, it proves that they belong to Christ. If they belong to Christ they share the benefits of Christ, which Paul makes patently clear as pertaining to the guarantee of eternal life that conquers death. This has already been proven in the resurrection of Christ (v. 11).

Therefore, the argument Paul commenced in Romans 6:1, and has forcefully argued through two and a half chapters, now concludes with this imperative: 'Therefore, brothers, we have an obligation – but it is not to the sinful nature, to live according to it. For if you live according to the sinful nature, you will die; but if by the Spirit you put to death the misdeeds of the body, you will live' (Rom. 8:12–13). Grace does not negate the moral imperative; on the contrary, it upholds it.

However, rather than sustaining it through a reliance on the law, the imperative is sustained in a non-nomistic manner, via the 'new' way of the Spirit. Presuming on the grace of God and commensurately living according to the sinful nature, or indeed attempting to live by the law, is the ultimate folly, because both yield nothing but death!

The only alternative, for Paul at least, is to live according to the Spirit, to allow the indwelling and empowering Spirit to conquer the power of *the flesh*. The flesh, which is the source of all sinful expression, was crucified with Christ. In Romans 5:20, Paul argued that though the law exposed sin and its greatness, grace abounded over it, enabling the justified person to be free. However, freedom is not freedom from God's authority, but a freedom from the law. It is a freedom in the Spirit, as Johnson affirms, 'The freedom given by the Holy Spirit, in other words, leads not to an abandonment of God's will as revealed in Torah but to the fulfilment of its righteous requirement.'[72] Those who are controlled by the Spirit put to death the deeds of the flesh and in so doing fulfil the law, thus validating the eternal life that Christ offers to those who embrace him by faith.

This 'living' by the Spirit transcends Spirit-empowered rule-keeping. Perhaps this paraphrase of Johnson's brilliant illustration allows us to capture this truth more clearly. Consider two children. The first child out of anxiety to maintain 'the right relationship' with a parent observes every one of the parent's commands – no less and no more. The child seeks to make the relationship entirely within the frame of the law: 'Tell me what you want and I'll do it.' The child clearly misses the entire point of such a relationship, which must be flexible and responsive. The 'keeping of the law' in this case is a rigid form of self-protection and extortion: 'You must reward me because I did everything you said perfectly.' By insisting on keeping everything a matter of rules, it suppresses the chance of spontaneous life occurring outside its self-imposed boundaries (much like the 'obedient' son in the parable of the prodigal son).

The second child focuses on the parent as a source of life and the loving giver of gifts, trusts in the parent, and responds obediently but flexibly to the parent's initiatives. While faithful responsiveness actually 'fulfils' all the rules laid down by the parent, the relationship is not rigidly defined by those rules. There are dozens of exchanges that take place every day that no rule can capture. As long as the child responds rightly, rules never come into it; in fact, rules are not the focus; the loving relationship is the focus. Because the relationship is right, because the child desires to walk in conformity with the parent, the burden of law / rules and guilt does not hang over them; they unconsciously fulfil it.[73] This second example more adequately represents life for the child of God who walks 'consistently' in the Spirit.

Conclusion

If the gospel is as powerful as Paul claims, then its reach must extend beyond the acquittal of sin's penalty. In arguing that the gospel counters the power of sin, Paul does not take the easy options of downgrading the gravity of sin, or upgrading the capacities of the human self. Rather, he introduces a radical new concept: 'union' with Christ. Through the Spirit's enabling the believer is effectively 'crucified and raised' with Christ, such that the old sin nature is considered dead!

Therefore, on the grounds of solidarity with Christ, the Christian life proceeds in the power of the Spirit – a 'new' way to live (Rom. 7:6). For those familiar with and reliant on Jewish law as an ethical guide, this would appear strange. However, by way of a convincing 'speech-in-character', Paul encourages his doubting audience to see that the law is quite incapable of enabling the emancipation from sin's power they so desperately seek. Through the Spirit, a new non-law way of animating morality has arrived; a way that operates outside of the legal code yet fulfils the very demands it once made. Paul opened his argument in Romans 6, stressing that grace does not dismiss morality, and he concludes it in Romans 8:13 by reinforcing that the obligation to address sin's power remains. However, overcoming sin's power to fulfil this obligation is no longer attempted by way of the law, which was ultimately futile, but by way of the Spirit – the Spirit of power.

5

Adoption and Spirit: Conquering Sin's Presence

Family is very important to God, and for those estranged from God, receiving the gospel effectively translates as being welcomed back into the family of God. In escaping from the slavery of sin, forgiven sinners are embraced 'in' Christ, through the power of the Spirit, by the love of God the Father, who bestows on them all the privileges of divine sonship. No longer carrying the shame of a conquered slave, they now qualify as 'sons'; *more than conquerors* over the habitual bondage of sin that once enslaved them. All too often, Christians, hesitant in claiming this victorious reality, fail to realize the value of their new privileged status and commensurate state, in Christ. However, the Spirit, in bringing a substantive change that simply cannot be ignored, creates a reality that Paul describes as *being a new creation in Christ*. In being *existentially present,* the Spirit effectively represents a 'deposit', guaranteeing to the believer the final experience of eternal blessing as God's adopted child. Without this life-transforming and hope-inspiring Spirit, the ultimate experience of salvation would not be practically conceivable. In stressing this particular dimension of the gospel, Paul reminds his readers in Romans 8:14–39 of the blessings and benefits of their new familial situation; fashioning his teaching around the powerful metaphor of adoption.

Perfection: Penultimate or Permanent

The gospel enables the believer to be free from not only the power of sin, but its presence. However, such a claim does not suggest absolute perfection. The *terminus* of the gospel, at least from a human perspective, is the restoration of God's redeemed people in unbroken fellowship with their Creator, Redeemer and Lord, in the new heavens and earth. Of course, the gospel's crowning focus is the full revelation of the kingdom of God where Christ will be forever honoured as king, and God the Creator gloried. However, many present-day presentations of the gospel lose sight of this eternal and ultimate emphasis, finding the gospel's full and ultimate application in the 'here and now'. Although we must affirm that the gospel does bring real transformation here and now, we must acknowledge an ultimate transformation, where that which is provisionally manifested will give way to unbounded glory beyond our limited human imagination.

Yet, some Christians in losing sight of God's ultimate goal are content to settle for penultimate realities. If the gospel is considered on this premise, the potential foci of the gospel's *terminus* are potentially limitless. Themes such as political liberation, social improvement, eradicating poverty, environmental transformation, material prosperity and religious self-fulfilment (in various forms) are all potential candidates of the gospel's principal focus. Of course we accept, when the gospel of Jesus Christ is embraced, that it will invariably result in transformed lives, more harmonious families, better communities, growing churches and even morally upright nations. But is the primary goal of the gospel simply a better world? Could it be that in settling for 'lesser' temporal goals, many Christians are content to get off the gospel train one stop too soon? In seeking to provide a 'general' answer to these questions, we will examine one of these 'penultimate' applications of the gospel – moral perfectionism.

Immature Christians easily become impatient. Having embraced the gospel through faith in Jesus Christ, and gained a glimpse of the everlasting glory that accompanies it, there is a deep longing to 'actually' experience this glory. Just as human taste buds, having tasted something sweet, crave more of that sweetness, so the Christian who has tasted glory through the Spirit's application of Christ now longs for a permanence of that experience. Of course, on one level this is perfectly valid. I believe Christians should long for their heavenly home and the company of their Saviour. However, when a legitimate wish to experience heavenly glory becomes twisted by temporal motives, a refashioning of the Christian hope in the form of an over-realized eschatology begins to look more attractive. This over-realized eschatology is a theological phenomenon that brings forward eternal realities. In simple terms, it translates as a theologically legitimated attempt to claim the full conditions of heaven on earth, now!

One of the greatest frustrations of Christian experience is contending with the lingering sinful nature; a believer just wants sin to go away so life can be easier to get on with! Of course, there are those who wrongly propose that this *burdensome struggle* with the flesh is 'normative' and any degree of liberation from sin is only possible after death. As flawed as this view may be, the opposite view of moral perfectionism is equally questionable. This claims that 'all' of sin's presence can be wiped out and full perfection can be fully experienced now. In its more nefarious manifestations, this perfection ideology is supplemented by a belief that happiness abounds in the enjoyment of this life's material benefits – prosperity theology. Therefore, the opening line of an *over-realized eschatological manifesto* might read something like this: 'Why can't I be free from this mortal coil, with all its trials and temptations; why can't I experience "all" the blessings of heaven now? I can!'

Stephen Neill suggests, 'Almost all "holiness movements", "higher life movements" and "perfectionist movements" of our time show plainly, if not always validly, their family kinship with that which began in the experience of John and Charles Wesley.'[1] However, while Wesley composed a theology stemming from his own experience, it is perhaps more accurate to suggest that he was heavily influenced by German pietism, through Moravian connections. After coming under the influence of practical mysticism in 1725, John Wesley became preoccupied with 'perfection', which would come to occupy a central role within his soteriology.[2] Synonymous with the idea of *entire sanctification*, perfectionism represents a higher plane of moral existence in the Christian life. Based on Wesley's own experience, sanctification is not regarded 'exclusively' as a process (though it involves that), but entails separate remarkable experience(s). Hence the popular notions of *the second blessing* and *entire sanctification*. In this scheme, the Christian begins the walk of faith as a carnal believer, but through a subsequent 'prominent' encounter of the Spirit reaches a higher plane of existence in which perfection actually becomes possible.

Wesley's view of perfection may be considered from both positive and negative points of view. First, it may be positively judged as a perfect love toward God and having an untainted desire to do his will. Second, perfection may also be viewed negatively, in the sense that it is perfect deliverance from the control and influence of conscious sin. Moreover, this deliverance from sin is not simply deliverance from 'sins', but encompasses deliverance from deeply rooted evil thoughts and temperaments. Lindstrom summarizes Wesley's view as follows:

> In his sermon on Perfection (1788) it is defined in the following terms. It means: 1. To love God with all one's heart and one's neighbour as oneself; 2. The mind that is in Christ; 3. The fruits of the spirit (in accordance with Galatians 5) unified; 4. The image of God, a recovery of man to the moral image of God, which consists of "righteousness and true holiness"; 5. Inward and outward righteousness, sanctity of life issuing from sanctity of heart; 6. God sanctifying of man in spirit, soul, and body; 7. Man's own perfect consecration to God; 8. A continuous presentation through Jesus of man's thoughts and words and actions as a sacrifice to God of praise and thanksgiving; 9. Salvation from all sin.[3]

As we can see, some of the attributes outlined in Wesley's scheme are qualities that many Christians of Augustinian heritage would judge as valid realities 'only' in eternity.

However, in fairness, John Wesley did not 'actually' believe in *absolute* perfection in the Christian life: '[Christians] are not perfect in knowledge. They are not free from ignorance; no, nor from mistake. We are no more to expect any living man to be infallible, than to be omniscient. They are not free from infirmities, such as weakness or slowness of understanding, irregular quickness or heaviness of imagination.'[4] For Wesley, perfection is analogical with reference to God's perfection. It is both unlike and like divine perfection. It is unlike divine perfection, as far as the Christian cannot arrive at the absolute perfection of God. Yet it is like perfection as far as the Christian transformed by the Holy Spirit displays the character traits of God consistent with his will.

Gaining perfection then should not be misinterpreted to mean the Christian can become a fourth person of the Trinity, an angel, or regain the Edenic state; but rather it refers to becoming morally 'like' God.[5] Furthermore, Wesley never proposes that the Christian cannot fall into sin again. So, when Wesley speaks of perfection, he principally has in mind perfection of the human affections or the perfection of love: 'By perfection I mean the humble, gentle, patient love of God, and our neighbour, ruling our tempers, words, and actions.'[6] Simply put, this is to be as perfect as one can be, with respect to fulfilling the intention of God's law. However, Wesley's notion of *perfect love* or *entire sanctification is* problematic because of its subjective / existential point of reference. What standard may a Christian person use to know what perfect love is? How do they know when they have arrived? What is considered perfect love for an immature believer may be considered by a more mature believer to be a life of sinful ignorance! This appears less problematic if you are measuring perfect with 'intention' but, again, how do you measure intentions? Even good intentions can be misguided. Of course, Wesley feels the need to 'do justice' to passages such as: 'attaining to the whole measure of the fullness of Christ' (Eph. 4:13). However, the whole measure is a different size according to differences of maturity.

By way of personal experience, I can say that the more mature I become, the greater becomes the awareness of the depths of my own shortfall before God's standard. As my 'measure' grows with maturity, a greater awareness of my emptiness follows. This then incites a greater submission to Christ, to 'fill it up', and so it goes on. In truth, however, Wesley probably means by pure love: being as perfect as you are capable of, under the conviction of the Holy Spirit at any given time. The *real problem* emerges when this 'subjective' theology of experience then becomes absolutized as a dogmatic norm. Movements such as the higher life laid heavy stress on the notion of second blessing; thus putting pressure on adherents to manifest perfection thereafter, in some cases reverting to forms of legalism. In fact, this school of thought has often nurtured ideas that Christians can no longer be sick or sinful in any way, even in the least degree, as these things are simply incompatible with the fullness of life in Christ.[7]

Thus, the greatest confusion in perfectionism comes when Wesley's theological project is simply misunderstood. Wesley espouses a dynamic practical theology (a theory of lived experience), rather than a logically tight, ontological formulation of a Christian engagement with sin. This is not necessarily bad in itself, but these kinds of theologies can easily lead to confusion in the wrong hands. In this regard, he is prone to be misunderstood by two groups: those who stand against perfectionism in all its forms, and those who want to embrace it in its extreme. With respect to the latter, Wesley himself was fully aware of this. Following a revival in London in 1762, Wesley foresaw the dangers of 'pride and enthusiasm': 'But almost as soon as I was gone enthusiasm broke in . . . Soon after, the same persons, with a few more, ran into other extravagances; fancying they could not be tempted; that they should feel no more pain; and that they had the gift of prophecy, and of discerning of spirits.'[8]

As we can see, Wesley and those true to his cause may have been able to limit the malevolent effects of perfectionism through a respect for scriptural authority and ecclesial sobriety. However, for many less-discerning adherents, the *idea of perfectionism* became a pretext for all kinds of outrageous claims. Many of those outrageous claims and forms still exist today.

It is true to say that the apostle Paul was also interested in perfection, and saw the gospel as the means to attaining it. In fact, he strove to attain it. For the apostle, the quest for perfection was an endeavour of seeking to know Christ on an ever-increasing deeper level:

> I want to know Christ and the power of his resurrection and the fellowship of sharing in his sufferings, becoming like him in his death . . . Not that I have already obtained all this, or have already been made perfect, but I press on to take hold of that for which Christ Jesus took hold of me . . . Forgetting what is behind and straining towards what is ahead, I press on towards the goal to win the prize . . . All of us who are mature should take such a view of things.
>
> (Phil 3:10–15)

If ever there were a Christian that could attain *entire sanctification* in this life, then surely the apostle Paul would have qualified. Yet as the text above suggests, there is no sense of Paul 'having arrived'. On the contrary, he views the quest for perfection (which is synonymous with the quest for knowing Christ) as a continuing endeavour. Paul never presumes to have 'arrived' at perfection in this life; indeed such a claim would be folly at heart; an open door for pride, which invariably precedes a moral fall. For Paul, the onward quest to 'know' Christ is ground in this life for striving for perfection, making the goal all the richer at its attainment, only in eternity. Indeed, no one ever achieves perfection by focusing on perfection. If a Christian could 'hypothetically' grasp perfection in this life, then it would only be commensurate to the degree that the person focuses on the source of perfection – Christ.

More importantly than the wish to have the presence of sin removed, is the *deep sense of hope* granted by the Spirit, hope that the blight of sin will be finally removed. In impatiently seeking to remove sin, many Christians rob themselves of the opportunity to know the power of God in human weakness. In seeking a shallow form of perfectionism they give up the opportunity to deepen their knowledge of Christ. The irony of this perfection search is that perfection (as far as it is possible in this life) is experienced 'only' when perfecting the self is not the conscious object of the search – knowing Christ is. Only in seeking to know Christ, who is perfect, does the Christian make great strides toward the goal of perfection!

Of course, having *the penalty of sin cancelled* by Christ, and *the power of sin broken* by virtue of union with Christ, Christians must look for and expect *a diminishing presence of sin* in their lives. In desiring this, they must continue to focus on Christ through the Spirit's power. Indeed, as a Christian becomes more like Christ, a deeper awareness of personal sin(s) follows, which further prompts Spirit-enabled repentance, leading to further transformation – reified as maturity. Of course, this is a continuous journey, and the non-attainment of complete perfection is not a just ground to give up hope. On the contrary, if perfection could be gained in this imperfect world, what would the Christian have to look forward to? For Paul, perfection is invariably linked to hope; as B.B. Warfield suggests, 'It is clear, therefore, Paul though promising this perfection as the certain heritage of every Christian man, presents it as a matter of hope, not yet seen; not as a matter of experience, already enjoyed.'[9]

Despite human ambitions to grasp perfection in the here and now, the gospel places it 'just' out of grasp. Yes, with good reason! Indeed, the gospel may substantively transform lives, but perfecting this world is not where God's gospel of salvation finds its ultimate *terminus*. In fact, rather than creating a perfect life 'here and now', the gospel may actually make matters worse (more imperfect) for its adherents. In this regard, Jesus' admonition is relevant: 'Do not suppose that I have come to bring peace to the earth. I did not come to bring peace, but a sword' (Matt. 10:34). The truth of the gospel may cause: a crisis of conscience, divisions in families, strife in communities, conflicts in societies, and may (initially) have little, no or even a negative impact on the material environment.

The gospel's supreme goal remains valid. The transformation that the gospel brings to 'this' world is strictly of a provisional nature. It foreshadows the perfection of eternity. It is penultimate, not ultimate. The perfection God offers through the gospel transcends this present age, and anticipates a 'new' heavens and 'new' earth where the perfection sought will be fully complete. Yet Christians should not infer that 'this' world has no value, or their work in it is simply pointless – assuming their material bodies are receptacles for their soon-to-be disembodied souls. Christians' provisional transformation is very much tied up with the ultimate transformation that God will enact with the ushering in of the new ultimate reality. It is true to say that what happens here does echo in eternity.

Spirit, Sonship and Inheritance (Romans 8:14–16)

The Spirit applies the reality of divine adoption to the believer in Christ, and ushers believers into an entirely new standing, where they no longer grace the heavenly Father's presence as 'slaves' of sin, but as privileged 'sons' of righteousness. Those controlled by the Spirit, having being united with Christ by faith, now validate that union by conducting themselves in the manner of 'sons'; worthy recipients of the 'family name' – those who abide within the privileged family domain. Moreover, the term 'son' should not be seen to exclude women – Paul uses the term 'sons' to include the women and men in his audience because in the Jewish, Greek and Roman cultures of his day it was usually the sons and not the daughters who were eligible to inherit the estate. For Paul, the Spirit that powerfully raised Jesus from the dead is the same Spirit that vivifies the mortal body: 'And if the Spirit of him who raised Jesus from the dead is living in you, he who raised Christ from the dead will also give life to your mortal bodies through his Spirit, who lives in you' (Rom. 8:11). This divine Spirit-presence, in adoptively embracing believers, endows them with a moral desire commensurate with their new privileged status: 'Therefore, brothers, we have an obligation – but it is not to the sinful nature, to live according to it' (Rom. 8:12).

This means that Christians, having been united to Christ through the indwelling Spirit, should no longer view themselves under the yoke of slavery, pessimistically approaching the subject of the ongoing Christian life with a *mindset of bondage.* Though in Romans 6:16 Paul has said that believers should consider themselves slaves to obedience, we need to recognize that even there he was uncomfortable with the servile connotation, and qualifies his statement in Romans 6:19. Now in Romans 8 he develops his argument by turning to an adoption metaphor that indicates that God desires believers to be 'sons' – the children who would be full heirs of a father's blessings. If a Christian lives under the sway of the natural self, the consequence will invariably lead to and result in 'death'. Paul is not implying natural death, as Thomas Schreiner rightly suggests, 'The death contemplated here is not merely physical death, for Rom 8:10-11 has already indicated that those who are in the spirit will all experience physical death. The death that is threatened, therefore, is death in the fullest theological sense; the death that is the wages of sin.'[10] Sonship then implies life, and a conduct commensurate with this new life!

What Paul is stating, and indeed has been working toward, is the necessary link between the status of justification and the ethical life. This is not a humanly contrived link, but one divinely initiated and empowered. The Spirit, in Christ, sets the believer free from the slavery of sin. But this is not simply freedom to express human desires, unabated by any moral necessity, as John Barclay rightly stresses, 'The flesh would certainly exploit this absolute freedom . . . But the spirit provides a counteracting force which motivates and directs them to exclude the flesh'[11] and act out a freedom consistent with the Spirit's moral presence.

The Spirit does not work in abstraction but, as Schweitzer intimates, animates an ethic that represents the spiritual reality of being-in-Christ, taken from the point of view of the will.[12] The Spirit then enables the indwelling Christ to empower the ethical life, such that all true ethical conduct is Christ-conduct. Moreover, as the Spirit empowers the ethical will, the human role in its working is, at 'the source' of this engagement, passive. This makes sense of Paul's use of the passive rendering of 'being led' in Romans 8:14, as Schreiner astutely points out, 'The Spirit is the primary agent in Christian obedience, that is, it is his work in believers that accounts for their obedience.'[13] Thus, the indwelling Christ, present as the Spirit, counters and excludes the flesh, nullifies the power of sin and establishes the presence of Christ-likeness. The Spirit is validating that such a person is a bona fide 'son' of God.

The presence of the Spirit is indispensable for qualifying one of Paul's most important salvific concepts – sonship. Importantly, by applying the notion of 'sonship' as a correlate of the adoption metaphor, Paul actually allows this familial term to do a lot of the theological 'heavy-lifting'. The theological content embedded in the notion of 'sonship' has significance for Christians from both Jewish and Roman backgrounds. The terms 'sons of God' or 'children of God' were used in the Old Testament to refer to God's people, Israel, and their inherent privilege.[14] In relating the idea of sonship to the associated concept of inheritance (v. 17), Paul is also drawing on Old Testament precedents.[15]

Indeed, there is merit in Thomas Tobin's argument that the Jewish emphasis is important here: 'What all these passages indicate is that words and phrases of this sort would inevitably conjure up in the mind of Paul's Roman Christian audience Israel and its ultimate fate.'[16] Paul is employing this language to win over those 'weak' believers with a Jewish heritage. He wants to convince them that, although Paul's gospel is non-law, it isn't anti-Jew, even though his Galatians epistle might have given them that impression. In fact, Paul has already applied this 'sonship' concept in the Galatians correspondence, emphasizing being redeemed from 'under' the law through Christ, into the greater privileged status of a son (Gal. 4:5)!

However, the apostle has in mind more than an exclusively Jewish audience when bringing the idea of sonship to bear on this discussion. The Gentiles, too, had good grounds to connect with the substance and intent of Paul's argument. Paul's concept of the 'adopted son' functions well in the ancient Roman context, where it correlates with the cultural practices of the Greco-Roman household, and its laws of privilege and inheritance.[17] The 1959 epic movie drama *Ben-Hur* depicts the story of one Quintus Arrius. Quintus adopts a Jewish galley slave, Ben-Hur, and bestows on him the full privileges of a son (wealth, title, honour, authority). Though special circumstances, through an act of adoption, Ben-Hur rises from despised slave to honoured son. Though such a sharp ascension from galley slave to nobility would have been highly unlikely in Roman culture, this does not stop Paul alluding to the actuality of such a transfer within the context of faith in Christ that invariably leads to God's adoption of the forgiven sinner.

Within the Roman context, the adoption of an adult slave as a 'son' didn't allow or place the adopted son in a lower place of privilege than the natural son. In fact, the son's prerogative had little to do with it. What matters is the father's will, as Michael Peppard suggests, 'The ultimate factor determining who counts as a son is the father's judgment.'[18] Of course, such a notion accords well with Paul's soteriological emphasis on God's sovereign initiative and the resulting status granted by the granting of favour, being received *only* on the grounds of faith, and not merit. Furthermore, Peppard indicates that the inheritance gained by the son, which includes land, money and the family name, also includes a curious thing called the 'family spirit'.[19] What is this 'family spirit'? It seems that each family or household had its own household spirit (*lars*) that protected the house (a pagan equivalent of a guardian angel) and it was the role of the head of the family to maintain the shrine for the worship of this guardian 'spirit'.[20]

Familial concepts, then, provide the perfect vehicle for bearing this adoption metaphor and its relationship to the Spirit. In Romans 8:15, Paul emphasizes the 'new presence', in which believers now stand, on account of the Spirit's sanctifying action. He does so by drawing on this parallel concept of 'family spirit', resident in ancient Roman practice. Paul could have been referring to the fear of offending the 'family spirit', when noting the believer 'in Christ' has 'not' received a spirit of fear, but the Spirit of sonship – the Spirit that endows, endorses and protects sonship. Adopted sonship in the truly Christian sense is a 'spiritual' phenomenon. Becoming an adopted 'son', like the rest of God's salvific actions is never on the grounds of human initiative. The same Spirit that brings the conviction of sin, applies the atoning work of Christ by faith, empowers the life of moral conformity to Christ, and is the same Spirit that bestows the privilege of sonship by 'sealing' this divine act of adoption. Moreover, in reading Romans 8:15–16 correctly, one is given a strong impression that without the Spirit, there is no adoption at all; a point not lost on Trevor Burke: 'The spirit and adoption are not only closely connected, but they are in fact inseparable; stated in another way, they are reciprocally related.'[21]

Of course, as with justification, adoption is a legal metaphor. However, this should not be taken to mean that it is characterized by a lack of relational and/or existential sentiment. The regenerating power of the Spirit that awakens the sinner to the reality of the Father's gracious bestowal of sonship may also be described as existentially / subjectively felt. However, the Spirit's role in adoption may also be considered as an objective and formal realization of the benefit bestowed.[22] But, this legal formality does not infer remoteness in any way, as Paul describes the Spirit of sonship as the means by which the believer, now deemed a 'son', can cry out '*Abba*, Father'. *Abba* in Hebrew thought is a term of relational endearment (Rom. 8:15).

Despite, the term *Abba* being popularly translated as 'Daddy', which has a tendency to 'lighten' the gravity of its meaning, Mary D'Angelo suggests another interpretation: '[*Abba*] asserts not a childlike relation to God, but the privileged status of the adult son (not daughter) and heir.'[23] Though used as a term of endearment, even adult children might apply it in familial situations. As such, there is no lack of relational empathy even in the adult case, for every believer can personally cry out '*Abba*, Father'. This expression must also be understood in a relative way. From the impersonal status of *slavery*, from which the forgiven sinner has been emancipated, there is a new status to embrace – personal *sonship*. Whereas the slave has no personal grounds to appeal to the 'father' of the household, the [adopted] son has a special relational privilege that enables such an appeal; an appeal actualized by the Spirit's presence.

But how does the Spirit actually secure the intimate adoption that Paul so confidently asserts? There is a marked failure among those who rely on the logical constructs and confines of a 'rational firstworld' culture to grasp the mysterious or mystical dimensions of the Spirit's working in this regard. Paul is not bound by such limitations.

While he may describe the engagement of the Spirit with God's children in 'relatively' cogent terms; the apostle recognizes a necessarily 'mysterious' element to this engagement which cannot be rationally quantified: 'The Spirit himself testifies with our spirit that we are God's children' (Rom. 8:16). Of course, Paul is intimating that, given the fact we are dealing with a divine–human engagement, there must be a 'secret' Spirit-to-spirit relational connection that is ultimately incomprehensible to 'natural' reason. That said, it is no less 'valid' for its rational inexplicability. Indeed, this secret Spirit-connection represents the work of God's Spirit on both sides of the equation; note Paul's commentary here on spiritual discernment: 'The man without the Spirit does not accept the things that come from the Spirit of God, for they are foolishness to him, and he cannot understand them, because they are spiritually discerned' (1 Cor. 2:14). Therefore, it seems only the person with the Spirit can receive that which comes from the Spirit. Even as the Spirit of God communicates with the human spirit to bring the assurance of sonship, remarkably it is the Holy Spirit that also initiates and enables the connection, even from the human side!

Under the guidance of the Spirit, the apostle brings this metaphor to bear into the cultural psyche of his Gentile (and Jewish) readers to powerfully reinforce the personal hope of salvation. In fact, if for no other reason than the granting of an existential hope of a right standing with the Father, through their adoptive relationship, the believer's engagement with the Spirit is to be highly valued. Yet this personal assurance is linked to more than assuaging the pangs of 'inner' doubt. As already touched upon, the Spirit that endows sonship also empowers moral conduct in line with new familial status. It evokes a lifestyle marked by the removal of sin's enduring presence. Such removal necessarily implies that Christians now operate on Christ's behavioural agenda, setting them at odds with the world's agenda(s).

Yes, the genuine Christian person will share in the blessed inheritance of eternal life but, as the apostle qualifies, sharing in Christ's mutual sonship is also a sharing in his sufferings as well. Jesus said, 'If anyone would come after me, he must deny himself and take up his cross daily and follow me' (Luke 9:23). As we know, Christ's life was characterized by a holy devotion to God and his kingdom agenda; an agenda that entails seeking first (prioritizing) the kingdom of God and his righteousness. Christ's life necessarily entailed suffering, and this suffering (on account of union with Christ as a holy co-servant / co-heir) is an integral part of Paul's Christology: 'I want to know Christ and the power of his resurrection and the fellowship of sharing in his sufferings, becoming like him in his death' (Phil. 3:10).

In embracing the gospel, the believer is 'bound to Christ' by the Spirit and therefore must share in all the realities of this Christ-life. As such, authentic identity with Christ invariably results in co-suffering, as Jesus indicates, 'If the world hates you, keep in mind that it hated me first . . . As it is, you do not belong to the world, but I have chosen you out of the world. That is why the world hates you' (John 15:18–19). The believer who consistently stands out from the world, through a genuine devotion to Christ, proves a life where the 'habitual' presence of sin is principally absent (Rom. 8:12).[24] If this were not the case the world would endorse such a person. As it is, sinful humanity prefers to dwell in the darkness of sin, and only approves of those who prefer darkness (John 3:19–20; Rom 1:32). Being a child of God translates as being an heir of God's promised inheritance – a co-heir with Christ.

However, just as Paul's morality is based on union with Christ, the reception of this promised inheritance is contingent on 'sharing in' Christ's sufferings. In Paul's logic, the believer cannot expect to receive the eternal inheritance of a son without suffering for the Son, or like the Son! This is the nature of 'union with Christ' – you have all of Christ or none of him. Thus, the promise of sharing in Christ's glory is 'only' held out for those whose union with Christ is validated by their willingness to share in Christ's sufferings (Rom. 8:17).

Of course, sonship also ensures an inheritance, but not a cheap and easy inheritance. If Christ the 'firstborn' Son of God suffered through uncompromising devotion to his Father, so then adopted sons should expect the same fate of their elder brother and lord. However, the potential anguish of such suffering is only assuaged by a hope-filled appreciation of the greatness of the future glory awaiting the faithful child of God. In this, it is the eschatological 'comforting' ministry of the Spirit that relativizes any grief experienced in this present life; empowering hope and filling the soul with joy – even as the material body fades: 'For our light and momentary troubles are achieving for us an eternal glory that far outweighs them all. So we fix our eyes, not on what is seen, but on what is unseen. For what is seen is temporary, but what is unseen is eternal' (2 Cor. 4:17–18).

The Spirit's influence in breaking the power of sin manifests itself in the removal of the presence of sin by entering into a new status of sonship, conceptualized through the metaphor of adoption. Because the vivifying Spirit gives life to the mortal bodies of those who trust Christ, ordinarily under the sentence of death, these Spirit-regenerated believers are now under obligation to reflect this 'new life' and conform to Christ in every way. Yet this new moral life is not initiated or animated by human will power, or even begrudgingly taken up as a religious duty. On the contrary, it is enacted by the divine power of the Spirit, which enables mortification of 'the flesh' (Rom. 8:13). The Spirit displaces fear from the forgiven sinner and the Spirit removes them from the realms of 'fearful' slavery, placing them within the realm of loving sonship. Moreover, the Spirit confirms this new 'liberated' familial status by sealing them with an intuitive Spirit-to-spirit confirmation – the peace of God that passes understanding (8:16).

The Spirit and the Hope of Perfection (Romans 8:17–25)

Any understanding of moral perfection, as it relates to Paul's thinking, must be in terms of an eschatological tension. The Christian exists in a tension between what is seen and the unseen, what is transitory and the permanent, and what is temporal and the eternal. Indeed, the Christian is existentially torn between the exigencies of the present fallen world and the blissful existence of the next world. This existence may be described as an eschatological existence. What makes such a 'torn' existence conceivable, let alone practically sustainable, is the presence of the Holy Spirit. The Spirit actually dwells in both realms, and through God's abiding / comforting presence is able to bring the blessings of the 'not yet' into the 'now'.

Paul is patently aware of this tension, and through an understanding of the Spirit is able to comfort others with a future hope: 'I consider that our present sufferings are not worth comparing with the glory that will be revealed in us' (Rom. 8:18). Paul knows that to be a loyal follower of Christ requires suffering and self-denial, yet this self-denial transcends an ordinary grief-filled existence. As the human 'self' is denied, the Spirit's comforting presence fills any lack. The Spirit, in secretly ministering to the 'human spirit', brings a peace that passes human understanding (Phil. 4:7), a peace characteristic of the blessed future. The ministry of the Spirit enables the removal of sin in this present life, but this removal remains incomplete; an imperfect foretaste of what awaits those who persevere in Christ. In our explication of Romans, in this section we now direct our attention to what Paul has to say about the future orientation of the Spirit's ministry, and the power that enables the believer to manage the tension experienced between *the now* and *the not yet*.

Although this eschatological 'tension' is taken for granted by many Christians, we should acknowledge that this 'species' of eschatology is 'distinctly' Pauline. It represents a radical shift from conventional Jewish eschatologies of his day. Conventional Jewish eschatology viewed the messianic age culminating with the Day of Judgement. In this model, there is no two-stage reality-in-tension as with Paul; as Albert Schweitzer argues, 'The eschatology of Paul is therefore quite different from that of Jesus, a fact which has been hitherto never duly appreciated. Instead of thinking as Jesus did along the lines of the simple eschatology of the books of Daniel and Enoch . . .'[25]

In Paul's conceptualization, the last day had already dawned with the first advent of Christ and the divine judgement of humanity's sin through the cross being applied by the Spirit. Paul, with the knowledge of Christ and the presence of the Spirit is able, as N.T. Wright argues, to radically redraw previous Jewish expectations: 'The hope, which has been fulfilled, has also thereby been reshaped. The present judgment passed on sin, in the Messiah's crucifixion, points onto the future, ultimate judgment that will be passed on the last day.'[26] Within this eschatological framework, the penalty of sin has been acquitted, its power broken, and now its very presence provisionally removed is tangibly foreshadowed. It inspires those 'in Christ' with a forward-looking hope toward the completion of what has begun. Yet Paul's eschatology is far more than the 'old' human existence with a new outlook on a brighter future. The Spirit 'actually' brings eternity into the present – merging the two realities.

When Paul states that those 'in Christ' are a new creation (2 Cor. 5:17), he is not merely citing a slogan to encourage believers to take seriously a new moral lifestyle; he is actually stating an ontological fact! The Christian 'is' a radically different being, living a new life, in a different realm. Schweitzer again is helpful here: 'Paul's conception is, the believers in mysterious fashion share the dying and rising again of Christ, and in this way are swept away out of the ordinary mode of existence, and former special category of humanity.'[27] We must understand that the resurrection of Christ has changed everything. The supernatural world of the eternal kingdom is no longer simply anticipated, it is experienced 'in the Spirit' as a reality which we view with eternal eyes! For Paul it could be no other way: 'Paul, alone among the believers of his time, gave due weight to the consideration that the traditional eschatology could not maintain itself unchanged: the Messiah having already appeared in the flesh, having died, having risen again; the eschatological expectation had to recast itself to those facts.'[28]

However, Paul's eschatology concerns more than humans existentially embracing a hope of being evacuated to an ethereal heaven – far more. It also takes into account the 'material' cosmos as well. For the age to come includes this present world transformed; indeed, Richard Gaffin believes the present experience of the believer is not only eschatologically conceived but cosmically qualified: 'It is existence in the new creation, the age to come.'[29] The new creation 'in Christ', through Christ's resurrection power in the Spirit, is a down payment of a greater cosmic transformation that is on the cusp of breaking through. This then is how we must understand Paul's eschatology, and by extension the context and content of the Christian's life in the Spirit.

The Christian life then, if it represents anything, represents a life of hope. Paul wants to encourage within the Roman believers – who would have ordinarily seen themselves as temporally benefitting from or being exploited by a part of a large and dominant empire – a grand hope, that they are actually part of something even greater – God's kingdom. This eternal kingdom, in which God's adopted 'sons' will reign, is not immediately obvious to the naked eye (save in a provisional form as the church). However, it will be revealed, in a similar manner as the resurrected Christ was revealed – in a gloriously transformed state. This transformed state of God's sons and daughters necessarily involves the material creation: 'The creation waits in eager expectation for the sons of God to be revealed' (Rom. 8:19).

Significantly, Paul personifies the created order as 'waiting' and 'groaning'; thus revealing an eschatology that is far from static. Indeed, there is a constant progression toward the goal. Paul's use of the metaphor of pregnancy is applicable here. The pregnant mother burdened by her advanced state should not lose sight of the fact that her pregnancy will result in the joy of birth. Rather, she should take heart that the greater her burden and more anxious her state of waiting (in the advanced stages of pregnancy), then the closer the actual event of the birth is.[30] The pain of tension reinforces that joy is imminent; so too, for the Christian anticipating the ultimate reality.

Therefore, Paul's eschatology is dynamic, forward-looking and hope-inspiring. Michael Peppard suggests this forward look correlates with the metaphor Paul employs, 'Divine sonship for Paul did not look primarily backward to origins, but forward to inheritance – just as it did in Roman society.'[31] But why is there a delay in the revelation of this inheritance?

We need to understand that all things are tied to God's cosmic plan, and the created order has been subjected to a certain frustration, not by its own choice! That is to say, the created order is subject to the will of the one who subjected it (Rom. 8:20). Creation, like the sons of God, is subject to a higher will. Regarding this 'subjection', Brendan Byrne argues that this refers to the human subjection of creation into idolatry, as set out by Paul in Romans 1:18–23, which could be successfully argued in a derivative or secondary sense.[32]

As such, the subjection in view here relates to *the fall*, and the subjection of creation to futility, on account of God's curse on creation. This curse resulted from and is commensurate with God's curse on humanity for the sin in Eden: 'To Adam he said, "Because you listened to your wife and ate from the tree about which I commanded you, 'You must not eat of it,' Cursed is the ground because of you"' (Gen. 3:17). Through the over-arching metaphor of adoption, Paul is able to bring to bear the greater cosmic purposes of God, highlighting then the anticipated reversal of the fall condition. Just as God's first son, Adam, led the created order into a cursed futility, so Christ (the Son of God, confirmed by the resurrection power of the Spirit) will lead this, once futile, created order into a glorious reality in which the children of God experience a blessed freedom (Rom. 8:21). The great cosmic plan then is inexorably tied to a Spirit-inspired hope, resident in those destined for salvation.

The 'groaning' of creation and the commensurate 'groaning' of the believer within it (both of whom are caught in the 'childbirth' tension of the 'now and not yet' (v. 22), suggest far more than a hypothetical hope. For Paul, the *first fruits* of the Spirit enable the believer to eagerly and joyfully expect that which is anticipated.

In ancient cultures, the first fruits of the crops were gathered in and became a pledge of the full harvest that was abundantly anticipated. The notion of 'first fruits' carries with it a sense of surety that the whole crop is guaranteed, even if it is yet to be delivered. For Paul the existential presence of the Spirit represented the surety of the full experience of this abundance; guaranteed to be delivered when full salvation will be experienced, when the curtains of this temporal reality are closed; as Edwin Palmer signals, 'Paul implies, they will one day have full adoption with all of its inheritance, including the redemption of the body. Whereas the first fruits of the harvest are a promise of better things, so the initial possession of the Holy Spirit is a promise of greater things to come.'³³ In this regard the Spirit is rightly understood as a deposit, representing a hope of a future payment in full (Eph. 1:14; 2 Cor. 1:22).

In much the same way as science fiction might portray a person entering a time machine and experiencing the future, so the Spirit, in bestowing the peace of God that passes all understanding, seals eternity in the present. That is why Paul can confidently say, 'For in this hope we are saved' (Rom. 8:24a). Not 'wish to be saved', but 'are saved' as a present reality for, in the Spirit, eternity is 'virtually' now! What then is the nature of this Christian hope? When Paul speaks of a present reality of salvation, he is certainly not advocating an over-realized eschatology. He is not suggesting that Christian hope simply terminates in a *present experience* of salvation. For if the object of hope is fully realized in this life, then, at least in Paul's mind, it is really not valid hope at all! Although the Spirit brings eternity into the present, the Christian present does not 'become' eternity, but merely the 'down-payment' that anticipates it! That is why Paul uses 'first fruits' terminology.

Therefore, Paul's understanding of hope looks beyond: 'But hope that is seen is no hope at all. Who hopes for what he already has?' (Rom. 8:24b). Paul is angling toward what Douglas Moo describes as '[a] necessary and appropriate sense of incompleteness in our Christian experience and a consequent eager longing for the incompleteness to be overcome'.³⁴ As such, the Spirit brings us a substantive taste of salvation with a provisional experience of being free from the presence of sin. The same Spirit also empowers an eternity-oriented hope; a hope that is so substantive and real that it enables the Christian to patiently endure all manner of hardship. This endurance is bearable because of the full and complete emancipation guaranteed. The fact that Paul speaks of the experience of the Spirit as 'first fruits of the Spirit' suggests that he conceives the Spirit's role as being greater than merely empowering ecstatic spiritual experiences.³⁵

This hope is not subjectively contrived but historically grounded. In fact, Peter Stork argues, 'Christian hope, while it is objectively real because of the historical reality of the Christ-event, is subjectively experienced as confident expectation through faith, "underwritten" in the resurrection of Jesus Christ.'[36] The notion of the resurrection 'underwriting' Christian hope is simply a brilliant way of expressing the hope that Paul professes. However, it is more than a rationally cogent appreciation of a historical event embedded in the thought processes of the believer. The believers' *union with Christ*, through the Spirit, and their commensurate experience of salvation gives certitude to such historically situated underwriting, because with this certitude comes peace and patience to endure (Rom. 8:25) – the fruit of Spirit.

In the same manner, the Spirit instils patience to endure this life. The Spirit also assists the believer in overcoming the weaknesses of human frailty, assisting with the doubts of not knowing how to respond, act or live in the midst of difficulties. The peaceful patience that attends the life of hope, through the Spirit, enables the believer to rest in faith. Even when words fail them and knowledge is lacking, the Spirit is mediating on their behalf. There appears to be a Trinitarian operation in play here: the heart of the believer 'in Christ', through the Spirit, is known by God the Father and the Father knows the mind of the indwelling Spirit, who intercedes on the believer's behalf.

We are only given a 'taste' of perfection in this life. The removal of sin's presence can be provisionally experienced through the Spirit's abiding presence, but the full emancipation from the ravages of sin is yet to be fully realized. However, this should not be viewed with disappointment. On the contrary, it should be understood as God's way of developing the Christian person as they eagerly anticipate the future hoped for. If, for example, a believer came to faith in Christ and then was immediately taken into the presence of God, surely there would be a 'real' lack in appreciation of and love for Christ. This is why Paul, for whom 'to live is Christ', could confidently say:

> I want to know Christ and the power of his resurrection and the fellowship of sharing in his sufferings, becoming like him in his death, and so, somehow, to attain to the resurrection from the dead. Not that I have

already obtained all this, or have already been made perfect, but I press on to take hold of that for which Christ Jesus took hold of me.

(Phil. 3:10–12)

This 'taste' of perfection given by God in the gospel, through the Spirit's presence, goads the believer on through life's tribulations to experience life 'in Christ' and 'as Christ', attaining a richness of relationship hitherto unknown. If Paul's experience is anything to go by, fully attaining perfection in this life would only be short-changing any aspiration to fully know Christ. Seeking Christ in the midst of imperfection is a great blessing, as Paul states, 'That is why, for Christ's sake, I delight in weaknesses, in insults, in hardships, in persecutions, in difficulties. For when I am weak, then I am strong' (2 Cor. 12:10).

The Spirit and Confidence (Romans 8:26–39)

Insecurity and uncertainty, as Christopher Morse suggests, plague the human experience: 'Our greatest fear is being left with loss, whatever form it takes. We dread a loss of freedom, security, interest, strength, health, reputation, memory, landmarks, friends, even looks.'[37] As stable as the *Pax Romana* was, life in the Roman world was uncertain. A bad situation might be overturned; a disadvantaged person might gain greater privilege from a generous benefactor. Conversely, life could take a turn for the worse: a good benefactor dies and his estate is taken over by a cruel relative; perhaps the emperor decides to enact a law that threatens religious affiliations; invasion by unmerciful enemies occurs; or a plague outbreak decimates a part of the city. In the ancient world the most certain thing was uncertainty!

In fact, not unlike the lives of many in the developing world today, in the ancient world, the prospect of things getting worse usually outweighed the prospect of things getting better! Given the tenor of Paul's argument in the latter part of Romans 8, there is a good chance that many of Paul's readers were thinking along these lines vis-à-vis their security as God's adopted sons. Yes, God has granted his blessing 'in Christ', but how 'solid' was the guarantee underwriting it? Could God's favour be revoked? Could the circumstances of life threaten or change it? If things start going badly, does that mean God is reneging on his commitments? Just how secure is this adoption?

In the wake of these potential objections, Paul seeks to obviate doubts by highlighting one central truth: *God is for us, not against us*! From verse 28 on, the apostle offers an *a fortiori* argument concerning God's unwavering love and its value. He begins, 'And we know that in all things God works for the good of those who love him, who have been called according to his purpose' (Rom. 8:28).

No doctrine mitigates notions of uncertainty better than the doctrine of predestination. Paul wants to stress that, for those who love God, there is an abiding certainty that everything is ultimately working in their favour. For the apostle, the love of God that undergirds Christian adoption is not a fleeting emotion based on a whim. No greater guarantee can be offered to the doubter than the promise that their internal destiny has already been predetermined: 'And those he predestined, he also called; those he called, he also justified; those he justified, he also glorified' (Rom. 8:30). Predestination and glorification stand as parentheses around truths that believers now experience – calling and justification. This is Paul's point: if you have experienced a calling of God; if you have an experience of being justified by faith, confirmed by the Holy Spirit; then 'know' that these temporal experiences are bracketed by everlasting certainties. Called and justified believers know that they only experience these blessings because they have been predestined, because predestination must reveal itself in calling and justification, and finally in glorification.

However, ordering the logical sequence of salvation is not Paul's primary goal here; rather Paul is framing this entire discussion in a context of the 'new' Spirit-empowered life. In considering the *ordo salutis*, as sequential and independent events abstracted from Paul's overall argument in Romans 8, Richard Gaffin identifies this as a problem created by traditional theological constructs: 'Nothing distinguishes the traditional *ordo salutis* more than its insistence that the justification, adoption, and sanctification which occur at the inception of the application of redemption are separate acts. If our interpretation is correct, Paul views them not as distinct acts but as distinct aspects of a single act.'[38] Christian solidarity with Christ, in the Spirit, is the single act in which redemption occurs. The *ordo salutis* as presented by Paul is merely a logical way of describing the process and conditions under which the incorporation into Christ through the life-giving Spirit is validated.[39] And what is the logical conclusion of such a validation? Paul's answer comes in question form: 'If God is for us, who can be against us?' (Rom. 8:31). If God, who holds eternity in his hands and determines all things, is acting on our behalf for our salvation in Christ and through the Spirit, then who can possibly unravel this? Theoretically, there is only one that could stand against us: God himself! To this potential objection, Paul now turns his attention.

A characteristic of the adoption 'culture' of ancient Rome was that the authority of a father over a child could be used as a form of social capital. Occasionally adopting out children could be used for social gain or political manoeuvring, avoiding the responsibility of raising your own children, and even raising extra money, as David Williams suggests, 'The adoptive father effectively bought the child. And adoption also allowed the family to save money for the support of other children, dowering the girls' marriage and underwriting the boys' to public office, entries to which were subject to means tests.'[40] Given this cultural peculiarity, it is not difficult to conceptualize a context in which Paul addresses a potential objection about the nature of divine adoption. Could the heavenly Father decide to 'trade' his children in the manner that a human father might do so, to gain his own advantage? It would seem that it is against such a supposed objection that Paul structures his whole argument from verse 32 onwards. Effectively the apostle is arguing, 'Surely God, who has already made a "greater" investment on our behalf, is then willing to do the "lesser" thing of completing that which was begun.' If God has invested so much in the salvation of humanity; a salvation that is in lock-step with his eternal plans, why then would you possibly abandon the very objects of his grace – those destined to inherit the glory set aside for them?

If God the Father did not spare his own Son, surrendering him up to die on a Roman cross for the sake of humanity, then surely this benevolent Father will grant the recipients of his grace the lesser chattels pertaining to future heavenly glories? Because of the greater grace shown in the execution of salvation, the lesser graces of maintenance and completion of salvation are certainly assured. Given that adoption, like justification, is a legal metaphor, the structure of Paul's rhetoric from Romans 8:33–5 makes perfect sense: Who will bring a charge? Who will condemn? Who will separate? Many commentators interpret this line of logic as Schreiner does, 'Believers can face a day of judgment with confidence, for those whom God has chosen as his own will certainly not be accused on the last day of judgment.'[41]

However, better sense is made of this sequence of rhetorical questions when framed in a manner similar to the legal adoption / unadoption that might have occurred in ancient Rome. The argument, therefore, is reinforcing that adoption by the heavenly Father, in Christ, through the Spirit, cannot be legally undone, no matter who brings accusations! God is the one who has already justified so he won't bring a charge to undo that which he has ordained. Christ died on our behalf, he was raised for us and now intercedes for us in heaven – he won't condemn us. The material trials, reminiscent of the covenant curses of Leviticus 26:14–39 – trouble, hardship, persecution, famine, nakedness, danger or the sword – are not able to enact separation in this divinely decreed adoption. These temporal tribulations, as great as they may seem, cannot transcend eternal decrees.

So can the security of Christian adoption be jeopardized? The conclusion of Paul's rhetorical response is an emphatic no! In fact, the apostle is so confident that he draws on a military metaphor to affirm that those who have embraced the adoptive love of God are 'more than' conquerors. Peter Macky believes that military metaphors were part of Paul's stock-in-trade when it comes to affirming the Christian stance in confidently addressing life: 'He firmly believes that in the end God through Christ would triumph over all the forces of darkness, defeating all the enemies, even death, and Satan. As an expression of that confidence, Paul imagines himself and other believers already marching in God's triumphal procession.'[42]

Victory is clearly Paul's tone when it comes to the Christian life, and notions of defeat and negativity that some Christians sponsor are not found in Paul. A Roman military quest might result in conquest; however, in some cases it didn't and the conquerors were defeated. The suffering and agents of suffering that rail against Christians attempting to dissuade them from persevering in love have been, as Michael Gorman intimates, 'overwhelmingly conquered'.[43] The conquest Paul refers to covers every dimension: it is conquest over the trials of life and death; a conquest over the supernatural (angels and demons); a conquest over time (the present and future); a conquest over any power and authority; a conquest over the natural realm (height and depth); and any other thing in the created order. Because the victory is complete, the soldiers of Christ can have supreme confidence that they will not be separated from their commanding officer – the inalienable bond of love remains.

Paul wrote the immortal words, 'The greatest of these is love.' Love is one of the apostle's great themes, and it should not surprise us that love should come to the fore as Paul sums up his presentation of the gospel at the end of Romans 8. N.T. Wright argues that the theme of God's love has been running beneath Paul's argument since Romans 5 but now re-emerges in Romans 8, so as to reveal itself as a major theme of the entire gospel.[44] Love is highly significant when discussing the hope of a sure relationship with God, because above and beyond all the rational arguments that might be marshalled in favour of the certitude of divine adoption, there is *nothing more convincing or powerful than a knowledge about and experience of God's love.* After all, love is the supreme motivating force behind God's saving actions on humanity's behalf.

Every believer truly knows they are saved when they encounter this love in a personally meaningful way, as Paul explicitly says, 'And hope does not disappoint us, because God has poured out his love into our hearts by the Holy Spirit, whom he has given us' (Rom. 5:5).

The gospel of salvation is not merely a deity dispensing tickets to heaven but, above all, a restoration of the loving relationship that was broken in Eden. For Paul, to be reunited with God, 'in Christ', is to be restored into the family, regaining the lost love of the Father and experiencing what it truly is to be a child of God. This experience of God's love is only possible through the Spirit, for when a believer experiences this love, the bitterness of sin is suppressed, and the sweet taste of glory is savoured.

The indwelling Spirit gives the Christian the capacity to experience a removal of sin's presence. The degree to which believers are submissive to the Spirit is the degree to which the 'presence' of sin is tangibly extinguished from their lives. Yet the removal of sin's presence in this life is imperfect, because those 'in Christ' are caught in a tension. This tension is between this present evil age and the glorious age of the kingdom, where sin will be utterly vanquished. What enables an existence within this *realm of tension* is embracing the Spirit-endowed 'sonship' that God the Father bestows on believers. Believers then become God's chosen and adopted children, with all the privileges.

However, to be a child of God and fellow heir with Christ, within this realm of eschatological tension, necessarily results in suffering. This suffering is not something from which God's children should flee; on the contrary, it is something to be embraced. Suffering becomes the means of experiencing a deeper relationship with and greater dependency on Jesus Christ. Jesus suffered and instructed his disciples that a servant being no greater than his master should also expect to suffer. Suffering is a consequence of allowing the Spirit of God to consecrate the believer for a holy life, a life where the vanquished penalty, power and presence of sin express they are children of God. God's children stand out in a corrupt generation, and suffer for it. This is the normal Christian experience.

The believer experiences the powerful sustaining presence of Christ through the abiding presence of the Spirit, and in the midst of the trial *suffers for Christ, as Christ, and with Christ.* This deepened connectedness with Christ, through the Spirit, persuades the believer to forsake a dependency on human strength and allow weakness to become the conduit through which the power of Christ is manifest (2 Cor. 12, 13).

Suffering should never be interpreted as a sign of God's abandonment; on the contrary, suffering for Christ is a solid validation that one is genuinely a disciple of Christ, torn between the tension of the 'now and not yet'. Suffering then becomes the great validation of Christian authenticity and a great source of hope. Such a hope drives the believer away from grasping heaven-on-earth-now theologies, encouraging them to fix their true gaze on the heavenly reality, where one day the fullness of the removal of sin's presence will be experienced. God will not abandon his children. If he has done the greater thing of offering Jesus as an atoning sacrifice for them, surely the lesser thing of completing that is a foregone conclusion. Yes, God is for us and through the presence of the Spirit he pours his love into our hearts, confirming this fact and certifying eternity as our unshakable destiny.

Conclusion

Enabled by the Holy Spirit, we are granted the capacity to be transformed into a new people; to overcome the 'real' presence of sin – albeit imperfectly. Yet the Spirit's transformative work in this regard is transacted in two distinct stages: the first stage partial and temporal, the second stage complete and eternal. The former stage foreshadows the latter, anticipating an ultimate reality of perfection at the consummation of all things. While tempting to claim perfection 'now', we appreciate that lingering human imperfection has a positive role to play; it serves to deepen our dependency on Christ, better equipping us for eternity. In embracing the metaphor of adoption, Paul reminds us that we have been transferred from a *state of slavery* to a *state of sonship*. This adoptive state is revealed in the Holy Spirit's influence over our lives, instilling hope and peace. Moreover, the Holy Spirit brings the reality of the *eternal state* into the present, endowing believers with an experience of the eternal. This has great benefits, as it encourages believers to endure suffering as Christ – bolstered by a vision of heavenly glory. Yes, though Christians suffer in the tension between the 'now' and 'not yet', with all the pain that this entails, they know their salvation is absolutely secure as adopted children of God. Furthermore, Paul asserts that Christians can claim to be 'more than conquerors' in the face of the most arduous circumstances; confidently assured that God, who did the 'greater' thing of sending his Son to suffer and die for their redemption, will most assuredly accomplish the comparatively 'lesser thing' of completing what he began – their salvation.

6

The Righteous Shall Live by Faith

The primacy of faith makes the gospel truly unique. God expects nothing more from the penitent sinner than to respond to his free offer of deliverance with a simple trust. At face value, faith is so basic to human understanding that it scarcely warrants a mention, and yet more needs to be said. Of course, we cannot negate the value of simple faith, or suggest that a heartfelt trust in Jesus must 'first' be validated by *rational inquiry*. Indeed, that would be a contradiction of the first order. Yet the meaning of faith in the theological endeavour should not be taken for granted either. No doctrinal postulate is immune from distortion, even one as 'apparently' innocuous as faith. In fact, confusion leading to the degradation of the gospel's integrity is a greater risk when pivotal concepts within the scheme are confused, especially those *assumed* to be beyond confusion; and no concept exercises more leverage in the Christian soteriological scheme than that which represents *the means* of embracing the salvation offered. In Paul's estimation, faith, as the 'only' valid means of laying hold of the salvation prescribed, exercises leverage like no other concept. As important as faith 'itself' is, a correct estimation of its 'nature' must also be taken into account.

Saving Faith, Salvation and Righteousness

As we know, faith is crucial to Paul's definition of the gospel: 'I am not ashamed of the gospel, for it is the power of God for salvation, for everyone who *believes*' (Rom. 1:16). We have already considered the grounds of Paul's lack of shame with respect to the gospel. We have given credence to the power of God, with respect to the Holy Spirit. We have also taken into account the assumed role of the Father and the explicit role of the Son in procuring humanity's redemption. But the principal focus has been the Holy Spirit's 'powerful' role, exposing the problem of sin, acquitting the penalty of sin, overcoming the power of sin, and ultimately removing its presence. As we now come to the vital subject of how the penitent sinner *effectually* lays hold of this 'inclusive' salvation (including both Jews and Gentiles), reflecting on 'the nature' of faith simply cannot be avoided.

Simple faith, as the means of attaining salvation, may seem too good to be true. After all, it is not natural to expect to get something for nothing. In the ancient Roman context, the notion of salvation by faith may have seemed incredibly naive. To a devout law-keeping Jew, the idea of exclusive faith might have appeared somewhat inadequate. After all, in gaining and maintaining eternal salvation, surely something more would be required than simple faith? However the brilliance of Paul's gospel – as it reveals to us the gravity of the human plight, and God's absolute sufficiency in addressing it – convinces us that nothing 'but' faith will do in the attainment of salvation.

Romans 1:17 reminds us, that encapsulated within the message of salvation is the theme of *righteousness*. It highlights the incapacity of human righteousness in contrast with the abundance and sufficiency of divine righteousness. It also reinforces the manner in which God enables the transferral from one to the other. Paul qualifies the nature of the attainment of righteousness (by faith) with the expression 'from first to last'. He then proceeds to quote Habakkuk 2:4, 'The righteous will live by faith.' Now, there are three ideas worth reflecting on here: the first being 'the righteousness of / from God'; the second is the notion of faith 'from first to last'; and the third relating to the meaning of 'The righteous shall live by faith', as applied in this particular context.

Fundamentally, we can assume that critical for an understanding of the gospel is the notion of righteousness, and crucial to grasping righteousness is faith. However, what we cannot readily assume is the *nature of their relationship*. Is it that 'an act' of faith lays hold of the *righteousness* of Christ vis-à-vis justification, such that the believer can simply be *assured* of eternal life? Or does faith pertain to the nature of 'living out' this *righteousness* in a relationship with Christ? Or are we unnecessarily creating a false dichotomy, whereas we should really consider both postulates as concurrently valid?

The term, 'the righteousness of God' (*dikaiosune theou*) can refer to either a 'quality' of God or a 'status' that God bestows on humanity.[1] John Zeisler believes the term transcends any potential either / or designation, but has a distinctly *relational aspect,* implying that who God is directly impacts the status and the actions of those in relationship with him:

> In the O. T. *righteousness* is a relationship term, and quite apart from the fact that it normally refers to behaviour with relationship, a relationship to Yahweh is nearly always added. This relational stress is especially clear in Ezek 33:10ff, where righteousness is seen to exist from moment to moment, depending on one's present relation to God and His will. How one stands now determines whether they live or die; this is the forensic side. But how he stands before God is determined by how he stands in relationship to God's will; this is the ethical side.[2]

The righteousness of God is also related to God's saving activity: 'You heavens above, rain down righteousness; let the clouds shower it down. Let the earth open wide, let salvation spring up, let righteousness grow with it; I, the Lord , have created it' (Isa. 45:8). As we know, in the text of Romans 1:17 Paul implies that 'righteousness of God' is related to the saving activity of God in the gospel, a saving activity manifest through Jesus Christ who, in vindicating God's righteous demands against sinful humanity with his atoning death on the cross, enables believers to stand in God's righteous presence; endowed with Christ's own righteousness. Yet this *status* of righteousness demands a concomitant *state* of righteousness, by virtue of this relational connection or 'union' (Rom. 6).

As such, we must recognize that Jesus Christ is not simply an 'object' we assent to in order to gain a *legal pronouncement* of a justified status. Jesus Christ is a person who relationally reconnects us with our heavenly Father, by virtue of his union with us through the Spirit. In such a relationship, the Father expects his (adopted) children to display righteousness concomitant with their 'in Christ' standing. Indeed, Zeisler's argument is relevant here, 'This righteousness; this is both a demand and gift, as in Matt 5; it is the new life, the moral renewal of the believer, which *yet remains always God's righteousness*.'[3] You cannot receive a declaration of righteousness *disengaged from* a relational / moral existence: 'Be holy because I, the Lord your God, am holy' (Lev. 19:2).

Having apprehended a *status of righteousness* by faith, believers concurrently apprehend *a state that demands righteousness*, as Don Garlington suggests, 'Thus, there is more at stake than a changed status; those who had been dead are now alive; they are new creatures in a new creation. In this light, Paul's statement becomes an exhortation for Christians to live as those who are washed, sanctified and justified.'[4] The *righteousness of state* is inextricably dependent on the *righteousness of status*, because it is 'ultimately' God's righteousness which has implications for our understanding of the nature of *saving faith*.

Is saving faith simply 'an act' that lays hold of a righteous status, leaving believers to work out their righteousness? Or does *saving faith* have an enduring quality that encompasses righteous state, undergirded by the righteous status? Of direct relevance here is Paul's notion: 'from faith to faith' (*ek pistis eis pistin*, Rom. 1:17 margin). This can be interpreted as an *idiom of emphasis*, where Paul is signalling that salvation is 'utterly' by faith. Though superficially true, Charles Quarles insightfully observes that wherever the prepositional construction *ek . . . eis* was used in Paul, there is not one instance of an idiomatic use. Rather, it retains its basic meaning: 'from, out of . . . toward, to', and notes, 'In summary, the *ek . . . eis* propositional series often express range, duration, repetition, *source and destination, previous state and new state/progression*. It does not appear to function as an idiom of emphasis.'[5]

Mark Seifrid's appraisal also concurs: 'Faith is both the source and the goal of the righteousness of God, the means of "seeing" it and the demand which it lays upon us.'[6] Therefore, the phrase 'from faith to faith' suggests that saving faith encompasses more than, although not less than, a 'point-of-time' belief. This includes the idea that faith grows, is perpetually operative, broad in its scope, and comprehensive in encompassing both source and destination. Therefore, saving faith considered thus enables us to embrace its more comprehensive nature, indicating that saving faith holistically imbibes and encompasses Paul's soteriology, and not simply one element of it.

As such, *saving faith* should be viewed as more than a 'rational decision' or a mere attitude of mind, but can be also be viewed as a state-of-being 'in faith'; albeit originating from a divinely imitated act 'of faith', working itself out in Christian living (Rom. 14:23; Gal. 2:20; 3:5–6; Eph. 6:16; Col. 1:23; 2:7). Therefore, faith not only denotes a heartfelt trust that grasps the righteousness offered in the gospel but, taken in concert with the *relational nature of righteousness*, represents trust within a *righteous state*, derivative of the *righteous status* gained by an initial act of saving faith. Thus, the *righteousness of Christ* first embraced by faith is existentially manifested by a righteous state-of-being by virtue of the faith 'union with Christ'. This state-of-being is perpetually sustained by a Spirit-animated faith. In this way, we can say that 'salvation' is appropriated and sustained by faith – 'from first to last'.

But how shall we understand the term, 'the righteous will live by faith'? Quoted from Habakkuk 2:4 (literally: 'but the righteous one by his fidelity will live'), Paul seeks to conceptually apply the two concepts previously discussed. There may be some basis for the argument that Christ's 'own' faith (faithfulness) is in view (as in Heb. 12:2–4), but given this same verse is applied to 'personal' faith in both Galatians 3:11 and Hebrews 10:39 – 11:39, and given that this species of faith is clearly presented by Paul as the means of appropriating salvation, the *faith of the believer* is most likely in view.[7] But what does it mean to 'live' by faith? Is it an eschatological reference to eternal life (viz. shall receive eternal life), or a reference to the ongoing Christian life (viz. shall adopt a style of life animated by faith)?

Reading the verse 'exclusively' eschatologically does not do justice to the immediate concerns of the Jewish Christians, with their misunderstanding of Paul's law-free gospel. For them, 'going on with God' was an issue of paramount importance.

Interestingly, Paul S. Minear observes of the *ek pistis* construction in Romans, 'Paul is dealing with believers; *with those who have faith*. In all, the issue was the correct understanding of what proceeds from or does not proceed from their faith.'[8] Regarding what 'does or does not' proceed from faith, Minear is not referring just to eschatological righteousness, that is ultimate salvation or eternal life, but also this current life, 'There is not uncertainty about the fact that this epistle deals with false and true ideas of *the style of life which proceeds from faith*.'[9] In this view, the notion of life validly pertains to the ongoing Christian life, especially if correlated with another 'flagship' Pauline statement: 'I have been crucified with Christ and I no longer live, but Christ lives in me. *The life I live in the body, I live by faith* in the Son of God, who loved me and gave himself for me.' (Gal. 2:20)

As such, it seems that saving faith is completely integral to the gospel of salvation. As we have seen, Paul's view of 'salvation' is not defined around forensic metaphors alone, but engages other equally weighty metaphors to construct a comprehensive view of salvation. Therefore, we should not suppose that faith has no *crucial role* to play in these other dimensions of the gospel as well. Indeed, there is no need to partition off faith exclusively with justification, while abandoning ethics to the category of law / flesh / works; this would contradict Paul. Rather, righteousness, as it pertains to the gospel, can concurrently exist forensically and ethically, vis-à-vis faith.[10]

Therefore, the Spirit-endowed gift of faith is the premise of 'getting right', 'staying right', thus 'being right' with God, because its source and power is from God. Zeisler summarizes it well, 'The righteous-by-faith is he who is drawn into and shares in the saving righteousness of God . . . What matters is that God's saving righteousness does two things for men and does them inseparably: it restores their relationship with God, and makes them new (ethical, righteous) beings.'[11] It is the Spirit-endowed, divinely initiated faith that enables the sinner to embrace Christ and gain his righteous status. This same faith unites the believer 'in Christ', where the righteousness of Christ is manifest under the Spirit's sustaining power. Only a robust understanding of the Spirit enables the *righteous status* and the *righteous state* to coexist, within the realm of saving faith!

Saving Faith as Rational Assent

Faith can be portrayed in an overly rational light, being represented as *rational assent*, a reasoned acknowledgement of facts, or acceptance of propositions. In this paradigm of believing, even an agnostic may determine by reasoned faith there is a degree of truthfulness regarding Jesus' historical existence. They may go as far as acknowledging things about Jesus, which require belief in the supernatural: the incarnation, miracles, the resurrection and the ascension. This variety of faith simply assents to the veracity of propositions: belief in the possibility of, the reality of, or the potential for something beyond the 'believer'; which the mind can 'reasonably' give credence to. It acknowledges perceived 'truths' that are cogent to any reasonable person.

When then would Christians find *rational assent* an attractive way of representing saving faith? In many cases the driver is a reaction to varieties of faith that seem subjective or mystical in nature. The 'style' of faith being reacted against is usually deemed intransitive (without an object of focus), a kind of 'feeling' faith. Transitive faith, on the other hand, must have an object to be valid, even if the object may appear invalid to others, such as an idol: 'Half of the wood he burns in the fire; over it, he prepares his meal, he roasts his meat and eats his fill . . . From the rest he makes a god, his idol; he bows down to it and worships. He prays to it and says, "Save me; you are my god."' (Isa. 44:16–17).

In reaction to these 'intransitive' forms of faith, a version of saving faith is promoted that represents little more than *rational assent to propositions*. Gordon H. Clark is an advocate of this position: 'Mindless encounters and meaningless relationships are not saving faith.

Truth is propositional, and one is saved and sanctified only through believing true statements.'[12] In reaction to intransitive faith, Clark believes that many Christians are motivated by either irrational pragmatism or irrational mysticism.[13] In response, he advances a version of faith that by-passes anything 'vaguely' subjective: 'Faith is strictly limited to knowledge.'[14] In fact, Clark is even sceptical about Puritan thinkers like John Owen, who would maintain that the 'person' of Christ constitutes the object of saving faith.[15]

Of course, this view of faith is not without its champions; for example, theologians in the calibre of Thomas Aquinas.[16] A seminal thinker, Aquinas defined faith as 'assent' in the context of what B.A. Gerrish calls 'heavily intellectualist language'.[17] For Aquinas, 'faith' is reasoned assent, but where God plays a role: 'For the faith of which we are speaking, does not assent to anything, except because it is revealed by God.'[18] For Aquinas, saving faith must meet certain conditions to be valid. First, the 'things of faith' (objects) should be proposed to the believing subject, and second, the believer must assent to the things proposed.[19] Concerning the faith that assents to the proposition, Aquinas indicates a twofold cause: first, there is an external inducement (a miracle, a sermon etc.), and second, there is an 'internal' inducement of divine provenance which, as Aquinas suggests, 'is from God moving man inwardly by grace'.[20]

However, despite this talk of 'divine moving', Aquinas' view of assenting faith is limited by something that plagues all rationalist approaches to faith – the inherent value assigned to the human 'believer' in the process of believing: 'The intellect assenting to divine truth as the command of the will moved by the grace of God, so that is subject to the free will in relation to God; and consequently *the act of faith can be meritorious.*'[21] In Aquinas' conception, the believer 'augments' his or her own saving faith, within the faith process. Faith is not absolutely credited *extra nos* by God.

In this conception, human rational energies contribute to faith, albeit 'moved' by God, leaving us with the potential to contribute to the appropriation of our own salvation. Furthermore, faith as rational assent, with its reliance on the capacity of the believing subject's rational capacities, actually mirrors the 'style' of faith it often attempts to avoid. Transitive rational faith is as equally prone to self-generation as intransitive mystical faith; one is generated by the rational mind, the other by the irrational mind. In either case, the potential for the human subject to augment saving faith is equally prevalent.

Another weakness with a saving faith styled on rational assent is its proclivity to make the proposition (a translocated object) the object of saving faith, and not the God who does the saving. D.B. Knox, in commenting on William Tyndale's view of faith, notes, 'God's favour is made known to us by the word of God especially his promises . . . Saving faith has as its object the promises of God.'[22] Did you see it? In this formulation, the 'promises' are the object of saving faith. I imagine in this 'shorthand' definition that Tyndale is not seriously suggesting that propositions save us, or that abstract promises constitute the 'true' object of saving faith; however, such definitions do serve to illustrate potential flaws in translocating the object of faith. If taken 'rationally', the promises, conceived as propositions, subtly become the object of saving faith, with the 'ultimate' object of saving faith (Christ) supplanted by an 'idea' of him.

As previously alluded to, John Owen was patently aware of this flaw, carefully advocating that the 'person' of Christ should be the 'true' object of saving faith – the one toward whom all the promises point. Indeed, errors of translocated faith are avoidable, when the nature of faith is considered to constitute 'far more' than an act of the mind: 'Justifying faith must be alive and relational, requiring a lively and personal response to its object [Christ].'[23] Saving faith, which is personal and relational, is less disposed to suffer from object translocation, as a personal / relational faith cannot entrust itself to a proposition, which in and of itself cannot save!

Notwithstanding these flaws, the greatest weakness of *rational assent* as saving faith is its proclivity to 'remain in the mind'; a faith that feigns legitimacy without practical veracity. While rational assent may attest to the veracity of the 'thing' believed, it cannot actually 'prove' its veracity, and necessarily remains aloof. For example, a new product may be advertised. The advertisement may be 'reasonably' convincing. The consumer is then induced to assent to its value, thus affirming the possibility of a purchase. But at this point, the consumer's faith in the product remains 'aloof'; nothing more than recognition of its theoretical value. However, at the point of committing to purchase, this rational assent necessarily transforms into consenting trust; because it costs something, it requires action!

According to the testimony of Holy Scripture, genuine saving faith should *validate itself* through practical obedience. Consider the example of Zacchaeus. After a meaningful faith encounter with Jesus, he pledges to generously make amends, and in response: 'Jesus said to him, "Today salvation has come to this house, because this man, too, is a son of Abraham"' (Luke 19:9). James pastorally addresses the lack of what believers such as Zacchaeus embraced: 'What good is it, my brothers; if a man claims to have faith but has no deeds? Can such faith save him?' (Jas 2:14). For James saving faith that assents to truth, even toward orthodox truth (Jas 2:19), is invalid if not verified by concomitant action.

Of course, charity and good works have *no causal relationship* to Zacchaeus' salvation or the variety of saving faith James suggests. What the apostolic testimony actually argues for is a *necessary consequential relationship* between saving faith and good works. Without the 'fruit' of good works as a *consequence*, the legitimacy of the *cause* should be called into question. A lack of consequence (works) betrays a lack of genuine cause (faith). Thus, the veracity of saving faith is validated by, but not caused by, its works. It would seem, then, the absence of works provides an impetus for a careful examination into the causal legitimacy of the 'alleged' saving faith, especially in the form of rational assent.

Saving Faith as Faithfulness

If legitimate faith must be accompanied and confirmed by works, then logic might suggest that faithfulness might be a better way of conceptualizing saving faith. Faithfulness incorporates both the notion of trusting faith and the validating outworking of it. In fact, the attainment of salvation testified within the New Testament requires perseverance in 'faith', in order for salvation to be finally attained (1 Tim. 4:16; Heb. 10:36). Furthermore, following the 'great' chapter on faith in Hebrews 11, and on the 'basis' of its catalogue of *faith witnesses*, believers are exhorted to persevere: 'Therefore, since we are surrounded by such a great cloud of [faith] witnesses, let us throw off everything that hinders and the sin that so easily entangles, and let us run with perseverance the race marked out for us' (Heb. 12:1). Why would the author of Hebrews use 'perseverance' as the primary application for his chapter 11 faith argument, if faith did not have an enduring / validating element?

Without question, the notion of incorporating faithfulness under the rubric of saving faith sends alarm bells off in the minds of many Protestant Christians, for whom the doctrine of 'faith alone' is *sine qua non*. However, is the incorporation of faithfulness into the concept of saving faith valid?

N.T. Wright offers us some insights in this regard. Wright believes Jesus is the 'one true' faithful Israelite, through whom humanity is redeemed by his covenant faithfulness. In response to Jesus' *faithfulness*, believers render an *answering faith*: the 'badge' of a renewed covenant people.[24] Considered with particular reference to justification, Wright suggests the faith of the justified believer 'should' be maintained as a faithful life: 'I repeat, I have always said that the final justification, the final verdict, as opposed to the present justification, which is pronounced over faith alone, will be pronounced over the totality of a life lived . . . Not that any such life will be perfect (Phil 3: 13-14) but that it will be going in the right direction, "seeking the glory and honour and immortality" (Rom 2:7).'[25]

Wright posits that each person must ultimately give an account of his or her life, and that believer's final justification at the last day is on account of the life lived – in Christ. Wright further suggests this is not based on human merit, but the righteousness believers have *today* is based on the work of Christ *yesterday*, which gives these faithful saints confidence in Christ *tomorrow*: 'And "tomorrow", our own resurrection will constitute the final declaration which will correspond to those already given.'[26] Without promulgating works-righteousness, Wright is attempting to counter a narrowly forensic view of justification, and validly take into account the concomitant concept of faithful perseverance.

Of course, Wright is considering the subject of justification in its broader context, over and against the narrow conceptualizations of some traditional Protestant formulations. His views are set within the framework of a redemptive-historical scheme, in which he views justification in a triple *sense – past, present and future.* He is also attempting to deal more realistically with the wider biblical data, and thus considers justification more broadly than a *legal status conferred by imputation at the moment of faith.* While not suggesting that a believer is justified by human merit, it is not difficult to see how Wright's explication of his triple-sense perspective on justification is open to these suggestions. In seeking to incorporate faithfulness and/or perseverance within the scope of 'being right by faith' his *temporal framing* readily exposes his argument to the aforementioned allegations.

In response, a less confusing way of conceptualizing such a view of justification might be to consider it from an 'a-temporal' threefold perspective: *justification executed* (Christ's actual justifying work); *justification applied* (the believer's faith acceptance of Christ); and *justification vindicated* (the eternal validation of this reality). This posits 'not' three stages of justification (as Wright's position can be more easily interpreted as implying) but three 'a-temporal' logical dimensions. In such a formulation, there is no 'future justification' (as we might understand it temporally); merely an eternal vindication of its historical execution that has been temporally applied.[27] This conceptualization avoids the pitfalls of framing it within 'temporal / sequential' categories, which 'can' give the impression that one is striving 'on the way' to being justified. What is evident from this discussion is that there is a significant problem viewing saving faith as faithfulness, when it is considered progressively within the dimension of temporality (time).

Of course, the primary objection to considering saving faith as faithfulness is its proclivity to be interpreted as the possible grounds of human merit. This objection is largely founded on the misconception that salvation 'equates' with justification. However, those holding this position find themselves with a problem when having to consider the issues in a more nuanced way, as saving faith operates in a wider field, as Douglas Campbell suggests, 'The semantic range of "faith" – denoting at times the content of belief and at times the quality of human loyalty or fidelity – is problematic for justification theory.'[28]

For example, the author of Hebrews exhorts his readers to live by faith (faithfully): 'But my righteous one will live by faith. And if he shrinks back, I will not be pleased with him' (Heb. 10:38). Incorporating human fidelity within the semantic range of faith is not an insurmountable problem when oriented the right way around. However, it becomes problematic when associated with faithfulness and where faithfulness is deemed to operate in a 'causal' sense within the soteriological matrix, even beyond the narrow confines of forensic justification. Even if 'saving faith' is interpreted as faithfulness within the metaphorical category of 'slavery' (Rom. 6 – 8) where Paul explicates victory over the power of sin (sanctification), there is always the potential for it to be misinterpreted, leading to the idea that 'my faithfulness *keeps me right* with God'!

I would suggest then, that faithfulness, as located within the soteriological matrix, is most properly categorized as the concomitant by-product of a faith adherence to Christ. Indeed, Paul describes faithfulness as the *fruit of the Spirit*, in a similar way that goodness, gentleness and self-control are (Gal. 5:22).[29] Faithfulness constitutes a human-related 'action' that flows out of the justified state – an outworking of faith. For Paul, saving faith (in its justification application) is located in a different category from works (of the law): 'For we maintain that a man is justified by faith *apart from* observing the law' (Rom. 3:28). He also adds, 'However, to *the man who does not work* but trusts God who justifies the wicked, his faith is credited as righteousness' (Rom. 4:5). It follows then, that 'saving faith', within its justification application, represents a God-initiated act of self-denying trust in God that appropriates righteousness, separate from any human-related action.

Faithfulness is a human-oriented action that flows out of saving faith. In fact, even perceived outside of forensic categories, saving faith equally represents self-abandonment and equally cannot be deemed as faithfulness. Faith that 'gets one right with God', must also 'keep one right with God'! Saving faith then, even in the broadest sense, must represent an abandonment of self-trust in favour of adhering to Christ, encapsulating the life-in-Christ, in its entirety (Gal. 2:20). Faithfulness, on the other hand, necessarily flows out of saving faith. Though having no value in gaining and/or maintaining the righteous 'status' in Christ, it does have ultimate value in proving the legitimacy of saving faith, in much the same way as fruit proves the legitimacy of a fruit tree.

Saving Faith as Perpetual Trust

So far we have considered *saving faith* as rational assent, and *saving faith* as faithfulness. The primary limitation of the former is its predisposition to represent faith as a mere intellectual recognition of facts, a point-of-time assent that lacks ongoing legitimizing proof. The latter alternative of faithfulness, has the obvious limitation of potentially incorporating ongoing human effort into faith – effectively making it a 'work'. What then is required is an understanding of saving faith that is verifiable by fidelity; but the verification process avoids becoming or being interpreted as being causal in any way.

In his Colossians letter, Paul encourages his readers to 'continue on their faith' and not be moved away (presumably by false doctrine) from the hope held out in the gospel (Col. 1:23). Thus, we see here the notion of 'continuing' in faith. This continuing should not, necessarily, be deemed as active faithfulness, but more as a perpetuation of the faith status. How then is continuation possible? Paul's Galatians correspondence offers a clue in this regard: 'But by faith we eagerly await through the Spirit the righteousness for which we hope' (Gal. 5:5). The Spirit, then, enables this endurance. Thus, in Paul's estimation, the Spirit *enables a perpetual state of faith*, in which the believer patiently waits for the goal of their hope – their salvation.

Of course, in seeking to understand faith as a *perpetual state of trust*, it is first essential to recognize that saving faith is not attributable to human energy in any way. When considered as faithfulness, the potential error of attributing human effort to faith is obvious. However, even faith that is not overtly active in relation to works has the potential to be derivative of human effort. Karl Barth's observations unmask some of these potential errors:

> The man who boasts that he possesses something which justifies him before God and man, even if that something be his own insecurity and brokenness, still retains confidence in human self-justification . . . Nothing human which desires to more than a void and deprivation, a possibility and a sign-post, more than the most trivial thing in the midst of the phenomena of this world, survives; nothing which is not, like everything else in this world, dust and ashes – before God. Only faith survives: faith which is not a work, not even a negative work; not an achievement, not even the achievement of humility; not a thing which exist before God and man in its own right.[30]

The basis of saving faith is this: there is no human basis! Saving faith only begins with the prevenient action of God through the Spirit, awakening the 'blind' human consciousness to the reality that it is hopelessly lost in unrighteousness, without 'any' capacity for self-deliverance. In fact, Paul describes this human impotence as a status of being 'dead' (Eph. 2:5). Only by God's sovereign initiative is the capacity to respond 'in faith' even a possibility: 'For it is by grace you have been saved, through faith – and this not from yourselves; it is the gift of God – not by works, so that no-one can boast' (Eph. 2:8–9). Saving faith is a gift from God, a gift bestowed by means of the Spirit.

What then is the manner of this bestowal? Paul brought the gospel to the Corinthians without relying on the prevailing methods of logic or eloquence. Shrouded in human weakness he proclaimed a message of 'foolishness': Jesus Christ and him crucified. Yet the message came across with power; in demonstrations of the Spirit's power (either signs or preaching), that the Corinthians' 'faith' might not depend on a prior basis of human wisdom, only God's power (1 Cor. 2:1–5). Paul describes his gospel as 'God's secret wisdom'; wisdom unintelligible and unobtainable by 'natural' (non-spiritual) reason. Furthermore, Paul intimates that this 'secret wisdom' has been revealed exclusively, by the Spirit (v. 10).

In Paul's estimation, it is only the Spirit that enables the truth of the gospel to be believed and understood (v. 12). Indeed, he argues that the (gospel) words he speaks have a Spirit-derivation, and implies that these words can 'make sense' in any meaningful way to the person equally endowed with the Spirit (v. 14). Therefore, the Spirit provides both the means of the message's conveyance and the capacity for this 'naturally' incomprehensible message to be comprehended. This, of course, means that only the prevenient 'gift' of the Spirit can grant the capacity for the sinner to truly grasp 'by faith' the Spirit-derived content of the gospel. Yet understanding Christ as the object of faith is not as simple as one might think, for while this Spirit-generated faith may not be intransitive, it is not transitive in the ordinary sense either.

Yes, saving faith is oriented toward an 'object' that is able to save – Jesus Christ. However, this saving faith-act is not as simple as suggesting the Spirit generates a 'thing' deemed faith that enables the believer to adhere to Jesus Christ, who saves! Jesus is not simply an object of faith in any normal sense of the concept. Because the object of saving faith (the person of Christ) is so intimately bound to the means of generating the faith that saves (the person of the Spirit), to suggest that the role of the latter is 'merely' to generate faith in the work of the former is inadequate, even if it is true on face value.

For Paul, the empowering presence of the Spirit enables Christ, in his *post-resurrection state*, to become 'functionally' indistinguishable from the Spirit (2 Cor. 3:7–18); being 'spiritually' united to the believer such that the believer's life is animated by Christ (Gal. 2:20). In such a state, both Christ and the Spirit are intimately bound in the believer's faith experience. To be 'in Christ' is only possible by being 'in faith', being in faith is only possible by being 'in the Spirit';

all of which engenders a 'practical' life of perpetual faith in Christ. Therefore, through the Spirit, Christ operates as both the subject that causes faith, and the object toward which that faith is directed. He is faith's source and goal, even as the Spirit initiates and sustains the 'in Christ' status, by animating this perpetual faith in Christ.

This then sheds light on Paul's key statement portraying faith in a perpetuating sense: 'I have been crucified with Christ and I no longer live, but Christ lives in me. The life I live in the body, I live by faith in the Son of God, who loved me and gave himself for me' (Gal. 2:20). Through a Spirit-engendered faith in Christ, Paul is able to conceptualize the reality of 'union with Christ'. Through this, he can state that his old 'self' is dead – crucified with Christ, and through the Spirit, Paul is then able to grasp the reality that Christ 'actually' lives in him, animating his mind to comprehend his new reality (1 Cor. 2:16). With his 'old self' no longer animating his life, but with Christ (present as the Spirit), Paul is able to live out his new life by virtue of faith in Christ (the Son of God). This 'life of faith' represents a perpetual state of trusting Christ as he loves and gives in the service of Christ, as the Son of God loved him, and gave himself for him.

The point is simply this: saving faith cannot simply be reduced to a point-of-time decision vis-à-vis justification, even as justification does not 'equate' with salvation. The faith that justifies through Christ is also the faith that sustains through Christ, as Christ remains the focus of that ongoing life of faith. Saving faith, then, represents a perpetual state of trust in Christ, through the Spirit; where the Spirit makes Christ an ever-present reality in the believer's life experience – the perpetual subject / object of trust.

This being the case, we now have the key to understanding Paul's summation of faith in the opening chapter of Romans: 'For in the gospel a righteousness from God is revealed, a righteousness that is by faith from first to last, just as it is written: "The righteous will live by faith"' (Rom. 1:17). The apostle is` therefore stating that in the gospel a way of being 'set right' with God is revealed that is from 'first to last'; surely this can mean nothing else other than the all-encompassing perpetual value of faith, within salvation. By this, I take it he means that faith is not only the grounds of acquitting sin's penalty through justification; not only the basis of breaking sin's power through life in the Spirit; but also the means of overcoming sin's presence, and sustaining the believer until salvation is complete.

Therefore, saving faith is not something that merely initiates a relationship with God, only to be set aside in favour of reason, religion or law. Saving faith is the phenomenon that gains and sustains salvation from beginning to end, in Paul's words – from first to last! Indeed, Calvin astutely noted this in countering erroneous notions that Christian salvation might begin with faith, but then continue with meritorious works: 'Similarly, when a prophet says, "The just shall live by faith", the statement does not apply to impious and profane persons, whom the Lord is turning them to faith may justify, but the utterance is directed to believers, and to them life is promised by faith.'[31]

With respect to the enduring nature of faith righteousness, Calvin further adds, 'Therefore, we must have this blessedness not just once but must hold to it throughout life. Finally, he [Paul] testifies that the embassy of free reconciliation with God is published not for one day or another, but is attested as perpetual in the church.'[32] Notwithstanding Calvin's particular sixteenth-century application, we recognize along with him the perpetual necessity of faith regarding the Christian life of righteousness. We may affirm then, that while a Spirit-enabled and sustained faith is present, faith, and never human merit, can be the only basis for a righteous standing before God – from beginning to end.

Indeed, it matters not whether we consider righteousness as a status or state. If the ground of righteousness is a perpetual Spirit-generated faith, then righteousness can 'never' be attributable to human merit! In avoiding the inherent flaws of saving faith as rational assent, and the different though equally flawed weaknesses, in its manifestation as faithfulness, we have come to a satisfactory appraisal of it. Saving faith is best understood as a perpetual state-of-being 'in faith'. It's not a point-of-time assent to a proposition about justification; not an enduring faithfulness 'on the way' to being set right with God, but a Spirit-enabled state-of-existence where absolute trust in God, generated by God, gains and sustains salvation. Saving faith is not something we conjure up, but a privilege God grants, enables and empowers. It is something we are invited into: initiated, sustained and completed by his divine power through the Spirit, all of him – none of us!

However, introducing a 'perpetual' quality into faith opens up the necessity to discuss temporality (time); one of the limitations of validating saving faith in terms of faithfulness. Faith, when considered as faithfulness, framed within reference to time and exercised in relation to a believing subject, is inherently biased toward an interpretation of faith that can develop into a human work. However, understanding saving faith as a 'perpetual state of trust' avoids this. This is not to suggest that faith or the believing subject do not exist within time; they certainly do, yet 'perpetual' saving faith is, in a sense, timeless – eternal in nature. How so? Because the Spirit that awakens faith, uniting the believer with Christ, brings the eternal reality into the present. That is why Paul can boldly state things like: 'And God raised us up with Christ and seated us with him in the heavenly realms in Christ Jesus' (Eph. 2:6). Of course, believers are not 'materially' seated with Christ, but through their spiritual state it becomes an 'actual' reality for them – as if eternity breaks into time.

Through a Spirit-generated state of perpetual trust, the Christian experience is eschatological, such that when sinners embrace the gospel by faith under the prompting of the Spirit, they enter into the domain of faith, the domain of the eternal God. Believers experience an eschatological reality where salvation is fully realized, even as it is 'yet to be' fully experienced. Remaining in a perpetual state of trust (in the Spirit) enables an existence within an 'a-temporal' (eschatological) state where the eternal reality is experienced, even while existing within concrete time. Douglas Campbell is therefore right in affirming: '"Faith" is a complex rather than simple notion, denoting both Christian belief and Christian endurance.'[33] Overcoming the limitations of 'faithfulness', and understanding saving faith in terms of a 'timeless' perpetual trust, I would suggest, fulfils both of Campbell's requirements.

Furthermore, in such a view, the Pauline concept of the 'obedience of faith' (Rom. 1:5; 16:26) is also logically purged of any malevolent notions of works-righteousness. For Paul, obedience has no role in 'working toward' a status of righteousness; rather it is the natural expression of a life in conformity with God's will, based on faith and not law. Faith in Christ is faith in the 'Lord' Jesus Christ, implying that faith must surrender to Christ in obedience, under the Spirit's motivation – as John McArthur suggests, 'God makes the believing heart an obedient heart.'[34] When a person enters into a relationship with the Lord Jesus through perpetual faith, they enter into a union that necessitates obedience to the 'character' with which they are united. This obedience is not deemed as *causal* but *consequential*; the fruitful expression of Christ's will animated by the Holy Spirit. We might say that, through the Spirit, the believer enters into a reality where perpetual faith necessitates perpetual obedience, where faith naturally consents to obedience and obedience naturally validates faith. And, because the 'Holy' Spirit animates this faith, the faith produced will invariably be holy!

These notions of the eternal impinging on the temporal, regarding faith as Spirit-enabled perpetual trust, can be difficult to understand, so perhaps this analogy might help. Most Christians have been to church conventions or camps. At these events there is usually a 'heightened sense' of God's presence; usually on account of rousing Christian music, inspiring teaching from the Bible, warm Christian fellowship, and a general 'spiritual' atmosphere. At these events, Christians can get so caught up in the experience that time appears to 'cease to exist'; they can temporarily forget that there is a reality outside the reality they are presently experiencing. In fact, many don't want it to end because it seems that heaven has come to earth and put time 'on hold'. If you have had this kind of experience, then you would be able to conceive of, even if only as a possibility, the notion that the Spirit can create an 'a-temporal' reality in the life of the believer where, although living in a world bound by time, their walk of faith is not conditioned by time, but by a Spirit-enabling 'eternity' that encroaches into 'their present'. This, I believe, is what the author of Hebrews 11:1 may have been alluding to when he wrote, 'Now faith is the substance [*hypostasis*] of what is hoped for.' For him, faith makes the eternal substance that is hoped for a present reality. By faith the perpetual eternal exists in time, while remaining unconditioned by it.

For Everyone Who Believes . . .

The gospel is not the exclusive possession of one group. This suggestion might seem obvious to the modern mind; however, the notion that a particular group should be included in God's favour at the expense of others was not so foreign to ancient ears. After all, wasn't Israel God's chosen nation? In a radical break from ideas of exclusivity, Paul was quite clear with respect to the gospel; it represented an offer of salvation to 'everyone' who believes – first to the Jew, then to the Gentile (Rom. 1:16). Such a statement must be understood in light of the fact that the gospel's universality might have led to the belief among some of a Jewish persuasion that the gospel might now lead to them being the excluded ones! In fact, given that Paul was speaking specifically to the Gentiles, there was reasonable scope to believe this.

Romans 9 – 11 represents Paul's primary appeal for the universality of the gospel with particular reference to the incorporation of the Jews. Paul sets any misunderstanding right. The gospel of salvation is just as much for the Jews as it is for Gentiles, as his impassioned plea suggests: 'I speak the truth in Christ – I am not lying, my conscience confirms it in the Holy Spirit – I have great sorrow and unceasing anguish in my heart. For I could wish that I myself were cursed and cut off from Christ for the sake of my brothers, those of my own race, the people of Israel' (Rom. 9:1–4a). However, the primary stumbling block for the Jews embracing the gospel was the matter of faith. The Gentiles received righteousness because they embraced it by faith; the Jews (as a socio-religious group) encountered resistance on account of their adherence to the Law.

God had not given up on his people. Nevertheless, Paul is resolute; he wants the Jews to embrace Christ, but he wants them to do it on the same basis as the Gentiles – that of faith! Paul's primary argument comes down to this summary statement: 'Christ is the end of the law so that there may be righteousness for everyone who believes' (Rom. 10:4). In Paul's thinking, the Christ-event represents the end of the Mosaic Law system and, despite his sympathies, even the most genuine or sincere Jew cannot expect to gain salvation unless they embrace Christ by faith.

Yes, the gospel is available to everyone, but it is only effective for those who embrace it by faith! And so to the Jew who wants to gain the benefits of salvation offered in Christ, Paul says this: 'If you confess with your mouth, "Jesus is Lord," and believe in your heart that God raised him from the dead, you will be saved. For it is with your heart that you believe and are justified, and is with your mouth that you confess and are saved' (Rom. 10:9–10). It seems these words were scripted specifically to assist the Jews in making their confession of faith in Christ. It was, as it were, 'the appeal' to come forward at the end of Paul's gospel sermon (Rom. 1 – 8)! To those who embraced it, this must have seemed revolutionary; no law to keep, no rules to follow, no religious requirements – simply trust!

There is no quarter for self-pity; the Jews have been given enough clues and now the offer of the gospel is before them, as it was plainly before them in the days of Jonah: 'Everyone who calls on the name of the Lord will be saved' (Rom. 10:13). However, the fault of some not responding does not rest with God. In defending God's faithfulness in this regard, Paul offers this hypothetical challenge, 'And how can they believe in the one of whom they have not heard?', but Paul's response suggests that the Jews are not guiltless with respect to hearing: 'But I ask: Did they not hear? Of course they did' (Rom. 10:18). Paul's point is simply this: God has given the Jews enough clues, signposts and indicators to reveal that faith is intimately involved with salvation. No, if there has been any rejection with respect to the gospel, it is not God's rejection of his historically favoured people, but 'their' rejection of him (of course, just as many Gentiles also reject the offer of the gospel).

Yet, Paul sees a positive side to this, for Israel's rejection has provided an opportunity for the Gentiles to come to faith, and is optimistic on behalf of the Jews, once again. God has provided the opportunity for them to be 're-grafted' back into the vine, by faith. God's favour still remains, but the gospel will not be compromised; only faith allows entry into God's favour – only faith delivers. Everyone who enters into a faith relationship with Jesus Christ and remains 'in Christ' by virtue of a Spirit-empowered perpetual faith will be saved.

Conclusion

Salvation by faith is truly a revolutionary idea. No one, neither privileged Jew nor noble Gentile, is set right with God in any other means. The divine granting of faith, by way of God's Spirit, precludes any capacity for human merit. Neither intellectual nor practical effort has any value in this regard. No one is set right with God by the agency of faithfulness (works of the law), nor are they justified by a notional apprehension of Christ's work (a rationalistic adherence to an idea). A sinner can only be established in a right relational standing with God, by God's own grace; on the grounds of Christ's work, purely and simply applied by the faith – faith that the Spirit powerfully endows. This being the case, a Christian's right standing with God is *perpetually valid* on the grounds of the Spirit's 'binding or uniting' them to Christ through a perpetual state of trust (faith). Indeed, what is true of their *status* before God is also true of their *state* with God. The faith that initiates their right standing with God sustains their righteousness until the completion of their salvation, and this faith is sustained by the indwelling presence of the Spirit.

Conclusion: Power and Glory

Paul defined the gospel in an atmosphere defined by power: the power of the flesh, the power of sin, the power of the law, the power of death and the powers of this dark world. Over and against these 'powers', Paul sets the power of God; a power that initiates, enables and sustains salvation. But why does God exercise his power to save humanity? Is the eternal happiness of redeemed humanity God's only concern? Of course, people are the beneficiaries of God's saving work; yet to claim the gospel has an exclusively human focus suggests that God is merely a servant of humanity – little more. However, when the meta-plot of God's salvific action is considered, we soon see that the ultimate 'end' of salvation extends beyond human deliverance. While human deliverance is very much in view, Romans intimates that the focus of the gospel is actually God himself and his glory (Rom. 1:23; 3:7,23; 4:10; 5:2; 6:4; 8:17; 9:4,23; 11:36; 16:27).

Of course, God's saving activity is motivated by divine love for lost humanity, and is designed to counter the problem that alienates them from him, yet as great as this 'alienation' is, the greater effect of humanity's moral deviation is its invidious distortion of the divine order, and the implication of this for God's identity. In effect, human sin robs God of what is rightfully his – glory. Through the gospel, God exercises his sovereign power to vindicate his name[1] and, in the process of redeeming humanity and the created order from futility, restores the universal order and his rightful place above it. For God to seek glory is to seek to reveal his glorious identity, that humanity might honour his boundless benevolence.

Sinful humanity has distorted the divine *order of things*, and consequently fallen short of their primary calling – the glorification of God. The gospel is ultimately concerned with the rectification of that fallen universal order, and represents an action that God the Father initiates, God the Son executes and God the Spirit empowers to accomplish this end. We might say that the gospel's goal is the *eternal restoration* of God, humanity and the created order in their 'right' orientation: God's people, in God's place, under God's rule (God's kingdom).[2] This is most evident in Romans 8:20–28. Therefore, the salvation of lost humanity, glorious as it may be to its beneficiaries, is principally designed for a higher goal – God's eternal honour. In this regard, the Spirit, through the gospel, exercises the power of God, for the glory of God.

As we have seen, the gospel reveals the problem of human unrighteousness. Yet to suggest the gospel simply exposes sin as moral disobedience is an oversimplification. Sin is much deeper than 'not doing what you are told'. When considered from God's view, sin directly affects his glory. God's wrath (divine justice) is set against all humanity, who in suppressing the truth of their Creator, failed to offer him the glory he deserved (Rom. 1:21). Claiming a wisdom above God's, humanity did the most odious thing imaginable: they exchanged God and his glory for artificial images, expressly *imagined* to redirect God's glory away from him (Rom. 1:23). Effectively, humanity stole 'the glory' from God, redirecting it toward themselves, through the agency of idolatry. Therefore, the essence of unrighteousness is displacing God from his rightful place, and assigning glory to the creation rather than the Creator. This is the great offence of sin; this is what the Spirit exposes through the gospel. As we have already seen, the heart of the issue is the human heart. Only the Spirit of God has the power to penetrate the depths of its wicked designs, exposing the real problem. That is why the apostle intimates that to be a true 'Jew' (one whom God favours), the heart must be 'circumcised', for without it no human can glorify God.

In proposing the solution to universal human unrighteousness, Paul presents a case, on God's behalf, to those who have confidence in law – actually using the law! The result: the over-confident defendants discover that the law, in which they placed all their confidence, actually condemns them. They are left defenceless, and as guilty as any Gentile: 'There is no difference, for all have sinned and fall short of the glory of God' (Rom. 3:22–3). Yes, even the most righteous Jew *falls short* of God's glory. Yet as we have seen, God provides an alternative: justification by faith in Jesus Christ. Having been 'justified' or set right with God on the grounds of Christ's atoning work with their sins acquitted, forgiven sinners have a new relationship toward God and his glory. No longer falling short of it, even idolatrously claiming it for themselves; but re-established in fellowship with God through the Spirit, they 'now' rejoice in the hope of the glory of God (Rom. 5:2). Indeed, the focus of this hope is not a self-indulgent existence in heaven, but an eternal existence devoted to God's intention for his redeemed people – the glorification of his name.

For God to acquit sin's penalty and do nothing about sin's power would be an express contradiction of the gospel's supreme purpose – the glory of God. Paul uses the metaphor of slavery to structure his discussion on how the subsequent disempowerment of the 'sin nature' is 'actually' possible through the gospel. Not through law, not through works, nor any other humanly augmented means, but through the radical notion of a Spirit-enabled 'identification' with Christ, is this life free from sin's power made possible. Crucified and raised with Christ, believers exist in a new *state of grace*; a life animated by the Spirit's power. In this state, Christ is both the source and goal of the life of faith (Gal. 2:20). Yet those who fail to grasp this will struggle under the burden of law morality, suffering the entrapment of the law's enduring condemnation. But through 'union with Christ' and its accompanying Spirit-empowerment, genuine believers are empowered to obediently walk in the 'new way' of the Spirit (Rom. 7:6). Indeed, a person controlled by a sinful nature cannot please God, but those controlled by the Spirit, who 'walk' in step with the Spirit, are enabled to bring glory to God through a life consistent with the gospel's ultimate goal.

For Paul, the leading of the Spirit is a confirming 'sign' that believers are 'sons' of God. In ancient Roman culture, those adopted into the family inherited all the privileges and blessings of the family. Through union with Christ, Christians have a 'guarantee' of sharing in a divine family inheritance, with all the attending benefits. Sonship

Conclusion: Power and Glory 183

means that the prior status of slavery has been nullified, implying a new status and an accompanying change in life. Yet all believers await the supreme experience of deliverance at the consummation of salvation, even suffering in the interim. Yet this suffering is not futile. As with Christ, suffering provokes a solid hope; the hope that the believer shares Christ's suffering, shares his glory (Rom. 8:17). Though torn between the temporal and eternal, the saints overcome their weaknesses, as the Spirit powerfully intercedes on their behalf (Rom. 8:23–7). Even despite the arduous nature of the Christian life, the Spirit grants believers the capacity to prevail. God's children are 'more than conquerors', those who finally share in the glory of God's conquest.

The gospel represents the power of God, to gain the righteousness of God, for the express purpose of the glory of God, appropriated by faith alone! Human works are powerless in attaining, maintaining, or completing the salvation offered. The faith that saves, cannot be reduced to rational assent, or extended to human faithfulness, but represents a Spirit-endowed perpetual state-of-trust in Christ; the subject / object of that saving faith. Through the Spirit's conviction, human unrighteousness is identified by faith alone. Through the Spirit's enabling, the sinner lays hold of God's justification by faith alone. Through the Spirit's empowerment, the believer walks in obedience by faith alone. Through the Spirit's deposit the believer is transformed in expectation of eternal glory by faith alone. No matter what dimension of the gospel of salvation is considered, no matter what metaphorical lens it is viewed through, the salvation offered is gained by faith alone – from beginning to end. That is why Paul describes saving faith in Romans 1:16 being from 'first to last'; it is comprehensive and extensive in its scope. Salvation is initiated by God, executed by Christ, empowered by the Holy Spirit, and appropriated by faith. Only interpreted this way can God's glory be rightfully imagined as the gospel's supreme goal.

If the crowning purpose of the gospel is the glory of God, and not simply human ends, it leaves us with this sobering challenge. Are we proclaiming the gospel for God's glory, or using it (and its associated ministries) for our glory? Many believers begin the Christian walk with good intentions, but as success in life and ministry ensues pride can so easily creep in and undermine their focus on the gospel. Subtly, the gospel can be distorted to become a means of human promotion, and with a selfish twist of motives the human ego can slowly displace the gospel's supreme goal. If the gospel becomes the means to promote 'my' reputation, career, popularity, influence and glory, then the very message that is designed to counter the effects of human sin and restore God's glory is hijacked, becoming subverted to the purposes of human glory. Surely this is akin to going back to Eden and stealing the glory from God, all over again! So it seems, that even within the process of promoting the gospel, the possibility of methodologically negating it is always at hand.

However, in keeping God's ultimate purpose in mind, we maintain our confidence that a prideful attachment to the idea of the gospel will not become our stumbling block. We confidently know that God exercises his power through the Spirit, to reveal Jesus Christ as the Saviour of fallen humanity, and fulfil his divine purposes through this revelation. Through the gospel of Jesus Christ, God acquits the penalty of sin, breaks the power of the sin nature, conquers the presence of sin, and offers the hope of eternal life to the redeemed sinner. This saving work of God reveals to humanity that God is worthy of all glory, and that the gospel's supreme purpose invariably transcends mere human deliverance to accomplish a grander purpose, where he will be enthroned above all. May the same Spirit that exposes our sin, enables our justification, empowers our sanctification and instils us with the hope of glorification empower us to exalt our God, glorifying him through a lifestyle of conformity to Christ. Above all, may the Spirit empower us to remain perennially vigilant toward the gospel's true goal and ultimate purpose – the glory of God: 'For from him and through him and to him are all things. To him be the glory for ever! Amen' (Rom. 11:36).

Bibliography

Adkins, Lesley, and Roy A. Adkins. *Handbook to Life in Ancient Rome* (Oxford: Oxford University Press, 1998).

Allen, R. Michael. *Justification and the Gospel* (Grand Rapids: Baker Academic, 2013).

Aquinas, Thomas. *Summa Theologiae, Secunda Secundae, 1-91* (trans. Laurence Shapcote; ed. John Mortensen and Enrique Alarcon Vol. 17, Lander: The Aquinas Institute for the Study of Sacred Doctrine, 2012).

—. *Summa Theologica* (trans. Fathers of the English Dominican Province; London: R.T. Washbourne, 1911).

Augustine. 'On the Merits and Forgiveness of Sin, and on the Baptism of Infants' (trans. Peter Holmes). Pages 15–78 in *Nicene and Post Nicene Fathers*, vol. 5 (ed. Philip Schaff; Grand Rapids: Eerdmans, 1886).

—. *A Treatise on Nature and Grace* (trans. Dr Holmes). Pages 121–51 in *Nicene and Post-Nicene Fathers*, vol. 5 (ed. Philip Schaff; Grand Rapids: Eerdmans, 1886).

Avis, Paul. *God and the Creative Imagination: Metaphor, Symbol, and Myth in Religion and Theology* (London: Routledge, 1999).

Ballentine, Samuel E. *The Torah's Vision of Worship* (Minneapolis: Fortress Press, 1999).

Barclay, John M.G. *Obeying the Truth: Paul's Ethics in Galatians* (Minneapolis: Fortress Press, 1988).

Barrett, C.K. *A Commentary on the Epistle to the Romans* (Black's New Testament Commentaries; ed. Henry Chadwick; London: A&C Black, 1991).

Barth, Karl. *The Epistle to the Romans* (trans. Edwyn C. Hoskyns; London: Oxford University Press, 1957).

Bavinck, Herman. *Reformed Dogmatics: Sin and Salvation in Christ* (trans. John Vriend; ed. John Bolt; 4 vols; Grand Rapids: Baker Academic, 2006).

Beker, J. Christiaan. *Paul the Apostle: The Triumph of God in Life and Thought* (Minneapolis: Fortress Press, 1980).

Berger, Peter L. *The Sacred Canopy: Elements of a Sociological Theory of Religion* (New York: Doubleday, 1969).

Billings, J. Todd. *Calvin, Participation, and the Gift: The Activity of Believers in Union with Christ* (Oxford: Oxford University Press, 2007).

Bird, Michael. *The Saving Righteousness of God* (Eugene: Wipf & Stock, 2007).

Bounds, Christopher T. 'Augustine's Interpretation of Romans 7:14-25, His Ordo Salutis and His Consistent Belief in a Christian's Victory over Sin'. *Ashbury Journal* 62, no. 2 (2009): pp. 20–35.

Branick, Vincent P. *Understanding Paul and His Letters* (New York: Paulist Press, 2009).

Burke, Trevor J. *Adopted into God's Family: Exploring a Pauline Metaphor* (New Studies in Biblical Theology; ed. D.A. Carson; Downers Grove: InterVarsity Press, 2006).

Byrne, Brendan. *Romans* (Sacra Pagina Series; ed. Daniel J. Harrington; Collegeville: Liturgical Press, 1996).

Calvin, John. *Commentaries on the Epistle of Paul the Apostle to the Romans* (trans. John Owen; Grand Rapids: Eerdmans, 1959).

—. *Institutes of the Christian Religion* (trans. Ford Lewis Battles; Library of Christian Classics; ed. John T. McNeill; 2 vols; Philadelphia: Westminster Press, 1960).

Campbell, Constantine R. *Paul and Union with Christ: An Exegetical and Theological Study* (Grand Rapids: Zondervan, 2012).

Campbell, Douglas A. *The Deliverance of God* (Grand Rapids: Eerdmans, 2009).

Campbell, William S. *Paul and the Creation of Christian Identity* (London: T&T Clark, 2008).

Caragounis, C.C. 'Romans 5:15-16 in the Context of 5:12-21: Contrast or Comparison?' *New Testament Studies* 31 (1985): pp. 142–8.

Carson, D.A. 'The Vindication of Imputation: On Fields of Discourse and Semantic Fields'. Pages 46–78 in *Justification: What's at Stake in the Current Debates* (ed. Mark Husbands and Daniel J. Treier; Downers Grove: InterVarsity Press, 2004).

Cartwright, Mark. 'Slavery in the Ancient World'. *Ancient History Encyclopedia* (2013) http://www.ancient.eu/article/629/ (published electronically 1 Nov. 2013).

Clark, Gordon H. *Faith and Saving Faith* (Jefferson: Trinity Foundation, 1983).

Colijn, Brenda B. *Images of Salvation in the New Testament* (Downers Grove: InterVarsity Press Academic, 2010).

Collins, Raymond F. *The Power of Images in Paul* (Collegeville: Liturgical Press, 2008).

Colon-Emeric, Edgardo A. *Wesley, Aquinas and Christian Perfection: An Ecumenical Dialogue* (Waco: Baylor University Press, 2009).

Constantineanu, Corneliu. *The Social Significance of Reconciliation in Paul's Theology* (Library of New Testament Studies; ed. Mark Goodacre; London: T&T Clark, 2010).

Cranfield, C.E.B. *The Epistle to the Romans* (International Critical Commentary; ed. J.A. Emerton, C.E.B. Cranfield and G.N. Stanton; 2 vols. Edinburgh: T&T Clark, 1975).

D'Angelo, Mary Rose. 'Abba and "Father": Imperial Theology and the Jesus Traditions'. *Journal of Biblical Literature* 111, no. 4 (1992): pp. 615–16.

Das, Andrew A. *Solving the Romans Debate* (Minneapolis: Fortress Press, 2007).

Davies, Glenn N. *Faith and Obedience in Romans* (Sheffield: Sheffield Academic Press, 1990).

Davies, W.D. *Invitation to the New Testament: A Guide to Its Main Witnesses* (London: Darton, Longman & Todd, 1967).

DeBruyn, Theodore, ed. *Pelagius' Commentary on St Paul's Epistle to the Romans* (Oxford: Clarendon Press, 1993).

Dieter, Theodor. 'Justification and Sanctification in Luther'. Pages 87–96 in *Justification and Sanctification: In the Traditions of the Reformation* (ed. M. Opocensky and P. Reamonn; Geneva: World Alliance of Reformed Churches, 1999).

Donfried, Karl P. 'Introduction 1977: The Nature and Scope of the Romans Debate'. Pages 61–72 in *The Romans Debate* (ed. Karl P. Donfried; Edinburgh: T&T Clark, 1991).

Douglas, E. Jane Demsey. *Justification in Late Medieval Preaching* (Leiden: Brill, 1966).

Dunn, J.D.G. *The New Perspective on Paul: Collected Essays* (Tubingen: Mohr Siebeck, 2005).

Eichler, J 'Logizomai'. Pages 822–6 in *The New International Dictionary of New Testament Theology* (ed. Colin Brown; Carlisle: Paternoster Press, 1992).

Fee, Gordon D. *God's Empowering Presence* (Peabody: Hendrickson, 1994).

Foerster, Werner. 'Soteria'. Pages 992–4 in *Theological Dictionary of the New Testament* (ed. Gerhard Friedrich and Geoffrey W. Bromiley; Grand Rapids: Eerdmans, 1999).

Foord, Martin. *The 16th Century Protestant Doctrine of the Gospel in Systematic Theology* (unpublished thesis: Australian College of Theology, 2012).

Fredrickson, Paula. 'Judaizing the Nations: The Ritual Demands of Paul's Gospel'. Pages 327–54 in *Paul's Jewish Matrix* (ed. Thomas

G. Casey and Justin Taylor; Rome: Gregorian and Biblical Press, 2011).

Furnish, Victor Paul. *Theology and Ethics in Paul* (Nashville: Abingdon Press, 1968).

Garlington, Don. 'A Study of Justification by Faith'. Pages 285–300 in *Exegetical Essays* (Eugene: Wipf & Stock, 2003).

Gay, Craig M. *The Way of the Modern World* (Grand Rapids: Eerdmans, 1998).

Gerrish, B.A. *Saving and Secular Faith* (Minneapolis: Fortress Press, 1999).

Gilbert, Gregory D. *What Is the Gospel?* (Wheaton: Crossway, 2010).

Given, Mark D. *Paul's True Rhetoric: Ambiguity, Cunning, and Deception in Greece and Rome* (Harrisburg: Trinity Press International, 2001).

Goldsworthy, Graeme. *Gospel and Kingdom* (Exeter: Paternoster Press, 1984).

Gorman, Michael J. *Cruciformity: Paul's Narrative Spirituality of the Cross* (Grand Rapids: Eerdmans, 2001).

Gunton, Colin E. *The Actuality of the Atonement* (Edinburgh: T&T Clark, 1988).

Haacker, Klaus. *The Theology of Paul's Letter to the Romans* (Cambridge: Cambridge University Press, 2003).

Hahn, Hans Christoph. 'Circumcision'. Pages 307–11 in *The New International Dictionary of New Testament Theology* (ed. Colin Brown; Carlisle: Paternoster Press, 1986).

Harries, Jill. 'Courts and the Judicial System'. Pages 85–101 in *The Oxford Handbook of Jewish Daily Life in Roman Palestine* (ed. Catherine Hezser; Oxford: Oxford University Press, 2010).

Hays, Richard B. *The Conversion of the Imagination: Paul as Interpreter of Israel's Scripture* (Grand Rapids: Eerdmans, 2005).

—. *The Moral Vision of the New Testament* (San Francisco: HarperSanFrancisco, 1996).

Heidland, H.W. 'Logizomai'. Pages 284–92 in *Theological Dictionary of the New Testament* (trans. G.W. Bromiley; ed. Gerhard Kittel and Gerhard Friedrich; Grand Rapids: Eerdmans, 1999).

Heyer, C.J. Den. *Paul: A Man of Two Worlds* (London: SCM Press, 1998).

Hodge, Charles. *Systematic Theology* (3 vols; London: James Clarke, 1960).

Holder, R. Ward. 'Romans in Light of Reformation Receptions'. Pages 1–9 in *Reformation Readings of Romans* (ed. Kathy Ehrensperger and R. Ward Holder; New York: T&T Clark, 2008).

Hooker, Morna D. 'Paul and "Covenantal Nomism"' in *Paul and Paulinism: Essays in Honour of C.K Barrett* (ed. M.D. Hooker and J.B. Wilson; London: SPCK, 1982).

Horton, Michael S. 'The Law & the Gospel' (1996). http://www.whitehorseinn.org/free-articles/the-law-the-gospel-by-michael-horton.html (published electronically 1996).

Jervis, L. Ann. 'God's Obedient Messiah and the End of the Law: Richard N. Longenecker's Understanding of Paul's Gospel'. Pages 22–35 in *Gospel in Paul: Studies in Corinthians, Galatians, and Romans for Richard N. Longenecker* (ed. L. Ann Jervis and Peter Richardson; Sheffield: Sheffield Academic Press, 1994).

—. 'The Spirit Brings Christ's Life to Life'. Pages 139–56 in *Reading Paul's Letter to the Romans* (ed. Jerry L. Sumney; Atlanta: Society of Biblical Literature, 2012).

Johnson, Luke Timothy. *Reading Romans* (Macon: Smyth & Helwys, 2001).

Kapic, Kelly M. *Communion with God: The Divine and the Human in the Theology of John Owen* (Grand Rapids: Baker Academic, 2007).

Kasemann, Ernst. *Commentary on Romans* (London: SCM Press, 1980).

Knox, David Broughton. *The Doctrine of Faith: In the Reign of Henry VIII* (London: James Clarke, 1961).

Lane, Anthony N.S. 'Twofold Righteousness: A Key to the Doctrine of Justification?' Pages 205–24 in *Justification: What's at Stake in the Current Debates* (ed. Mark Husbands and Daniel J. Treier; Downers Grove: InterVarsity Press, 2004).

Larsen, Timothy, and Daniel J. Treier, eds. *Evangelical Theology* (Cambridge: Cambridge University Press, 2007).

Lincicum, David. *Paul and the Early Jewish Encounter with Deuteronomy* (Grand Rapids: Baker Academic, 2010).

Lindberg, Carter. 'Do Lutherans Shout Justification but Whisper Sanctification?' Pages 97–112 in *Justification and Sanctification in the Traditions of the Reformation* (ed. M. Opocensky and P. Reamonn; Geneva: World Alliance of Reformed Churches, 1999).

Lindstrom, Harald. *Wesley and Sanctification* (London: Epworth Press, 1946).

Louis, Paul. *Ancient Rome at Work: An Economic History of Rome from the Origins to the Empire* (London: Kegan Paul, Trench, Trubner & Co., 1927).

Lowrie, Walter. 'About "Justification by Faith Alone"'. *Journal of Religion* 32, no. 4 (1952): pp. 231–41.

Luther, Martin. *Commentary on the Epistle to the Galatians* (ed. Philip S. Watson; London: James Clarke, 1953).

—. *Commentary on the Epistle to the Romans* (trans. J.T. Mueller; Grand Rapids: Zondervan, 1954).

—. *Lectures on Romans* (Luther's Works; ed. Hilton C. Oswald; 55 vols; Saint Louis: Concordia, 1972).

Lyman, Rebecca. *Early Christian Traditions* (Cambridge: Cowley, 1999).

MacArthur, John F. *Faith Works: The Gospel According to the Apostles* (Dallas: Word, 1993).

Macky, Peter W. *St. Paul's Cosmic War Myth: A Military Version of the Gospel* (New York: Peter Lange, 1998).

Malherbe, Abraham J. *Social Aspects of Early Christianity* (Philadelphia: Fortress Press, 1983).

Marshall, I. Howard. *Aspects of the Atonement: Cross and Resurrection in the Reconciling of God and Humanity* (Milton Keynes: Paternoster, 2007).

Matera, Frank J. *Romans* (Grand Rapids: Baker Academic, 2010).

McCormack, Bruce L. 'What's at Stake in the Current Debates over Justification?' Pages 81–117 in *Justification: What's at Stake in the Current Debates* (ed. Mark Husbands and Daniel J. Treier; Downers Grove: InterVarsity Press, 2004).

McFarland, Orrey Wayne. *The God Who Gives: Philo and Paul in Conversation* (Durham: Durham University, 2013).

McGrath, A.E. 'Justification'. Pages 522–3 in *Dictionary of Paul and His Letters* (ed. G.F. Hawthorne, R.P. Martin and D.G. Reid; Downers Grove: InterVarsity Press, 1993).

—. 'Forerunners of the Reformation? A Critical Examination of the Evidence for Precursors of the Reformation Doctrines of Justification'. *Harvard Theological Review* 75, no. 2 (1982): pp. 219–42.

—. *Luther's Theology of the Cross* (Oxford: Blackwell, 1994).

—. *Iustitia Dei: A History of the Christian Doctrine of Justification* (Cambridge: Cambridge University Press, 1998).

Meeks, Wayne A. *The Moral World of the First Christians* (Philadelphia: Westminster Press, 1986).

Minear, Paul S. *The Obedience of Faith* (London: SCM Press, 1971).

Moo, Douglas J. *The Epistle to the Romans* (New International Commentary on the New Testament; ed. G.D. Fee; Grand Rapids: Eerdmans, 1996).

Morse, Christopher. *The Difference Heaven Makes* (New York: T&T Clark, 2010).

Murray, John. *The Epistle to the Romans* (New International Commentary on the New Testament; ed. F.F. Bruce; Grand Rapids: Eerdmans, 1987).

Nee, Watchman. *The Normal Christian Life* (Bombay: Gospel Literature Service, 1957).

Neill, Stephen. *Christian Holiness* (London: Lutterworth Press, 1960).

Newbigin, Lesslie. *Foolishness to the Greeks* (Grand Rapids: Eerdmans, 1986).

Osborn, Eric. *Ethical Patterns in Early Christian Thought* (Cambridge: Cambridge University Press, 1976).

Palmer, Edwin H. *The Holy Spirit* (Philadelphia: Presbyterian and Reformed Publishing Company, 1964).

Peppard, Michael. *The Son of God in the Roman World* (Oxford: Oxford University Press, 2011).

Porter, Stanley E. 'A Functional Letter Perspective: Towards a Grammar of Epistolary Form'. Pages 9–32 in *Paul and the Ancient Letter Form* (ed. Stanley E. Porter and Sean A. Adams; Leiden: Brill, 2010).

Quarles, Charles L. 'From Faith to Faith: A Fresh Examination of the Prepositional Series in Romans 1:17'. *Novum Testamentum* 45, no. 1 (2003): pp. 1–21.

Rabens, Volker. *The Holy Spirit and Ethics in Paul: Transformation and Empowering for Religious-Ethical Life* (Minneapolis: Fortress Press, 2013).

Reasoner, Mark. *Romans in Full Circle* (Louisville: Westminster John Knox Press, 2005).

Richard, B. Gaffin, Jr. *The Centrality of the Resurrection: A Study in Paul's Soteriology* (Grand Rapids: Baker, 1978).

Rupprecht, A.A. 'Legal System, Roman'. Pages 546–50 in *Dictionary of Paul and His Letters* (ed. G.F. Hawthorne, R.P. Martin and D.G. Reid; Downers Grove: InterVarsity Press, 1993).

Schreiner, Thomas R. *Romans* (Grand Rapids: Baker Academic, 1998).

Schweitzer, Albert. *The Mysticism of the Apostle Paul* (London: Adam & Charles Black, 1931).

Schwobel, Christoph. 'Reconciliation: From Biblical Observations to Dogmatic Reconstruction'. Pages 13–38 in *The Theology of Reconciliation* (ed. Colin E. Gunton; London: T&T Clark, 2003).

Scott, Ian W. *Implicit Epistemology in the Letters of Paul* (Tubingen: Mohr Siebeck, 2005).

Seifrid, Mark A. *Christ Our Righteousness: Paul's Theology of Justification* (Leicester: Apollos, 2000).

—. 'Luther, Melancthon and Paul on the Question of Imputation: Recommendations on a Current Debate'. Pages 137–52 in *Justification: What's at Stake in the Current Debates* (ed. Mark Husbands and Daniel J. Treier; Downers Grove: InterVarsity Press, 2004).

Sider, Ronald. 'The Scandal of the Evangelical Conscience'. *Christianity Today* (2005). http://www.ctlibrary.com/bc/2005/ (accessed 3 January 2007).

Smith, Preserved. 'Luther's Development of the Doctrine of Justification by Faith Only'. *Harvard Theological Review* 6, no. 4 (1913): pp. 407–25.

Soskice, Janet Martin. *Metaphor and Religious Language* (Oxford: Oxford University Press, 1985).

Spence, Alan J. *Justification: A Guide for the Perplexed* (New York: T&T Clark, 2012).

Stirewalt Jr, M. Luther. *Paul, the Letter Writer* (Grand Rapids: Eerdmans, 2003).

Stork, Peter. 'Hope-Essential and Abundant'. *Australian eJournal of Theology* 15, no. 1 (2010).

Stowers, Stanley K. *A Rereading of Romans: Justice, Jews, and Gentiles* (New Haven: Yale University Press, 1994).

Stuhlmacher, Peter. 'The Purpose of Romans'. Pages 231–44 in *The Romans Debate* (ed. Karl P. Donfried; Edinburgh: T&T Clark, 1991).

Tan, Seng-Kong. 'Calvin's Doctrine of Our Union with Christ'. *Quodlibet Journal* 5 (2003): www.quodlibet.net/tan-union.shtml.

Tannehill, Robert C. *Dying and Rising with Christ: A Study in Pauline Theology* (Berlin: Verlag Alfred Topelmann, 1967).

Taylor, Charles. *A Secular Age* (Cambridge: Belknap Press of Harvard University Press, 2007).

TeSelle, Eugene. 'Exploring the Inner Conflict: Augustine's Sermons on Romans 7 and 8'. Pages 313–46 in *Engaging Augustine on Romans* (ed. Daniel Patte and Eugene TeSelle; Harrisburg: Trinity Press International, 2002).

Thompson, Deanna A. 'Letting the Word Run Free: Luther, Romans, and the Call to Reform'. Pages 27–36 in *Reformation Readings of Romans* (ed. Kathy Ehrensperger and R. Ward Holder; New York: T&T Clark, 2008).

Tobin, Thomas H. *Paul's Rhetoric in Its Contexts: The Argument of Romans* (Peabody: Hendrickson, 2004).

Wallace, Daniel B. 'Some Initial Reflections on Slavery in the New Testament'. *Bible.org* (2004). https://bible.org/article/some-initial-reflections-slavery-new-testament (published electronically 30 June 2004).

Walton, John H. *The Lost World of Genesis One: Ancient Cosmologies and the Origins Debate* (Downers Grove: InterVarsity Press, 2009).

Warfield, Benjamin Breckinridge. *Perfectionism* (Philadelphia: Presbyterian and Reformed Publishing Company, 1967).

Watson, Francis. *Paul, Judaism, and the Gentiles* (Grand Rapids: Eerdmans, 2007).

Weinrich, Michael, and John P. Burgess. 'Justification in a Reformed Perspective: Key Theses'. Pages 1–7 in *What Is Justification About? Reformed Contributions to an Ecumenical Theme* (ed. Michael Weinrich and John P. Burgess; Grand Rapids: Eerdmans, 2009).

Wesley, John. *A Plain Account of Christian Perfection* (The Works of John Wesley; ed. Thomas Jackson; 14 vols; London: Wesleyan Conference Office, 1872).

Williams, David J. *Paul's Metaphors: Their Context and Character* (Peabody: Hendrickson, 1999).

Witherington III, Ben. *Paul's Letter to the Romans: A Socio-Rhetorical Commentary* (Grand Rapids: Eerdmans, 2004).

—. *The Problem with Evangelical Theology* (Waco: Baylor University Press, 2005).

Wright, N.T. 'Justification: Yesterday, Today, and Forever'. *Journal of the Evangelical Theological Society*, no. 54 (2011): pp. 49–63.

—. *Paul and the Faithfulness of God* (Christian Origins and the Question of God; 2 vols; Minneapolis: Fortress Press, 2013).

—. *Pauline Perspectives: Essays on Paul 1978-2013* (Minneapolis: Fortress Press, 2013).

Zeisler, J.A. *The Meaning of Righteousness in Paul: A Linguistic and Theological Inquiry* (Cambridge: Cambridge University Press, 1972).

Endnotes

Introduction

[1] Throughout this book, law is largely conveyed in two ways: Law (capitalized) refers to the Mosaic Law as an entire system, and law (lower case) generally refers to the law as commandments – the moral component of that system.

1 Where Has the Power Gone?

[1] Wright argues, 'Paul was there to announce it [the Messiah's rule] and to make it a reality. This cannot be other than politically subversive.' N.T. Wright, *Paul and the Faithfulness of God* (2 vols; Christian Origins and the Question of God; Minneapolis: Fortress Press, 2013), 2:1281.
[2] Timothy Larsen and Daniel J. Treier, eds, *Evangelical Theology* (Cambridge: CUP, 2007), p. 18.
[3] Ronald Sider, 'The Scandal of the Evangelical Conscience', *Christianity Today* (2005), http://www.ctlibrary.com/bc/2005/ (accessed 3 January 2007).
[4] Craig M. Gay, *The Way of the Modern World* (Grand Rapids: Eerdmans, 1998), p. 2.
[5] Charles Taylor, *A Secular Age* (Cambridge: Belknap Press of Harvard University Press, 2007), p. 25.
[6] Peter L. Berger, *The Sacred Canopy: Elements of a Sociological Theory of Religion* (New York: Doubleday, 1969), p. 110.

7. Taylor, *Secular Age*, p. 41.
8. Taylor, *Secular Age*, p. 67.
9. Taylor, *Secular Age*, p. 69.
10. Taylor, *Secular Age*, p. 75.
11. Peter Berger argues, 'At the risk of some simplification, it can be said that Protestantism divested itself as much as possible from the three most ancient and most powerful concomitants of the sacred – mystery, miracle, and magic.' Berger, *Sacred Canopy*, p. 111.
12. Taylor notes the effect this has toward secularization, 'This is the context in which we have to see the transformation which does away with the enchanted world, and brings on stage the first viable forms of exclusive humanism.' Taylor, *Secular Age*, p. 88.
13. Berger, *Sacred Canopy*, pp. 128–9.
14. Gay, *Way of the Modern World*, p. 190.
15. Lesslie Newbigin, *Foolishness to the Greeks* (Grand Rapids: Eerdmans, 1986), p. 36.
16. Taylor, *Secular Age*, p. 38.
17. 'Concerns about our culture's preoccupation with therapies of self-help converge with similar concerns that have been voiced about the exaggerated importance modern Western society and culture has assigned to *individuality*.' Gay, *Way of the Modern World*, p. 17.
18. Augustine writes of grace in the justified life, 'We ourselves bring it to pass; that is to say, we ourselves justify our own selves. In this matter, no doubt, we do ourselves to work; but we are fellow-workers with Him who does the work, because His mercy anticipates us . . . Now the Scriptures refer to both these operations of grace.' Augustine, 'A Treatise on Nature and Grace' (trans. Dr Holmes; ed. Philip Schaff; vol. 5; *Nicene and Post-Nicene Fathers* (Grand Rapids: Eerdmans, 1886), chap. 35.
19. Spence argues, 'For Augustine the doctrine of justification is a comprehensive theology of salvation developed within an understanding of the human predicament, which included the intransigence of human sinfulness, the inability of the will to choose what is right and the dreadful prospect of a final reckoning before God.' Alan J. Spence, *Justification: A Guide for the Perplexed* (New York: T&T Clark, 2012), p. 42.
20. Thomas Aquinas, *Summa Theologica* (trans. Fathers of the English Dominican Province; London: R.T. Washbourne, 1913), I: II/ Q 113:6.
21. Spence, *Justification*, p. 48.
22. Aquinas writes, 'It denotes the habit of perseverance, considered as a virtue. In this way it needs the gift of habitual grace, even as the other infused virtues. Secondly, it may be taken to denote the act of perseverance

enduring until death: and in this sense it needs not only habitual grace, but also the gratuitous help of God sustaining man in good until the end of life.' Aquinas, *Summa Theologica*, II: II / Q 137:4.

23 Bruce L. McCormack, 'What's at Stake in the Current Debates over Justification?', in *Justification: What's at Stake in the Current Debates* (ed. Mark Husbands and Daniel J. Treier; Downers Grove: InterVarsity Press, 2004), p. 89.

24 Smith claims that Luther borrowed this doctrine largely from the French scholar, Lefevre. 'Justification by faith only was also pointed out by him in the clearest terms. There are two ways of righteousness, "that of the law and that of faith, one of works, the other of Grace, one human, the other divine."' Preserved Smith, 'Luther's Development of the Doctrine of Justification by Faith Only', *Harvard Theological Review* 6, no. 4 (1913): p. 413.

25 Smith, 'Luther's Development', p. 409.

26 Mark Reasoner, *Romans in Full Circle* (Louisville: Westminster John Knox Press, 2005), p. 34.

27 Spence, *Justification*, p. 29.

28 Alister E. McGrath, *Luther's Theology of the Cross* (Oxford: Blackwell, 1994), p. 56.

29 E. Jane Demsey Douglas, *Justification in Late Medieval Preaching* (Leiden: Brill, 1966), p. 133.

30 McGrath, *Luther's Theology*, p. 135.

31 Alister McGrath, *Iustitia Dei: A History of the Christian Doctrine of Justification* (Cambridge: CUP, 1998), p. 182.

32 McGrath, *Iustitia Dei*, p. 203.

33 McGrath, *Iustitia Dei*, p. 205.

34 What I am objecting to here is the notion that such a slogan could be interpreted to mean that 'faith only' is all that matters in the Christian life, thus diminishing the notion of holiness.

35 This is truer of Luther's later position, conditioned by polemics, where he made a sharp distinction between justification and works.

36 Walter Lowrie, 'About "Justification by Faith Alone"', *Journal of Religion* 32, no. 4 (1952): p. 232.

37 Quoting Luther, WA 56: 287, 16–24; LW25, pp. 274ff., in Theodor Dieter, 'Justification and Sanctification in Luther', in *Justification and Sanctification: In the Traditions of the Reformation* (Geneva: World Alliance of Reformed Churches, 1999), p. 87.

38 Martin Luther, *Commentary on the Epistle to the Galatians* (ed. Philip S. Watson; London: James Clarke, 1953), p. 24.

39 Dieter, 'Justification and Sanctification in Luther', p. 91.

40 Dieter, 'Justification and Sanctification in Luther', p. 92.
41 Luther, *Commentary on the Epistle to the Galatians*, p. 24.
42 Martin Luther, LW 12:328–29, quoted from Carter Lindberg, 'Do Lutherans Shout Justification but Whisper Sanctification?' in *Justification and Sanctification in the Traditions of the Reformation* (Geneva: World Alliance of Reformed Churches, 1999), p. 98.
43 John Calvin, *Institutes of the Christian Religion* (trans. Ford Lewis Battles; ed. John T. McNeill; 2 vols, Library of Christian Classics; Philadelphia, Westminster Press, 1960), 1:III:16.1.
44 Calvin, *Institutes*, p. 725.
45 Bruce McCormack observes, 'It should be noted that it is the role played by the imputation of Christ's righteousness in justification . . . which makes possible the Protestant distinction between justification and sanctification.' McCormack, 'What's at Stake', p. 92.
46 Calvin, *Institutes*, 1:III:16.1.
47 Spence, *Justification*, p. 86.
48 D.A. Carson, 'The Biblical Gospel', in *For Such a Time as This: Perspectives on Evangelicalism, Past, Present and Future* (ed. Steve Brady and Harold Rowdon; London: Evangelical Alliance, 1996), p. 1.
49 Gerhard Ebeling, *The Nature of Faith* (trans. Ronald Gregor Smith; London: Collins, 1966), p. 150.
50 Gregory D. Gilbert, *What Is the Gospel?* (Wheaton: Crossway, 2010), p. 28.
51 Gilbert, *What Is the Gospel?*, p. 31.
52 Also clearly indicated by Michael Horton's assessment, 'Too often we confuse the fruit or effects with the gospel itself. Nothing that happens within us is, properly speaking, "gospel," but it is the gospel's effect.' Michael S. Horton, 'The Law & the Gospel' (1996). http://www.whitehorseinn.org/free-articles/the-law-the-gospel-by-michael-horton.html (published electronically 1996).
53 Wright, *Paul and the Faithfulness of God*, 2:1096.
54 Werner Foerster, 'Soteria', in *Theological Dictionary of the New Testament* (ed. Gerhard Friedrich and Geoffrey W. Bromiley; Grand Rapids: Eerdmans, 1999), pp. 992–3.
55 Brenda B. Colijn, *Images of Salvation in the New Testament* (Downers Grove: InterVarsity Press Academic, 2010), p. 141.
56 Richard B. Gaffin Jr, *The Centrality of the Resurrection: A Study in Paul's Soteriology* (Grand Rapids: Baker, 1978), p. 140.
57 R. Michael Allen, *Justification and the Gospel* (Grand Rapids: Baker Academic, 2013), p. 7.

58 Martin Foord, *The 16th Century Protestant Doctrine of the Gospel in Systematic Theology* (unpublished thesis, Australian College of Theology, 2012), p. 95.
59 Foord, *16th Century Protestant Doctrine*, p. 96.
60 Foord, *16th Century Protestant Doctrine*, p. 100.
61 Foord, *16th Century Protestant Doctrine*, p. 105.
62 While elements of this Spirit-oriented framing of soteriology will be drawn out in this particular book, the greater issue of the 'framing' of soteriology with reference to the Law or Spirit requires a larger and more detailed work, currently under consideration.
63 Calvin, *Institutes*, 1.III:1.4.
64 Ben Witherington III, *The Problem with Evangelical Theology* (Waco: Baylor University Press, 2005), p. 229.
65 Peter Stuhlmacher, 'The Purpose of Romans' in *The Romans Debate* (ed. Karl P. Donfried; Edinburgh: T&T Clark, 1991), p. 229.
66 Stanley K. Stowers, *A Rereading of Romans: Justice, Jews, and Gentiles* (New Haven: Yale University Press, 1994), p. 2.
67 Raymond F. Collins, *The Power of Images in Paul* (Collegeville: Liturgical Press, 2008), p. 185.
68 Mark D. Given, *Paul's True Rhetoric: Ambiguity, Cunning, and Deception in Greece and Rome* (Harrisburg: Trinity Press International, 2001), p. 141.
69 M. Luther Stirewalt Jr, *Paul, the Letter Writer* (Grand Rapids: Eerdmans, 2003), p. 112.
70 Francis Watson, *Paul, Judaism, and the Gentiles* (Grand Rapids: Eerdmans, 2007), p. 166.
71 Watson, *Paul, Judaism, and the Gentiles*, p. 174.
72 Watson, *Paul, Judaism, and the Gentiles*, p. 179.
73 Watson, *Paul, Judaism, and the Gentiles*, p. 186.
74 Given, *Paul's True Rhetoric*, p. 142.
75 This term appears nowhere else in the New Testament; Branick insightfully argues, 'The term "spirit of Holiness" (1:4), instead of the more usual poor line expression, "holy spirit," has a Semitic ring to it. The "of" expression as used here is a Semitic way of expressing an adjective.' Vincent P. Branick, *Understanding Paul and His Letters* (New York: Paulist Press, 2009), p. 247.
76 Porter observes, 'The elaboration of him in terms of how his apostolic calling is grounded in the work of God through Jesus Christ and ratified by the spirit promotes the seriousness of his ministry to the Gentiles, of whom the Romans are part.' Stanley E. Porter, 'A Functional Letter

Perspective: Towards a Grammar of Epistolary Form', in *Paul and the Ancient Letter Form* (ed. Stanley E. Porter and Sean A. Adams; Leiden: Brill, 2010), p. 22.
77 Glenn N. Davies, *Faith and Obedience in Romans* (Sheffield: Sheffield Academic Press, 1990), p. 25. It should also be noted that an alternative interpretation advocates that this section was a later addition (Dunn, Fitsmyer, Jewett).
78 Douglas J. Moo, *The Epistle to the Romans* (ed. G.D. Fee, New International Commentary on the New Testament; Grand Rapids: Eerdmans, 1996), p. 44.
79 Martin Luther, *Lectures on Romans* (ed. Hilton C. Oswald; Luther's Works; Saint Louis: Concordia Publishing House, 1972), 25:5. 'That is so that all the Gentiles should become obedient and submit themselves to faith.'
80 G.N. Davies, *Faith and Obedience*, p. 27.
81 G.N. Davies, *Faith and Obedience*, p. 27.
82 Note, Luther's view can also be interpreted this way.
83 Ernst Kasemann, *Commentary on Romans* (London: SCM Press, 1980), p. 14.
84 Thomas R. Schreiner, *Romans* (Grand Rapids: Baker Academic, 1998), p. 35.
85 Branick's assessment mirrors the conventional interpretation, 'The play on "flesh" and "spirit" clearly refers to the combined human descent and divine role of Jesus.' Branick, *Understanding Paul*, p. 246.
86 Gordon D. Fee, *God's Empowering Presence* (Peabody: Hendrickson Publishers, 1994), pp. 483–4.

2 Temple and Spirit: Revealing Unrighteousness

1 Karl P. Donfried, 'Introduction 1977: The Nature and Scope of the Romans Debate', in *The Romans Debate* (ed. Karl P. Donfried; Edinburgh: T&T Clark, 1991), p. xli.
2 Andrew A. Das, *Solving the Romans Debate* (Minneapolis: Fortress Press, 2007), p. 204.
3 Deanna A. Thompson, 'Letting the Word Run Free: Luther, Romans, and the Call to Reform', in *Reformation Readings of Romans* (ed. Kathy Ehrensperger and R. Ward Holder; New York: T&T Clark, 2008), pp. 26–8.
4 Francis Watson, *Paul, Judaism, and the Gentiles* (Grand Rapids: Eerdmans, 2007), p. 3.

5. Peter Stuhlmacher, 'The Purpose of Romans', in *The Romans Debate* (ed. Karl P. Donfried; Edinburgh: T&T Clark, 1991), p. 229.
6. Mark Reasoner, *Romans in Full Circle* (Louisville: Westminster John Knox Press, 2005), p. xxvi.
7. W.D. Davies, *Invitation to the New Testament: A Guide to Its Main Witnesses* (London: Darton, Longman & Todd, 1967), pp. 245–251.
8. W.D. Davies, *Invitation to the New Testament*, p. 259.
9. Stanley K. Stowers, *A Rereading of Romans: Justice, Jews, and Gentiles* (New Haven: Yale University Press, 1994), p. 24.
10. Stowers, *A Rereading of Romans*, p. 36.
11. Watson, *Paul, Judaism, and the Gentiles*, p. 51.
12. Watson, *Paul, Judaism, and the Gentiles*, p. 55.
13. Watson, *Paul, Judaism, and the Gentiles*, p. 87.
14. Watson, *Paul, Judaism, and the Gentiles*, p. 123.
15. Watson, *Paul, Judaism, and the Gentiles*, p. 163.
16. Watson, *Paul, Judaism, and the Gentiles*, p. 186.
17. J. Christiaan Beker, *Paul the Apostle: The Triumph of God in Life and Thought* (Minneapolis: Fortress Press, 1980), p. 13.
18. However, due consideration must be given to the contribution of John Calvin, for whom the doctrine of 'union with Christ' was not insignificant to his theological formulations.
19. Albert Schweitzer, *The Mysticism of the Apostle Paul* (London: Adam & Charles Black, 1931), p. 221.
20. Schweitzer, *Mysticism*, p. 222.
21. Schweitzer, *Mysticism*, p. 223.
22. Schweitzer, *Mysticism*, p. 223.
23. Schweitzer, *Mysticism*, p. 225.
24. Beker, *Paul the Apostle*, p. 14.
25. Beker, *Paul the Apostle*, p. 15.
26. Beker, *Paul the Apostle*, p. 18.
27. Beker, *Paul the Apostle*, p. 16.
28. Herman Bavinck, *Reformed Dogmatics: Sin and Salvation in Christ* (trans. John Vriend, ed. John Bolt; 4 vols; Grand Rapids: Baker Academic, 2006), 3:383.
29. Bavinck, *Reformed Dogmatics*, 3:384.
30. David J. Williams, *Paul's Metaphors: Their Context and Character* (Peabody: Hendrickson Publishers, 1999), p. 2.
31. Janet Martin Soskice, *Metaphor and Religious Language* (Oxford: OUP, 1985), p. 15.
32. Williams, *Paul's Metaphors*, p. 1.

[33] Paul Avis, *God and the Creative Imagination: Metaphor, Symbol, and Myth in Religion and Theology* (London: Routledge, 1999), p. 4.
[34] Avis, *God and the Creative Imagination*, p. 4.
[35] Avis, *God and the Creative Imagination*, p. 3.
[36] Avis, *God and the Creative Imagination*, p. 56.
[37] Avis, *God and the Creative Imagination*, p. 78.
[38] Richard B. Hays, *The Conversion of the Imagination: Paul as Interpreter of Israel's Scripture* (Grand Rapids: Eerdmans, 2005), p. xvi.
[39] Paula Fredrickson, 'Judaizing the Nations: The Ritual Demands of Paul's Gospel', in *Paul's Jewish Matrix* (ed. Thomas G. Casey and Justin Taylor; Rome: Gregorian and Biblical Press, 2011), pp. 346, 351.
[40] John H. Walton, *The Lost World of Genesis One: Ancient Cosmologies and the Origins Debate* (Downers Grove: InterVarsity Press, 2009), p. 82.
[41] As Ballentine suggests, 'In the tabernacle and the worship associated with it, the Torah conceives the community of faith as empowered to create a ritual world of space, time, and status that mirrors God's cosmic design.' Samuel E. Ballentine, *The Torah's Vision of Worship* (Minneapolis: Fortress Press, 1999), p. 64.
[42] Thomas H. Tobin, *Paul's Rhetoric in Its Contexts: The Argument of Romans* (Peabody: Hendrickson Publishers, 2004), p. 68.
[43] 'Given the public nature of Paul's letter writing, they would also have been aware, in some detail, of Paul's responses in those conflicts.' Tobin, *Paul's Rhetoric*, p. 69.
[44] Tobin, *Paul's Rhetoric*, p. 17, quoting Suetonius, Claud. 25.4 (GLAJJ 2:307). It is largely accepted among scholars that 'Chrestus' was a reference to Christ, and the conflicts revolved around a clash of Christian and Jewish ideals.
[45] The list of the names in Romans 16 indicates that most of the people in the church / churches were Gentiles, probably 20 per cent were Jews.
[46] Various Roman writers noticed the influence Jewish laws had on non-Jewish inhabitants of Rome: Horace, Valerius Maximus, Seneca the Younger, Tacitus and Juvenal, e.g. Seneca complained that 'the way of life of this accursed race (the Jews) has gained such influence that it is now received throughout the world; the vanquished have given laws to their victors.' Tobin, *Paul's Rhetoric*. Tobin also notes, 'That the Roman Jewish community itself already had a self-understanding that strongly emphasized the superiority of the Mosaic Law over other codes of law and the superiority of Jews' observance of their law

over other people's non-observance of their own laws'. Tobin, *Paul's Rhetoric*, p. 30.

47 It should be noted, at this point, that the interrelationship of right believing and right living is not the only issue in Romans. Paul also desired to show that the Jews no longer had exclusive access to God, or any advantage over the Gentiles: but without rejecting them as a people – or God's inclusion of them in his future kingdom. He wants to uphold obedience of life, but an obedience that relied on an absolute trust in God's way, the way of the Spirit. And he sought to show the freedom of flexibility of life in the Spirit without rejecting love for one's fellows and respect for the governing authorities. Romans was written to address issues, of which, the issue of 'righteous' living was one of the most significant.

48 William S. Campbell, *Paul and the Creation of Christian Identity* (London: T&T Clark, 2008), p. 107.

49 Brendan Byrne argues it this way: 'Moreover, the opening section, 1:18–32, which at first sight appears to target the alienation of the Gentile world, has its own rhetorical role to play within the wider block, 1:18 – 3:20. It catches the Jewish dialogue partner in a rhetorical "trap" designed to drive home more effectively the thesis that there is no righteousness to be had on the basis of the law.' Brendan Byrne, *Romans* (Sacra Pagina Series; ed. Daniel J. Harrington; Collegeville: Liturgical Press, 1996), p. 63.

50 Scott, *Implicit Epistemology*, p. 19.

51 Byrne, *Romans*, p. 65.

52 Byrne, *Romans*, p. 80.

53 Frank J. Matera, *Romans* (Grand Rapids: Baker Academic 2010), p. 67.

54 Hans-Christoph Hahn, 'Circumcision', in *The New International Dictionary of New Testament Theology* (ed. Colin Brown; Carlisle: Paternoster Press, 1986), p. 308.

55 Hahn, 'Circumcision', p. 310.

56 Hahn, 'Circumcision', p. 310.

57 Byrne, *Romans*, p. 102.

58 'The physical circumcision of Genesis 17 has already been reinterpreted within the Old Testament itself, though generally in the direction of polemicizing against those who are not circumcised in heart in addition to the flesh rather than holding out circumcision of the heart as an alternative to physical circumcision.' David Lincicum, *Paul and the Early Jewish Encounter with Deuteronomy* (Grand Rapids: Baker Academic, 2010), p. 150.

59 John Calvin, *Commentaries on the Epistle of Paul the Apostle to the Romans* (trans. John Owen; Grand Rapids: Eerdmans, 1959), p. 112.
60 Thomas R. Schreiner, *Romans* (Grand Rapids: Baker Academic, 1998), p. 142.
61 Lincicum, *Paul*, p. 153.
62 Schreiner, *Romans*, p. 143.
63 Byrne, *Romans*, p. 104 (italics added).
64 Gordon D. Fee, *God's Empowering Presence* (Peabody: Hendrickson Publishers, 1994), p. 493.

3 Law Court and Spirit: Acquitting Sin's Penalty

1 C.J. Den Heyer, *Paul: A Man of Two Worlds* (London: SCM Press, 1998), p. 244.
2 Raymond F. Collins, *The Power of Images in Paul* (Collegeville: Liturgical Press, 2008), p. 196.
3 Collins, *Power of Images*, p. 197.
4 A.A. Rupprecht, 'Legal System, Roman', in *Dictionary of Paul and His Letters* (ed. G.F. Hawthorne, R.P. Martin and D.G. Reid; Downers Grove: InterVarsity Press, 1993), p. 546.
5 Jill Harries, 'Courts and the Judicial System', in *The Oxford Handbook of Jewish Daily Life in Roman Palestine* (ed. Catherine Hezser; Oxford: OUP, 2010), p. 89.
6 Harries, 'Courts and the Judicial System', p. 90.
7 Harries, 'Courts and the Judicial System', p. 93.
8 C.K. Barrett, *A Commentary on the Epistle to the Romans* (Black's New Testament Commentaries; ed. Henry Chadwick; London: A&C Black, 1991), p. 67.
9 John Calvin, *Commentaries on the Epistle of Paul the Apostle to the Romans* (trans. John Owen; Grand Rapids: Eerdmans, 1959), p. 130.
10 Martin Luther, *Commentary on the Epistle to the Romans* (trans. J.T. Mueller; Grand Rapids: Zondervan, 1954), p. 30.
11 Douglas J. Moo, *The Epistle to the Romans* (ed. G.D. Fee, New International Commentary on the New Testament; Grand Rapids: Eerdmans, 1996), p. 208.
12 Barrett, *Commentary on the Epistle to the Romans*, p. 68.
13 L. Ann Jervis, 'God's Obedient Messiah and the End of the Law: Richard N. Longenecker's Understanding of Paul's Gospel', in *Gospel in Paul: Studies in*

Corinthians, Galatians, and Romans for Richard N. Longenecker (ed. L. Ann Jervis and Peter Richardson; Sheffield: Sheffield Academic Press, 1994), p. 30.

[14] Thomas H. Tobin, *Paul's Rhetoric in Its Contexts: The Argument of Romans* (Peabody: Hendrickson, 2004), p. 130.

[15] N.T. Wright, *Paul and the Faithfulness of God* (2 vols; Christian Origins and the Question of God; Minneapolis: Fortress Press, 2013), 2:914.

[16] Wright, *Paul and the Faithfulness of God*, 2:997.

[17] Mark Reasoner, *Romans in Full Circle* (Louisville: Westminster John Knox Press, 2005), p. 32.

[18] A.E. McGrath, 'Justification', in *Dictionary of Paul and His Letters* (ed. G.F. Hawthorne, R.P. Martin and D.G. Reid; Downers Grove: InterVarsity Press, 1993), p. 518.

[19] J.D.G. Dunn, *The New Perspective on Paul: Collected Essays* (Tubingen: Mohr Siebeck, 2005), p. 200.

[20] Don Garlington, 'A Study of Justification by Faith', in *Exegetical Essays* (Eugene: Wipf & Stock, 2003), p. 282.

[21] The following subject of faith and its meaning, if engaged on a technical level, could be quite lengthy; however, for the purposes of brevity our discussion here shall be limited to essential points. The nature of saving faith will be discussed at length in the last chapter.

[22] Dunn, *New Perspective on Paul*, p. 190.

[23] Francis Watson, *Paul, Judaism, and the Gentiles* (Grand Rapids: Eerdmans, 2007), p. 244.

[24] Stanley K. Stowers, *A Rereading of Romans: Justice, Jews, and Gentiles* (New Haven: Yale University Press, 1994), p. 196.

[25] Stowers, *A Rereading of Romans*, p. 201.

[26] Watson, *Paul, Judaism, and the Gentiles*, p. 44.

[27] Wright, *Paul and the Faithfulness of God*, 2:967.

[28] Watson, *Paul, Judaism, and the Gentiles*, p. 232.

[29] 'Paul's righteousness terminology is wholly conditioned by the faith/law antithesis.' Watson, *Paul, Judaism, and the Gentiles*, p. 233.

[30] Stowers, *A Rereading of Romans*, p. 207.

[31] Stowers, *A Rereading of Romans*, p. 208.

[32] Calvin, *Commentaries*, p. 147.

[33] Tobin, *Paul's Rhetoric*, p. 152.

[34] H.W. Heidland, 'Logizomai', in *Theological Dictionary of the New Testament* (ed. Gerhard Kittel and Gerhard Friedrich; Grand Rapids: Eerdmans, 1999), p. 284.

[35] J. Eichler, 'Logizomai', in *The New International Dictionary of New Testament Theology* (ed. Colin Brown; Carlisle: Paternoster Press, 1992), p. 823.

36 Michael Bird, *The Saving Righteousness of God* (Eugene: Wipf & Stock, 2007), p. 61.
37 Alister E. McGrath, 'Forerunners of the Reformation? A Critical Examination of the Evidence for Precursors of the Reformation Doctrines of Justification', *Harvard Theological Review* 75, no. 2 (1982): p. 226.
38 Bird, *Saving Righteousness of God*, p. 76.
39 Charles Hodge, *Systematic Theology* (3 vols; London: James Clarke, 1960), 3:145.
40 Bird, *Saving Righteousness of God*, p. 110.
41 Martin Luther, *Commentary on the Epistle to the Galatians* (ed. Philip S. Watson; London: James Clarke, 1953), p. 137.
42 Mark A. Seifrid, 'Luther, Melancthon and Paul on the Question of Imputation: Recommendations on a Current Debate', in *Justification: What's at Stake in the Current Debates* (ed. Mark Husbands and Daniel J. Treier; Downers Grove: InterVarsity Press, 2004), p. 151.
43 Luther, *Commentary on the Epistle to the Galatians*, p. 137.
44 Calvin, *Institutes*, 1.537.
45 Calvin, *Institutes*, 1.540.
46 Calvin, *Institutes*, 1.553 (emphasis added).
47 C.E.B. Cranfield, *The Epistle to the Romans* (ed. J.A. Emerton, C.E.B. Cranfield, and G.N. Stanton; 2 vols; International Critical Commentary; Edinburgh: T&T Clark, 1975), 1:253.
48 John Murray, *The Epistle to the Romans* (New International Commentary on the New Testament; ed. F.F. Bruce; Grand Rapids: Eerdmans, 1987), p. 179.
49 Schreiner, *Romans*.
50 Byrne, *Romans*, p. 163.
51 I. Howard Marshall, *Aspects of the Atonement: Cross and Resurrection in the Reconciling of God and Humanity* (Milton Keynes: Paternoster, 2007), p. 108.
52 Christoph Schwöbel, 'Reconciliation: From Biblical Observations to Dogmatic Reconstruction', in *The Theology of Reconciliation* (ed. Colin E. Gunton; London: T&T Clark, 2003), p. 34.
53 Colin E. Gunton, *The Actuality of the Atonement* (Edinburgh: T&T Clark, 1988), p. 179.
54 Note: this love is not causal, but consequential; a product of the Spirit's endowment – its fruit.
55 Constantineanu writes of a horizontal dimension as well, 'Thus, we could infer from the above argument that Paul does not refer simply to peace/reconciliation between the individual believers in God. Rather, this is being incorporated in the discussion of a particular life of the Christian community gathered "in Christ". To have "peace with God" means to

live out that peace with joy, hope and love, whatever the circumstances.' Corneliu Constantineanu, *The Social Significance of Reconciliation in Paul's Theology* (Library of New Testament Studies; ed. Mark Goodacre; London: T&T Clark, 2010), p. 126.
56 Elsewhere in 2 Cor. 1:22; 5:5; and Eph. 1:14 Paul speaks of the Spirit as a deposit that guarantees the inheritance offered in Christ.
57 Marshall, *Aspects of the Atonement*, p. 128.
58 Marshall, *Aspects of the Atonement*, p. 104.
59 Orrey Wayne McFarland, *The God Who Gives: Philo and Paul in Conversation* (Durham: Durham University, 2013), p. 136.
60 C.C. Caragounis, 'Romans 5:15-16 in the Context of 5:12-21: Contrast or Comparison?', *New Testament Studies* 31 (1985). The particle ou'/ oux when used in rhetorical question form anticipates an affirmative answer.
61 McFarland, *The God Who Gives*, p. 140.
62 McFarland, *The God Who Gives*, p. 222.
63 McFarland, *The God Who Gives*, p. 224.
64 Michael Weinrich and John P. Burgess, 'Justification in a Reformed Perspective: Key Theses', in *What Is Justification About? Reformed Contributions to an Ecumenical Theme* (ed. Michael Weinrich and John P. Burgess; Grand Rapids: Eerdmans, 2009), p. 6.
65 Anthony N.S. Lane, 'Twofold Righteousness: A Key to the Doctrine of Justification?', in *Justification: What's at Stake in the Current Debates* (ed. Mark Husbands and Daniel J. Treier; Downers Grove: InterVarsity Press, 2004), p. 212.
66 Lane, 'Twofold Righteousness', p. 213.
67 Calvin writes, 'Christ was given to us by God's generosity, to be grasped and possessed by us in faith. By partaking of him, we principally receive a double grace: namely, that having been reconciled to God through Christ's blamelessness, we may have in heaven instead of a judge a gracious Father; and secondly, that sanctified by Christ's spirit we may cultivate blamelessness and purity of life.' Calvin, *Institutes*, 1.725.
68 Volker Rabens, *The Holy Spirit and Ethics in Paul: Transformation and Empowering for Religious-Ethical Life* (Minneapolis: Fortress Press, 2013), p. 23.
69 Rabens, *Holy Spirit*, p. 137.
70 Rabens, *Holy Spirit*, pp. 202–3.

4 Slavery and Spirit: Emancipating from Sin's Power

1 'Be imitators of God, therefore, as dearly loved children and live a life of love, just as Christ loved us and gave himself up for us as a fragrant

offering and sacrifice to God. But among you there must not be even a hint of sexual immorality, or of any kind of impurity, or of greed, because these are improper for God's holy people. Nor should there be obscenity, foolish talk or coarse joking, which are out of place, but rather thanksgiving. *For of this you can be sure: No immoral, impure or greedy person – such a man is an idolater – has any inheritance in the kingdom of Christ and of God*' (Eph. 5:1–5, emphasis added).

[2] Richard B. Hays, *The Moral Vision of the New Testament* (San Francisco: HarperSanFrancisco, 1996), p. 37.
[3] Eric Osborn, *Ethical Patterns in Early Christian Thought* (Cambridge: CUP, 1976), p. 29.
[4] Osborn, *Ethical Patterns*, p. 29.
[5] Victor Paul Furnish, *Theology and Ethics in Paul* (Nashville: Abingdon Press, 1968), p. 172.
[6] Watchman Nee, *The Normal Christian Life* (Bombay: Gospel Literature Service, 1957), p. 48.
[7] Constantine R. Campbell, *Paul and Union with Christ: An Exegetical and Theological Study* (Grand Rapids: Zondervan, 2102), p. 334.
[8] Robert C. Tannehill, *Dying and Rising with Christ: A Study in Pauline Theology* (Berlin: Verlag Alfred Topelmann, 1967), p. 12.
[9] C.R. Campbell, *Paul and Union with Christ*, p. 361.
[10] Rebecca Lyman, *Early Christian Traditions* (Cambridge: Cowley, 1999), p. 24.
[11] McCormack states, 'The problem with refusing to engage ontological questions as an essential part of the dogmatic task is that we all too easily make ourselves the unwitting servants of the ontology that is embedded in the older theological rhetoric we borrow – and so it was with Calvin.' Bruce L. McCormack, 'What's at Stake in the Current Debates over Justification?' in *Justification: What's at Stake in the Current Debates* (ed. Mark Husbands and Daniel J. Treier; Downers Grove: InterVarsity Press, 2004), pp. 104–5.
[12] He is arguing from a position that favours the Reformation point of view on justification.
[13] McCormack, 'What's at Stake', p. 115.
[14] Although I believe McCormack's 'unity of the wills' does not completely account for the notion of 'union with Christ', I acknowledge that a correspondence of wills is nevertheless involved here, especially given Paul's statement in Rom. 6:11, 'In the same way, count yourselves dead to sin.'
[15] Calvin, *Institutes*, 1.III:1.3, 541.
[16] Calvin, *Institutes*, III:11.5, 730.

17 J.Todd Billings, *Calvin, Participation, and the Gift: The Activity of Believers in Union with Christ* (Oxford: OUP, 2007), p. 61.
18 Seng-Kong Tan, 'Calvin's Doctrine of Our Union with Christ', in *Quodlibet Journal* (2003).
19 Daniel B. Wallace, 'Some Initial Reflections on Slavery in the New Testament'. *Bible.org* (2004), https://bible.org/article/some-initial-reflections-slavery-new-testament (published electronically 30 June 2004).
20 Paul Louis argues, 'Slavery is the basis of the whole economic system of the States in antiquity . . . Without slavery Roman society is as unthinkable as would have been the Greek societies without it.' Paul Louis, *Ancient Rome at Work: An Economic History of Rome from the Origins to the Empire* (London: Kegan Paul, Trench, Trubner & Co., 1927), p. 37.
21 Mark Cartwright, 'Slavery in the Ancient World', *Ancient History Encyclopedia* (2013), http://www.ancient.eu/article/629/ (published electronically 1 Nov. 2013).
22 Abraham J. Malherbe, *Social Aspects of Early Christianity* (Philadelphia: Fortress Press, 1983), p. 86.
23 Malherbe, *Social Aspects*, p. 17.
24 Malherbe, *Social Aspects*, p. 87.
25 Wayne A. Meeks, *The Moral World of the First Christians* (Philadelphia: Westminster Press, 1986), p. 13.
26 Tannehill, *Dying and Rising with Christ*, p. 7.
27 Tannehill, *Dying and Rising with Christ*, p. 17.
28 Hays, *Moral Vision*, p. 39.
29 Luke Timothy Johnson, *Reading Romans* (Macon: Smyth & Helwys, 2001), p. 113.
30 Augustine held this position from around ad 394/395. Christopher T. Bounds, 'Augustine's Interpretation of Romans 7:14-25, His Ordo Salutis and His Consistent Belief in a Christian's Victory over Sin', *Ashbury Journal* 62, no. 2 (2009): p. 20.
31 Eugene TeSelle, 'Exploring the Inner Conflict: Augustine's Sermons on Romans 7 and 8', in *Engaging Augustine on Romans* (ed. Daniel Patte and Eugene TeSelle; Harrisburg: Trinity Press International, 2002), p. 112.
32 Augustine, 'On the Merits and Forgiveness of Sin, and on the Baptism of Infants', in *The Complete Works of St Augustine* (ed. Philip Schaff; Grand Rapids: Eerdmans, 1886), II:17.
33 Theodore DeBruyn, ed. *Pelagius' Commentary on St Paul's Epistle to the Romans* (Oxford: Clarendon Press, 1993), p. 102.
34 DeBruyn, *Pelagius' Commentary*, p. 105.
35 Bounds, 'Augustine's Interpretation', p. 21.

[36] Bounds, 'Augustine's Interpretation', pp. 20ff.
[37] Bounds, 'Augustine's Interpretation', p. 23.
[38] TeSelle, 'Exploring the Inner Conflict', p. 121.
[39] '[Augustine] sees the three meanings of law (the law of works or the letter, the law of sin and death, and the law of the Spirit of life) as the key to the entire section.' TeSelle, 'Exploring the Inner Conflict', p. 114.
[40] Although I would contend that even this interpretation is too dogmatically 'loaded'.
[41] John Calvin, *Commentaries on the Epistle of Paul the Apostle to the Romans* (trans. John Owen; Grand Rapids: Eerdmans, 1959), 7:15.
[42] R. Ward Holder, 'Romans in Light of Reformation Receptions', in *Reformation Readings of Romans* (ed. Kathy Ehrensperger and R. Ward Holder; New York: T&T Clark, 2008), p. 98.
[43] 'We can firmly establish that Calvin was thinking about Chrysostom's exegesis of Paul at the very time that he was avoiding the Greek father in his interpretation of Romans. Chrysostom did not slip from Calvin's mind; the evidence points instead to the conclusion that Calvin rejected Chrysostom.' Holder, 'Romans in Light of Reformation Receptions', p. 104.
[44] Holder, 'Romans in Light of Reformation Receptions', p. 108.
[45] Francis Watson, *Paul, Judaism, and the Gentiles* (Grand Rapids: Eerdmans, 2007), p. 288.
[46] Brendan Byrne, *Romans* (Sacra Pagina Series; ed. Daniel J. Harrington; Collegeville: Liturgical Press, 1996), p. 209.
[47] Byrne, *Romans*, p. 209.
[48] Johnson, *Reading Romans*, p. 115.
[49] Francis Watson sees Paul's explication of covetousness as referring back to Genesis: Far from providing a defence against sin, the law is deeply implicated in sin's origins. It is primarily the Genesis story that accounts for Paul's presentation of a personalized sin that finds its opportunity to reproduce itself in the good commandment of God. Watson, *Paul, Judaism, and the Gentiles*, p. 284.
[50] Douglas Moo helpfully adds in this regard, 'All law, is unable to deliver us from the power of sin; the multiplication of rules and commands, so much a tendency in some Christian circles, will be more likely to drive us deeper into frustration than to improve the quality of our walk with Christ.' Douglas J. Moo, *The Epistle to the Romans* (ed. G.D. Fee, New International Commentary on the New Testament; Grand Rapids: Eerdmans, 1996), p. 477.
[51] Klaus Haacker, *The Theology of Paul's Letter to the Romans* (Cambridge: CUP, 2003), p. 66.

52 Ben Witherington III, *Paul's Letter to the Romans: A Socio-Rhetorical Commentary* (Grand Rapids: Eerdmans, 2004), p. 207.
53 Byrne, *Romans*, p. 236.
54 Despite the Reformed 'categories', Murray's assessment is valid: 'In this context, as will be shown later, the apostle is not dealing with justification and the expiatory aspect of Christ's work, but with sanctification and with what God has done in Christ to deliver us from the power of sin. Hence what is thrust into the foreground in terms of "no condemnation" is not only freedom from the guilt but also freedom from the enslaving power of sin.' John Murray, *The Epistle to the Romans* (New International Commentary on the New Testament; ed. F.F. Bruce; Grand Rapids: Eerdmans, 1987), p. 275.
55 Thomas R. Schreiner, *Romans* (Grand Rapids: Baker Academic, 1998), p. 400.
56 Witherington, *Paul's Letter*, p. 212.
57 Murray observes, 'Since the wages of sin is death "the law of sin" must also be the "Law of death". The word "law" is used in this connection as a regulating and actuating power as well as a legislating authority. In view, therefore, of this contrast the "law of the spirit of life" should be understood as a regulating and actuating power of the Holy Spirit as a spirit of life'. Murray, *Epistle to the Romans*, p. 276.
58 Byrne, *Romans*, p. 236.
59 Murray, *Epistle to the Romans*, p. 282.
60 Let the reader be aware that fulfilment of the Law's requirements is not simply 'keeping the rules' but through the Spirit actually accomplishing what the Law demands; but in an unconscious non-nomistic manner.
61 Calvin, *Commentaries*, 8:4.
62 Moo, *Epistle to the Romans*, p. 516.
63 Moo, *Epistle to the Romans*, p. 517.
64 Schreiner, *Romans*, p. 404.
65 Schreiner, *Romans*, p. 405.
66 Albert Schweitzer, *The Mysticism of the Apostle Paul* (London: Adam & Charles Black, 1931), p. 295.
67 Schweitzer, *Mysticism*, p. 3.
68 L. Ann Jervis, 'The Spirit Brings Christ's Life to Life', in *Reading Paul's Letter to the Romans* (ed. Jerry L. Sumney; Atlanta: Society of Biblical Literature, 2012), p. 142.
69 Jervis, 'The Spirit Brings Christ's Life to Life', p. 144.
70 Murray observes here, 'The apostle has prepared us for this prediction. Christ himself is a resurrection and the life . . . It must be observed,

however, that when the spirit is said to be "life" it is life as overcoming and delivering from death that is in view, the Holy Spirit as life in the consummating act of redemption, namely, the resurrection. This explains what is meant when it is said that "the spirit is life because of righteousness". The Holy Spirit is not life in the redemptive sphere apart from accomplishment of redemption by Christ.' Murray, *Epistle to the Romans*, p. 290.

Schreiner's summary is also worth noting, 'The spirit indwells believers and they are no longer slaves of sin, yet they still die because of sin. Sin is no longer the master over believers, but this does not mean that sin is non-existent. The physical body of believers (which includes the whole person) indicates that Christians are still part of the old age, even though they possess the new age gift of the spirit. Full redemption will come at the day of resurrection when all sin and weakness will be left behind. But the cause we are examining is not the main point of verse 10.' Schreiner, *Romans*, p. 414.

[71] Johnson, *Reading Romans*, p. 131.
[72] Johnson, *Reading Romans*, p. 129.
[73] Johnson, *Reading Romans*, p. 120.

5 Adoption and Spirit: Removing Sin's Presence

[1] Stephen Neill, *Christian Holiness* (London: Lutterworth Press, 1960), p. 31.
[2] Harald Lindstrom, *Wesley and Sanctification* (London: The Epworth Press, 1946), p. 1278.
[3] Lindstrom, *Wesley and Sanctification*, p. 132.
[4] John Wesley, *A Plain Account of Christian Perfection* (ed. Thomas Jackson; The Works of John Wesley; 14 vols; London: Wesleyan Conference Office, 1872), 11:366–446.
[5] Edgardo A. Colon-Emeric, *Wesley, Aquinas and Christian Perfection: An Ecumenical Dialogue* (Waco: Baylor University Press, 2009), p. 25.
[6] Wesley, *Plain Account*, 11:366–446.
[7] Benjamin Breckinridge Warfield, *Perfectionism* (Philadelphia: Presbyterian and Reformed Publishing Company, 1967), p. 243.
[8] Wesley, *Plain Account*, 11:366–446.
[9] Warfield, *Perfectionism* p. 462.
[10] Thomas R. Schreiner, *Romans* (Grand Rapids: Baker Academic, 1998), p. 420.

[11] John M.G. Barclay, *Obeying the Truth: Paul's Ethics in Galatians* (Minneapolis: Fortress Press, 1988), p. 115.
[12] Albert Schweitzer, *The Mysticism of the Apostle Paul* (London: Adam & Charles Black, 1931), p. 296.
[13] Schreiner, *Romans*, p. 422.
[14] Exod. 4:22–3; Deut. 14:1–2; 32:5–6; 31:19–22; Isa. 1:24; Hos. 1:10.
[15] Gen. 21:10; Deut. 4:20; 9:26; Ps. 33:12; 74:2; Isa. 63:17; Mic. 7:18.
[16] Tobin, Thomas H. *Paul's Rhetoric in Its Contexts: The Argument of Romans* (Peabody: Hendrickson, 2004), p. 286.
[17] Michael Peppard, *The Son of God in the Roman World* (Oxford: OUP, 2011), p. 135.
[18] Peppard, *Son of God*, p. 136.
[19] Peppard, *Son of God*, p. 136.
[20] Lesley Adkins and Roy A. Adkins, *Handbook to Life in Ancient Rome* (Oxford: OUP, 1998), p. 274.
[21] Trevor J. Burke, *Adopted into God's Family: Exploring a Pauline Metaphor* (New Studies in Biblical Theology; ed. D.A. Carson; Downers Grove: InterVarsity Press, 2006), p. 143.
[22] Edwin H. Palmer, *The Holy Spirit* (Philadelphia: Presbyterian and Reformed Publishing Company, 1964), p. 125.
[23] Mary Rose D'Angelo, 'Abba and "Father": Imperial Theology and the Jesus Traditions', *Journal of Biblical Literature* 111, no. 4 (1992): p. 615–6.
[24] I am not advocating perfectionism, but merely indicating that a holy life must be consistently evident in those who yield to Christ and deny themselves like him, commensurate with the relationship to him.
[25] Schweitzer, *Mysticism*, p. 90.
[26] Wright, *Paul and the Faithfulness of God*, 2:1094.
[27] Schweitzer, *Mysticism*, p. 97.
[28] Schweitzer, *Mysticism*, p. 100.
[29] Gaffin, *Centrality of the Resurrection*, p. 138.
[30] Brendan Byrne confirms this by noting, 'It allows Paul to view the sufferings of the present time, not as a threat to salvation, but as a sign that the long for deliverance is actually close at hand'. Byrne, *Romans*, p. 256.
[31] Peppard, *The Son of God in the Roman World*, p. 136.
[32] Byrne, *Romans*, p. 258.
[33] Palmer, *The Holy Spirit*, p. 129.
[34] Moo, *The Epistle to the Romans*, p. 547.
[35] Ibid., p. 557.
[36] Peter Stork, "Hope-Essential and Abundant," *Australian eJournal of Theology* 15, no. 1 (2010): p. 8.

37 Christopher Morse, *The Difference Heaven Makes* (New York: T&T Clark, 2010), p. 102.
38 Gaffin, *Centrality of the Resurrection*, p. 140.
39 Gaffin, *Centrality of the Resurrection*, p. 141.
40 David J. Williams, *Paul's Metaphors: Their Context and Character* (Peabody: Hendrickson Publishers, 1999), p. 64.
41 Thomas R. Schreiner, *Romans* (Grand Rapids: Baker Academic, 1998), p. 462.
42 Peter W. Macky, *St. Paul's Cosmic War Myth: A Military Version of the Gospel* (New York: Peter Lange, 1998), p. 185.
43 Michael J. Gorman, *Cruciformity: Paul's Narrative Spirituality of the Cross* (Grand Rapids: Eerdmans, 2001), p. 328.
44 N.T. Wright, *Pauline Perspectives: Essays on Paul 1978-2013* (Minneapolis: Fortress Press, 2013), p. 115.

6 The Righteous Shall Live by Faith

1 C.E.B. Cranfield, *The Epistle to the Romans* (ed. J.A. Emerton, C.E.B. Cranfield, and G.N. Stanton; 2 vols; International Critical Commentary; Edinburgh: T&T Clark, 1975), 1:96.
2 J.A. Zeisler, *The Meaning of Righteousness in Paul: A Linguistic and Theological Inquiry* (Cambridge: CUP, 1972), p. 35 (emphasis added).
3 Zeisler, *Meaning of Righteousness*, p. 188 (emphasis added).
4 Don Garlington, 'A Study of Justification by Faith', in *Exegetical Essays* (Eugene: Wipf & Stock, 2003), p. 282.
5 Charles L. Quarles, 'From Faith to Faith: A Fresh Examination of the Prepositional Series in Romans 1:17', *Novum Testamentum* 45, no. 1 (2003): p. 13.
6 Mark A. Seifrid, *Christ Our Righteousness: Paul's Theology of Justification* (Leicester: Apollos, 2000), p. 38.
7 Several clues suggest that Paul utilized the Old Testament quote to confirm that the Old Testament prophets saw human faith as the means toward righteousness, which results in life; although the translator of Hab. 2:4 in the Septuagint regarded the passage as a reference to divine faithfulness as is shown by his use of the first person singular pronoun (*ek pistis mou*) instead of the third person singular pronominal suffix that appears in the Hebrew text. However, citations of the passage in Galatians and Hebrews suggest that Paul and his contemporaries generally adopted the

interpretation suggested by the MT. In Gal. 3:11 Habakkuk's statement is used to demonstrate that righteousness before God is the result of personal faith rather than obedience to the Law. Heb. 10:39 – 11:39 clearly states that the author of Hebrews regarded Habakkuk's statement as a reference to human faith. (Quarles, 'From Faith to Faith', pp. 16–17.)

8 Paul S. Minear, *The Obedience of Faith* (London: SCM Press, 1971), p. 41.
9 Minear, *Obedience of Faith*, p. 43 (emphasis added).
10 Moreover, when Christian ethics is predicated on the notion of 'union with Christ', as it is in this book, in which the believer 'died' with Christ, the ethical life then is really Christ working through the believer by faith, empowered by the Spirit. Understood thus, Christian ethics cannot be predisposed to work's righteousness.
11 Zeisler, *Meaning of Righteousness*, p. 189 (emphasis added). Note: I want to qualify Zeisler's statement that the 'saving righteousness' does two things inseparably; by this I take it to mean that they are not logically inseparable (but remain two distinct realities); however from a temporal point of view regarding the 'actual' working of the Spirit, they cannot be separated practically.
12 Gordon H. Clark, *Faith and Saving Faith* (Jefferson: Trinity Foundation, 1983), p. vii.
13 Clark, *Faith and Saving Faith*, p. 5.
14 Clark, *Faith and Saving Faith*, p. 21.
15 Clark, *Faith and Saving Faith*, p. 57.
16 Thomas Aquinas (1225–74), structured his magnum opus *Summa Theologica* on Aristotelian logic, and its highly rationalistic categories and methods.
17 B.A. Gerrish, *Saving and Secular Faith* (Minneapolis: Fortress Press, 1999), p. 6.
18 Thomas Aquinas, *Summa Theologiae, Secunda Secundae, 1-91* (trans. Laurence Shapcote; ed. John Mortensen and Enrique Alarcon, *Summa Theologiae*; vol. 17; Lander: Aquinas Institute for the Study of Sacred Doctrine, 2012), p. 4.
19 Aquinas, *Summa Theologiae*, p. 67.
20 Aquinas, *Summa Theologiae*, p. 68.
21 Aquinas, *Summa Theologiae*, p. 36 (emphasis added).
22 David Broughton Knox, *The Doctrine of Faith: In the Reign of Henry VIII* (London: James Clarke, 1961), p. 8.
23 Kelly M. Kapic, *Communion with God: The Divine and the Human in the Theology of John Owen* (Grand Rapids: Baker Academic, 2007), p. 117.

24 N.T. Wright, 'Justification: Yesterday, Today, and Forever', *JETS*, no. 54 (2011): p. 57.
25 Wright, 'Justification', p. 60.
26 Wright, 'Justification', p. 63.
27 This may well be saying what Wright means; however I cannot be sure he would agree with my 'a-temporal' framing.
28 Douglas A. Campbell, *The Deliverance of God* (Grand Rapids: Eerdmans, 2009), p. 80.
29 It should be noted that faithfulness in Gal. 5:22 is translated from *pistis*, which can also be simply translated as 'faith'.
30 Karl Barth, *The Epistle to the Romans* (trans. Edwyn C. Hoskyns; London: OUP, 1957), p. 110.
31 John Calvin, *Institutes of the Christian Religion* (trans. Ford Lewis Battles; ed. John T. McNeill; 2 vols; Library of Christian Classics; Philadelphia, Westminster Press, 1960), 1:III:XIV.11. 778.
32 Calvin, *Institutes of the Christian Religion*, 1:III:XIV.11. 779.
33 Campbell, *Deliverance of God*, p. 79.
34 John F. MacArthur, *Faith Works: The Gospel According to the Apostles* (Dallas: Word, 1993), p. 58.

Conclusion

1 'It is not for your sake, people of Israel, that I am going to do these things, but for the sake of my holy name' (Ezek. 36:22).
2 Graeme Goldsworthy, *Gospel and Kingdom* (Exeter: Paternoster Press, 1984), p. 47.

www.ingramcontent.com/pod-product-compliance
Lightning Source LLC
Chambersburg PA
CBHW070656100426
42735CB00039B/2169